DIGITAL SPACE

Designing Virtual Environments

DIGITAL SPACE
Designing Virtual Environments

Peter Weishar

McGraw-Hill
New York   San Francisco Washington, D.C.   Auckland   Bogotá
Caracas   Lisbon Madrid Mexico City   Milan
Montreal   New Delhi   San Juan   Singapore
Sydney   Tokyo   Toronto

McGraw-Hill

A Division of The McGraw-Hill Companies

1234567890 DOC/DOC 90321098

ISBN 0-07-069611-X

The sponsoring editor for this book was Wendy Lochner, the editing supervisor was Penny Linskey, and the production supervisor was Pamela Pelton. It was set in Stemple Garamond and Gil Sans by Peter Weishar.

Printed and bound by R.R. Donnelley & Sons Company.

McGraw-Hill books are available at special quantity discounts to use as premiums and sales promotions, or for use in corporate training programs. For more information, please write to the Director of Special Sales, McGraw-Hill, 11 West 19th Street, New York, NY 10011. Or contact your local bookstore.

 This book is printed on recycled, acid-free paper containing a minimum of 50% recycled, de-inked fiber.

To my wife Donna
for putting up with me even before
I started writing this book.

ACKNOWLEDGMENTS

I would like to thank some of the many people whose foresight and support throughout my career made this book possible;

Wendy Lochner, my editor at McGraw-Hill Publishing for her insightful and creative input and faith in a first-time author.

Professor John Canemaker from New York University Film School, Red Burns, Chair of the Interactive Telecommunications Program at New York University, Dr. Mary Schmidt Campell, Dean of the Tisch School of the Arts at NYU for their daily encouragement and inspiration.

Chuck Carter, Robyn Miller from Cyan, Inc., Ron Thornton from Foundation Imaging, and Jon Kletzien and Richard Dubrow from Advanced Media Design for volunteering their time, expertise and beautiful images for the case studies and interviews in this book.

Maggie Webster-Shapiro, Penny Linskey, and Robin Gardner from McGraw-Hill Publishing for their professionalism and making the process of producing this book as painless as possible. Caren Anhder and Debbie Johnson from Strata, Inc., Sonya Palosaari from Epson America, Inc., Ronnie Banks and Melisa Bell from Kinetix, and Carl Ludwig from Bluesky/VIFX, as well individuals at Silicon Graphics, Inc., SoftImage, Inc., NewTek, NetPower, Inc., Apple Computer, Inc., LightScape, Alias|Wavefront, and many other companies who contributed their time and expertise to help make this book more complete and accurate.

My parents for their constant interest, support and caring throughout my education and career. My family for their encouragement and enthusiasm along with their trying very hard to understand what I do for a living.

Thank you to Bonita Rutigliano Engel, Kaori Eda, and Michelle Dwosken for their help creating some of the example illustrations.

Mostly, thank you to my wife Donna, my favorite editor, proofreader, typist, producer, writer, cheerleader and confidante who made this book possible.

Table of Contents

CHAPTER 1

Overview

A few years ago, three-dimensional computer graphics was relegated to a limited number of pioneers working with custom software on extremely expensive equipment, and the term "computer artist" was an oxymoron on the level of "military intelligence." At that time, there were a few visionaries who could predict the emergence of 3D design as a significant segment of the infant field of computer graphics. However, it would have taken a modern-day Nostradamus to foresee the birth of a ubiquitous new medium and a thriving, unique industry.

Digital Space: Designing Virtual Environments is written for the individual artist who is either taking the first steps into 3D computer graphics or wishes to understand more about the creation of computer-generated environments. This book will take the reader through the basics of planning, modeling, texture mapping, lighting, and rendering a 3D project from the point of view of an artist. There is also an extensive case study section where successful professionals explain the artistic process of 3D design in their own words. All of the basic terminology and techniques that you will need to start comfortably working in 3D are explained along with clear descriptions of the most common virtual set designs.

Every true artist has a uniqueness of vision, a way of combining familiar materials, imagery, and techniques into a personal and meaningful statement. When I was in art school, the entire class was given the same materials and the same exact subject matter; yet, there was an amazing divergence of artwork produced in one room with everyone using just pencil and paper. Yes, this was due in part to varying technical ability, but mostly it was due to the individuality of the students. Each person made literally thousands of decisions as they worked on their drawing. Students decided how dark the shadows should be, the length of a hatch mark, and the smoothness of texture all by adjusting the pressure of the pencil on the paper or perhaps by moving a finger a few millimeters one way or the other while drawing. These unique decisions, along with bolder ones such as the choice of composition and even how far to sit from the subject, comprised the essence of what made these drawings artwork.

The same process can exist with computer-generated art. Mid- and high-level 3D software packages are filled with a myriad of features, check boxes, and plug-ins that would confuse your average brain surgeon. It is not just the settings of these parameters that make a work unique, it is the choices the 3D artist makes as he or she works through the creative process. Most novices are surprised to find out that computer artists, just like painters, work with varying levels of detail and must choose which object or part of the composition should receive a higher level of accuracy and visual emphasis. A computer artist must learn to work with and take advantage of the digital medium just as a painter uses pigment and brush to eloquently suggest distant trees and mountains with a few skilled strokes.

With the fast pace of the computer industry, even monthly periodicals are hard pressed to provide accurate information about the newest developments in 3D computer graphics. It is best to take a step back and look at the industry as a whole rather than try to predict which software will have the most particle-effects features and who will make the fastest accelerator board.

SOFTWARE

HIGH-END PROGRAMS

There are two software programs which seesaw in feature sets as they vie for the top position in 3D animation: Alias and SoftImage. Both of these programs started out as UNIX-based software which only ran on Silicon Graphics computers. Alias Animator is owned by Silicon Graphics and still only runs on their proprietary computers running IRIX. SoftImage was bought by Microsoft who ported (rewrote) the code so it now runs on the original SGI platform and also on Windows NT workstations.

Currently, SoftImage has a stronger feature set for creating realistic character animations while Alias is the tool of choice for creating complex models. It is not uncommon for a production house to model a character in Alias and animate it in SoftImage.

Alias and SoftImage both require a serious investment. Although the specified requirements for a minimal system may be a little less, the combination of hardware and software will cost an average user anywhere from fourteen to nineteen thousand dollars (in 1998) for a basic system. That does not include a lot of extras like software plug-ins, disk arrays, and video in/out. I guess that's one reason why they call them high-end systems.

Alias, Inc. is currently porting their newest version of Alias Power Animator, named Maya, to run on Windows NT systems, but the cost of the hardware and software should stay about the same. Alias and SoftImage are professional tools which have an enormous amount of flexibility and power. However, they are probably a little too expensive and too hard to learn for those just starting out in 3D.

MID-RANGE PROGRAMS

If you have a more limited budget, there are a wealth of mid-range programs from which to choose. 3D Studio Max®, LightWave®, and ElectricImage® are three of the many programs which stand out in this category.

The most popular package by far is 3D Studio Max by Kinetix. Kinetix is the relatively newly formed multimedia arm of Autodesk which has been specializing in CAD applications since the beginning of time. 3D Studio started out as a DOS-based program that ran on a standard Intel machine. The system requirements were fairly low and if you didn't mind the somewhat archaic DOS interface, 3D Studio was a very solid choice. 3D Studio Max is much more than just an upgrade. It is a complete rewrite of the code. Max is optimized to run on Windows NT, but it will also do fine with Windows 95. Possibly because of its popularity, 3D Studio Max has around 200 plug-ins by third-party

Figures 1-1 and 1-2:
Two interface shots
from the latest version
of 3D Studio Max R2®
from Kinetix®.

companies which give the program a great deal of flexibility and features. The latest version is called 3D Studio Max R2 and it costs roughly half as much as Alias and SoftImage The standard retail price (srp) is about $3,500. To date, it is not used as much for feature film work, mostly because many of the high-end features are not as developed as they are with their more expensive high-end counterparts. Many CAD architects use Max for rendering because of its tight integration with AutoCAD (the most popular engineering and architecture program). 3D Studio Max is maturing very rapidly, and I expect to see a great deal more high-end film work produced with this software in the near future.

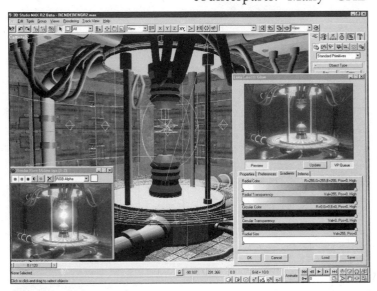

1-1

LightWave by NewTek, Inc. has the most interesting heritage of the bunch. Back in the stone age of personal computing, Commodore introduced an inexpensive computer which the consumer could hook up to their TV instead of a monitor. The Amiga computer developed from the original Commodore. Then a small company in Topeka, Kansas introduced the VideoToaster to work only on Amiga systems. The VideoToaster was a combination add-on board and software that produced near-production-quality video output and editing. The LightWave 3D modeler and renderer was part of that package. If anyone ever argues with you that the Amiga with the VideoToaster was not an

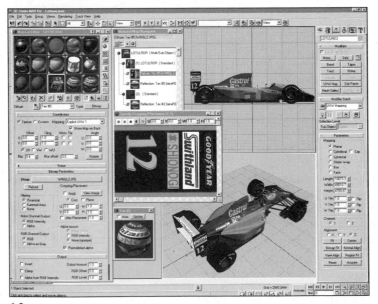

1-2

amazing piece of technology that was far ahead of its time, open this book to this page and hit them with it. The Amiga computer was, however, the victim of the most boneheaded marketing effort of all time and it has managed to virtually disappear from the PC market, although I'm told that the Amiga is still in limited production at the time of this writing.

NewTek, Inc., ported LightWave onto different platforms while the Amiga started its plunge into obscurity. LightWave is now a fully mature program running on many different platforms. There are versions for SGI, Windows, and Windows NT on Intel and Alpha-based computers, Macintosh, and of course, Amiga. Lightwave is the favorite of the television industry. There is a very long list of shows that use NewTek's software for everything from mythological beasts to space battles. LightWave has a reputation for being difficult to learn and use, mostly due to the legacy of the funky and often convoluted Amiga interface. However, the unwieldy working environment is becoming less and less of an issue with each new upgrade.

ElectricImage by Electric Image, Inc. is arguably the only high-end solution available on the Macintosh platform. ElectricImage started out as a rendering and animation tool only, with no 3D modeler. Artists usually used an excellent modeling program called Form•Z to create the geometry and then ported their models into ElectricImage. At that time, Form•Z cost about $1,500 (srp) and ElectricImage went for around $7,500 (srp). At those prices, many artists were faced with the difficult choice between spending about two times their hardware investment on new software or just turning to a more economical solution. But, ElectricImage had two things going for it: very attractive, high-end rendering features and the fastest rendering engine available on any platform. To answer the price problem, Electric Image released ElectricImage Broadcast® for about $2,500 (srp) which is identical to the expensive version except it does not render the high-resolution animations needed for film work. They have also released a fairly powerful modeling package so an artist need not rely on importing models. Perhaps in response, Form•Z has introduced a render engine to their model-only application.

ElectricImage on a Macintosh platform competes favorably against high-end workstations and is used a great deal for flying logos and special effects. ElectricImage has the peculiar advantage that many artists use exclusively Macintosh computers and they are fiercely loyal to that platform. It also has the disadvantage that its character animation and modeling tools are not as fully developed as its competitors. As I write this, ElectricImage is being ported to Windows NT and SGI.

LOWER PRICED PROGRAMS

There are many more offerings in the lower price point range of 3D software. Most of the companies producing these products would not categorize themselves as low-end developers, and indeed many of these packages have surprisingly advanced features. A 3D animation package fits within the low-end category if its street price is under or around $1,000 and it would not be a practical solution for film or extensive broadcast video production. However, many of these programs now have feature sets that are very similar to the Alias and SoftImage of just two or three years ago. Desktop computers of today are at about the same level as low-end workstations of that time, so I cannot emphasize enough that "low end" is just a relative term.

Although there are no exact figures, one of the most popular programs on the Macintosh platform is StudioPro® by Strata. StudioPro helped break open the multimedia revolution when it was used by Cyan, Inc. for the production of their blockbuster CD-ROM game, *Myst*. StudioPro had a well-rounded feature set and a beautifully designed interface which gave it a strong reputation for ease of use and made it an excellent tool to learn the medium. Strata has a terrific, but very slow raytrace renderer which makes it a solid choice for print and multimedia. For a long time, this software was the most popular and logical choice for Macintosh artists on a limited budget. However, while Strata relied on to its reputation, other Macintosh software packages like Infini-D® by MetaCreations and Macromedia's 3D Xtreme® (both of which are now available on Windows) continued to mature and develop more powerful features. With all of the problems plaguing the Macintosh platform and the increased competition in the 3D software industry, Strata has its work cut out to reestablish itself as a leader in this category.

Strata recently completely rewrote their StudioPro software (version 2.5) to include a very strong feature set and a new, innovative and elegant interface, as well as a wealth of "high-end" rendering features. In fact, many of the illustrations in this book were produced with StudioPro.

On the PC side Calgori's TrueSpace® is a popular program for artists on a limited budget. TrueSpace has matured a great deal from its limited origins to become a solid, all-around package good for 3D illustration. Infini-D and 3D Xtreme for the PC are also good tools with sophisticated modeling and lighting effects that are very often bundled with other software or sold for very low prices (from $99 competitive upgrade to around $400 stand alone).

Many professional 3D artists will summarily discount the lower end software because these packages lack either rendering speed or the latest feature sets. They are often designed for the novice and therefore will sometimes sacrifice high-end capabilities for ease of use and "friendly" icons. However, low-end software serves a

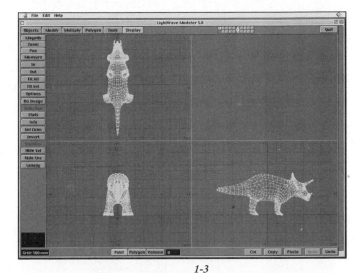

1-3

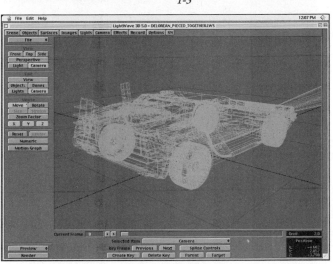

1-4

Figures 1-3 and 1-4: The interface for LightWave 5.0. LightWave has two modules, one for modeling (Figure 1-3) and one for animation and rendering (Figure 1-4).

very valuable purpose in the industry. It is frequently the first exposure most artists and students have to the medium and it is a very valuable tool for seasoned professionals on a budget. If you are a freelancer or own a small studio, a lower end package can pay for itself in a single project. I use one of these packages a great deal for my own work. When I'm at a client's office or the University, I'll sit in front of systems costing anywhere from $20,000 to $75,000. If I'm doing a simple print piece at home, the elaborate animation system is overkill. In any event, it's good for a 3D artist to know a range of packages. It makes you more employable and more flexible in different working situations.

HARDWARE AND EQUIPMENT

Keeping tabs on the computer hardware industry is very similar to being a weatherperson in Florida. The weather there can vary drastically every quarter mile at intervals of about five minutes. If you ever watch the local news in Florida, the beleaguered weatherperson spends most of his time talking about how unusual the weather was yesterday and then resigns himself to predicting 30 percent rain for tomorrow. Computer industry pundits are usually safe reporting that processor speed should double in the next year and hardware will drop in price. It is a difficult task for anyone to determine where the future of the industry will go and what hardware will turn out to be the best investment. If you have been in the industry for a few years, you have probably been burned once or twice by hardware which did not live up to the hype or was outmoded within a couple of minutes of purchase.

After making the above disclaimer, I will give a rundown of popular platforms and make a few hardware suggestions based on the current state of the industry.

PLATFORMS

While there are several platform choices, many artists prefer to work on SGI (Silicon Graphics, Inc.) systems because of their

1-5

custom graphics accelerators and "unified memory" which makes screen redraw very fast and
responsive. Silicon Graphics owns their own chip
design and manufacturing company which produces the MIP's brand processor. MIP's is a RISC
(Reduced Instruction Set Chip) processor so it is
designed to process many small calculations very
quickly. RISC processors perform very well with
graphics intensive applications. Most "old timers"
(computer artists who have been working for
roughly six years or more) like to work with the
UNIX-based system because of its power and flexibility. UNIX
has a reputation for being very difficult and arcane, although it is
improving with each new version of IRIX, the graphic interface
which sits on top of the UNIX shell.

Windows NT workstations are being sold to consumers as a
cheaper alternative to the SGI offerings With all the add-on cards
and whatnot that are needed to bring the performance on par with
an SGI, the price is still much higher than the average desktop PC.
Windows NT is gaining an advantage as many more hardware
manufacturers make NT workstations giving the consumer a
greater choice of systems and configurations.

Most NT systems run on a standard Intel processor or multiple
Intel processors, but in the wide range of offerings there are
exceptions to the rule. For example, the Alpha® chip by Digital
Equipment Corporation is an extremely fast processor that, when
combined with Windows NT, provides the best price/perfor-
mance ratio of any commercial chip. A properly configured DEC
Alpha computer makes an excellent rendering engine. However,
the chip is used only by a small percentage of the market and not
all software runs in its native format with the DEC Alpha.

The Apple Macintosh computer was once the obvious choice for
almost all digital artists. Its terrific interface, ease of use, and innovative hardware design once made Apple the industry leader in
desktop computing. Through a series of mishaps and shortsighted

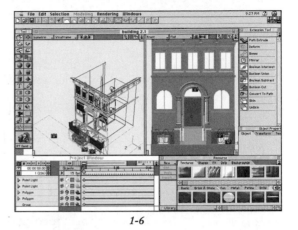

1-6

Figure 1-5:
Strata StudioPro.

Figure 1-6:
The interface for
Strata StudioPro 2.1.

management decisions Apple currently holds about 4 percent of the industry and looses marketshare every quarter. Even though the outlook is a bit bleak for the future of the Mac, it is still a viable system with a strong user base.

SGI

Figure 1-7:
A top of the line
Macintosh 9600 desktop
computer.

Figure 1-8:
The futuristically-styled
20th anniversary
Macintosh.

The entry-level Silicon Graphics workstation is called the O2. It is a great deal more powerful than the average entry-level desktop system. A good O2 system should have an internal 4 gig (gigabyte) drive, 128 megs (megabytes) of RAM, a 17 inch monitor, and video in/out. The O2 has a few innovative features like unified memory and extensive graphic subsystems for fast screen redraw. The combination of the IRIX operating system and either Alias or SoftImage with the proper swap space settings will take up to about 2 gigabytes of disk space and about 40 to 60 megs of RAM just to start up the program and stare at the screen, so it is not such a great idea to get just a base system which only comes with 64 megs of RAM and a 2 gig hard drive.

WINDOWS NT SYSTEMS

All Windows NT systems should have a 4 gigabyte internal drive, at least 128 megabytes of RAM and a 17 inch monitor. It is very helpful to get a fast/wide SCSI connection to peripheral drives to help with animation playback and video in/out.

Three of the software packages mentioned above can run on Windows NT: 3D Studio Max, LightWave, and SoftImage. Each of these packages will work just fine on a standard high-end system; however, if you wish to optimize your hardware to specific software, consider the following information:

3D Studio Max will see a significant performance boost from a multiprocessor machine and a video card that supports Heidi 3D or Open GL acceleration. Heidi and Open GL are both software graphics libraries which speed up the redraw of 3D objects on screen. A video card that "supports" these libraries has a specific chip set which can process the instructions from a graphics library at a very fast rate.

LightWave does not currently support multiprocessors, so a computer with a single, very fast chip would be a better use of your funds. LightWave's code takes up less hard disk space than most other 3D software packages, so you could get a smaller internal drive, but I do not think it is worth it.

SoftImage has a very well-designed interface that works best on a 19 inch monitor. It also works better with a lot of disk space and a high-end Open GL graphics card.

WINDOWS 95 SYSTEMS

Unlike NT, Windows 95 will only run on an Intel processor. 3D Studio Max does not support multi-reading (multiple processors) on Windows 95 and SoftImage will not run at all with this operating system, so there is a good chance you won't need a dual processor machine. Windows 95 requires less RAM than NT and it uses a little less disk space, so you can reduce some cost, but a serious 3D artist will have over 100 megs of RAM on his workstation.

MACINTOSH SYSTEMS

A PowerPC with a 604e, 225 megahertz processor or higher is essential for a Macintosh system. If you're not running ElectricImage, the Macintosh will have significantly slower render times than some of the PC or UNIX workstations. Although the processors themselves are very fast, the Macintosh operating system will slow down the "real world" functioning of your computer. A dual-processor configuration will add about one third more speed to the machine. Although all Apple Macintoshes have onboard video, it's a good idea to consider buying an accelerated QuickDraw 3D card if most of your work will be done in 3D. You should

1-7

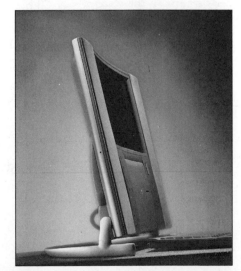

1-8

also have at least 100 megs of RAM, a 2 gigabyte internal drive, and a 17 inch monitor.

PERIPHERALS

No matter what system you buy, make sure you have a way of viewing your work on the intended delivery platform. If you are producing work for multimedia, you should have access to a standard PC. At the current time, a standard PC has a 133 to 233 MHz Intel Pentium processor, 15 inch to 17 inch 16-bit monitor, a 1 or 2 gigabyte hard drive, and a 56k modem. Remember, if you are using an SGI or a Macintosh the monitor will usually have less contrast and better color than a vanilla PC so your work may look very different to the majority of viewers than it did during production.

If you are producing video, you must have a way to get video out of your machine so you can view it on a standard NTSC television set at 30 frames per second. If you do not have one already, buy a good VCR with multiple AV in/out options. This will be a far cry from a real video editing set up, but you will be able to see how different your work looks when not viewed RGB.

1-9

Figure 1-9:
Image of the O2 desktop workstation with a CAD simulation of an underwater camera on the display. Underwater camera screen image courtesy of Katz Design, Image courtesy of Silicon Graphics, Inc.

There is a very dramatic difference between the screen and print versions of the same image. If you do any kind of print work, a high quality color printer is a necessity. I used to send out to service bureaus for Iris® or Fiery® proofs whenever I did a print job. Iris prints are so high quality that they are often used with archival quality paper and coatings to create permanent works of art. The drawback is the machines and materials are prohibitively expensive for a small studio. Matchprints and press proofs which use the separated film to create a four-color image are even more expensive. I recently started using an Epson Stylus printer which makes images on glossy paper at over 1,440 dpi (dots per inch). These printers create photographic quality images for a fraction of the cost of Iris and Fiery machines. This entire book was proofed with an Epson printer and, if you can't tell already, I believe these low cost inkjet printers are a significant advancement for computer artists who produce images for print.

If you are producing CG (computer-generated) artwork for the film industry, there is no simple or inexpensive way to convert your work to film. Many traditional filmmakers will edit live footage on nonlinear editing computer systems, but they have the option of going back to the film dailies to examine their work in fine detail. For a computer artist to do the same, the digital images must first be recorded onto film, which is a very expensive and time-consuming task. Some studios use very high-resolution widescreen televisions to view their computer animations in progress, but that is also a very expensive proposition. In short, creating 3D work for film production is not cheap. Even though a small studio or individual might be able to afford a high-end computer or two, the cost of high-end editing, compositing equipment, film recorders, and peripherals can make film production prohibitive.

1-10

Figure 1-10:
The top of the line Silicon Graphics Onyx2 family of computers. These ultra-expensive, ultra-fast machines are the pinnacle of graphics hardware.

No matter what the final delivery medium, or hardware and software configuration, you must have a strong back-up solution. Many animators will rely on DAT tape (digital tape) because of its extremely high storage capacity and low media costs. Tape can be a little cumbersome to work with because it is a linear medium, so the user must forward and rewind through the tape to access specific files. I wouldn't recommend using any media that can't store at least 100 megabytes on a single disk or tape. Optical disks, Jaz drives, and writable CD-ROM's are all popular forms of removable media. Zip disks are extremely popular, but they are not sufficient if you are looking to back up animations or very large files. Whichever medium you choose, you must remember that frequent back-up is an essential requirement for any computer artist. Telling

1-11

**Figure 1-11:
The Netpower Symetra 3
workstation. Netpower
makes an entire line of
Intel-based Windows NT
workstations aimed at
graphics professionals.**

a client that you lost your work to a computer glitch is the same unacceptable excuse as "the dog ate my homework."

THE INDUSTRY

3D computer graphics is maturing at a frantic pace. It is not just the proliferation of affordable hardware and software that drives the industry; it is the collective imagination, talent, and determination of the artists who have chosen to express themselves through this medium. It would be inaccurate to predict the future of 3D digital design by following the trends of hardware and software development alone, because these are only the tools of the artist. It would be like studying the history of painting by discussing the advancements in paint from fresco to egg tempera to oils and acrylics without taking into account artistic movements like the Renaissance, Impressionism, and Abstraction.

The field of 3D design can be broken up into several segments: realtime and virtual reality graphics, multimedia (CD-ROM) and print, architectural rendering, and film and television.

REALTIME 3D GRAPHICS

Realtime 3D graphics are essential to many arcade-style VR games. Arcade games are an entire industry unto themselves. Artists and programmers must try to generate the smallest possible size files so the computer processor can manipulate the images and display them quickly for the game player. The file sizes themselves are miniscule compared to prerendered graphics and animations, so there is a trade off in the quality and realism of the image.

VRML (Virtual Reality Modeling Language) is a form of realtime 3D that is designed to be viewed in a web browser. It is not as efficient as most 3D arcade games so it is not used for action games, but the code and graphics are relatively easy to use.

REALTIME DESKTOP 3D

Realtime desktop 3D has extreme limitations since frames must render in a fraction of a second. Therefore, most realtime environments have a very blocky, flat look that appears more primitive and crude than pre-rendered work. There are many exceptional realtime pieces that push the limits of the technology, but they are still far from the photorealistic look of most 3D artwork.

CD-ROM

CD-ROM was going to be the next big thing about three years ago. Many print and multimedia artists scrambled to learn the latest 3D programs to produce walkthrough, puzzle-solving games. There was a huge buzz in Hollywood for interactive titles, and eventually almost every major project had some interactive marketing or ancillary interactive product attached to it. But Hollywood and big money went about the CD-ROM business the same way they do everything else: they threw a lot of cash at inexperienced people regardless of talent and hoped something good would come out of it. (I sound bitter, don't I? Well, actually, I am.) When the public saw the amount of half-baked, expensive, and boring titles being produced, they basically said, "No thanks." The general (false) wisdom in the entertainment industry was CD-ROM was a dead medium and most of the money dried up. The bottom fell out of the industry and now there are only a handful of producers making CD-ROM walkthrough games.

There was a great deal of good that came out of the CD-ROM boom and bust. Some intelligently run, talented companies like Lucas Arts, Cyan, Trilobyte Studios, and ID software (for real-time "twitch" games) rose above the fray and still produce

Figure 1-12:
The interface for Virtus Walkthrough Pro, an excellent tool for the creation of VRML level I models.

excellent quality games. Many 3D artists were given their first real jobs producing commercial work. And, I believe the CD-ROM type game still has tremendous potential and will have a resurgence in the DVD format. Many of the artists and producers who cut their teeth on CD-ROM are now working on Internet development which is experiencing a more aggressive boom than the early days of CD-ROM.

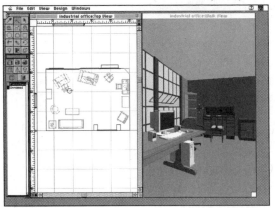

1-12

ARCHITECTURAL RENDERING

Architectural rendering is a field with relatively little hype where a 3D artist can produce very high quality work. Many of the artists working in this discipline have degrees in architecture or engineering, or are accomplished draftspeople.

In the past, the most popular CAD programs for architects had limited rendering and no animation capabilities. Computer-generated art looked very plastic and lifeless, so many architectural firms used CAD for the floor plans and then resorted to traditional rendering techniques for visualization and client presentations. Most of that has changed with better CAD rendering and easier file format transfers.

Architectural renderers differ a great deal from the 3D artists in entertainment because they are creating real spaces and they cannot cut corners to come up with designs that are attractive but impossible to build. Since architectural rendering is meant to visualize a concept as it will look in reality, it is often less flashy and dramatic than film or game special effects. It also grabs less of the public's attention because it is a less "sexy" discipline. However, there are currently many firms producing exceptional work in this field which rivals the artistry of any traditional architectural rendering.

FILM

Producing feature films and television is perhaps the most demanding area of 3D design. The artist is often asked to create fantastic effects that seam perfectly with live action. Careful attention must be paid to detail, lighting, and movement in order to make the work convincing. The most popular programs for this kind of work have "steep learning curves" (which means "really hard" in English) and usually have higher price tags.

Many artists consider film to be the most prestigious and challenging area of 3D design. Because of the enormous expense of the equipment and the huge budgets, there are not many small shops that can handle effects for a major production. Many smaller studios will get overflow work or an entire project that has limited special effects, but if you are looking to break into the field, your best bet is to try to get into one of the big production houses like Disney, Dreamworks, ILM, Rhythm and Hues, Digital Domain, Pixar, or RG/A. Many of these big shops use a combination of Alias, SoftImage, and their own proprietary software to create special effects that cannot be matched by small studios.

TELEVISION

Three-dimensional special effects for television has grown into a major segment of the 3D industry. A frame of video takes much less time to render than a frame of 35 mm film, and the budgets and equipment needed are far more reasonably priced. Small studios are able to effectively handle the effects work of a television series. The budgets are smaller than most Hollywood films, but so is the GNP of most countries. I recently read about a production house for a major syndicated show that uses freelance artists working from their own homes. The artists send the model files via e-mail to be rendered at the production house. It is unknown whether this kind of

**Figure 1-13:
The low cost Epson Stylus 3000 printer which makes photo-quality prints of digital images up to 17x22".**

1-13

decentralization will become a significant industry trend, but it may open up opportunities for artists who do not wish to move to New York or Los Angeles. 3D work for television is growing at a rapid rate and there are many affordable production solutions. Television is an excellent avenue if you are looking to get into a 3D animation studio and eventually do film work. Some of the well-known studios are starting to get more film work and this trend will probably continue.

GETTING A JOB

The industry has matured a great deal since its inception. As the field matures, the procedures for getting a job have become a little more structured and definable. Before there was widespread training in 3D design, post-production houses were recruiting artists who knew traditional animation methods yet did not know how to turn on a computer. The production houses would commonly absorb the cost of months of training on high-end equipment. There were stories of six-figure salaries offered to kids just out of college and astronomical fees of $400+ an hour for the production of 3D artwork. For a while it seemed like anyone with a portfolio and a plane ticket to California could make more money as a 3D artist than a successful lawyer. Of course, that was only half true, and the part that was true has changed.

Today, most studios will ask to see a reel or printouts of your work before they'll consider you for a job. This creates a paralyzing paradox for many would-be computer artists who cannot afford the high-end software the big studios are using to make a demo reel. You can't get into the studio without knowing the software and you can't learn the software without getting into a studio. If you just take a class or two you can't get on the computers long enough to make the reel.

Of course, getting enough experience to get that first job is a problem in almost any field. That problem is compounded when the experience must be gained on expensive equipment. The solution is actually simple. Make a demo reel or portfolio with the best software you can afford. You will have to spend money on equipment and software, but you won't have to buy the best that is out there. The important thing is to show art directors and producers that you can think and create in 3D. If you keep the focus on creativity and originality, your portfolio will open doors. It is, of course, a good thing to have knowledge of the program your potential employer uses, but at this point in time, most employers are willing to train 3D artists in specific software if they are looking to fill a staff position.

If you are not quite sure which area of 3D design you want to go into or you are looking to present a more general portfolio, you should show examples of different 3D disciplines. Below are a few ideas for portfolio or reel examples. There is no set rule as to what kind of work or how much work you should show. A lot of it depends on the kind of job you are looking for and your particular style.

ARCHITECTURE

For an architectural recreation, study a specific place or period and then pay careful attention to detail and proportion. This piece can be shown as a series of stills or a slow walkthrough. It is important to remember that you will be showing your modeling and set design skills in an architectural example. Don't make a fast flythrough filled with special effects. If you are applying for a job in an architectural firm, it would be a good idea to show renderings of your own designs, too.

MECHANICAL MODELING

Take a common tool or a recognizable object like a wrench, watch, or coffeemaker and create an accurate model from a few different points of view. Advertising agencies and print designers are often looking for artists to visualize products which are not in the market yet. The client is very often looking for variations or cutaways of a product that cannot be shown through photography, so make part of the coffeemaker semitransparent to show the inner workings, etc. The important thing here is to make the object look as attractive, understandable, and "heroic" as possible.

CAMERA MOVEMENT AND SPECIAL EFFECTS

Show some command of special effects like fire, water, or fog. The prospective employer will want to see intelligent camera movement along with attractive composition and an effective use of special effects.

CHARACTER ANIMATION

This has become an extremely popular area of 3D art. The most important thing to show here is either natural movement or a stylized, exaggerated movement of an animated character. If you haven't studied or worked with animation or film, you'll have a hard time creating unique character animations.

COMPOSITING

In the film industry, there is a great deal of work seaming 3D models with live action (like the dinosaurs tromping around *Jurassic Park*). Architects are also often asked to visualize a structure in its intended surroundings. This is all much harder than it sounds because the artist must consider things like the direction of the light in the live picture, and the reflections and shadows cast by the 3D object on the real background. Your ability to composite computer-generated and real elements will help you stand out from the pack.

PORTFOLIO DON'TS

Don't show your work on too many different formats. Presentation is very important, so if you are showing some work on VHS, some on Beta, a few pieces on CD-ROM, and the rest as printouts or chromes, your portfolio will have a slapped-together appearance. Try to convert as much as is practical to one format with brief titles or explanations. Keep in mind that the art, design, and entertainment industries all care a great deal about presentation and showmanship. You should present yourself in a slick and well-organized manner.

Don't move the camera around in wild, unnatural moves. Even though the virtual camera in your model can do anything or go anywhere, it is not a good idea to make it move in impossible ways. It often confuses the viewer and is a sure sign of a neophyte in computer animation.

 Don't get all of your ideas from existing 3D work. Stay away from hackneyed subject matter. A portfolio which consists of fighting robots and chrome spheres on checkered floors shows very little imagination. About a year ago I was interviewing some applicants for a job and three of them showed me reels with the same clip art model of a man with an applied chrome texture. Needless to say, the only thing that stood out about their work was its sameness.

 Don't try to be something you are not. If you have never studied or worked with character animation, don't think you have to rush through something just to round out your portfolio. If you know that your work will not be strong in certain areas, leave it out and let the good quality work speak for itself.

 Don't use too many stock textures and models that come with your software. If you are using a popular package like 3D Studio Max, an experienced production manager or art director will be able to spot the fact that you are using someone else's stock work as a short cut. An experienced animator is expected to show original and different work, especially in his or her portfolio.

 Don't overdo the special effects such as lens flares, fog, mist, lightning bolts and explosions. It's hard to pinpoint what is too much when it comes to effects, but a pretty good indicator is if you have never seen *anything* like it in reality. When the viewer does not have a frame of reference based upon actual visual experience, the piece will look "fake." If you are showing an abstraction or highly stylized piece, this may not be so bad, but if you are trying for photorealism or an architectural rendering job, over reliance on special effects will be distracting.

And finally, *don't* make it too long. We would expect to see a 15 minute reel from a major effects house like Industrial Light and Magic, but if you are just one person, 2 to 3 minutes of tape or 10 to 15 stills are plenty. Remember, you are not going to be there every time your work is shown so you can't stand next to the screen and make comments like "Um, like, you can skip this part. I did it, like, freshman year. The next clip is better."

There is a great deal of technical knowledge which must be acquired to become a professional 3D artist. There is no single book or even class that can cover all of the esoteric knowledge that you may need during your career. This book should give you a clear understanding of the general principles of computer graphics as well as provide you with various working methods, tips, techniques, and advice you will need to become a successful 3D artist. The latter part of this book is devoted to interviews and case studies with leading 3D artists, many of whom have had a significant impact on the industry. I've included the most extensive glossary that I know of for a book on this subject because many talented, intelligent artists are often intimidated by the jargon used in the computer graphics industry. A single source for translating many of the technical terms will go a long way to help you feel comfortable working in this field.

CHAPTER 2

Planning

If you eavesdropped on a couple of artists talking to each other about 3D modeling, you would hear so much technical jargon you would probably think you had tuned into a rerun of a bad episode of *Star Trek: The Next Generation*. The difference is, however, instead of complaining about "power fluctuations in the plasma conduits causing warp field destabilization" the 3D artists might be talking about "reversing the surface normals and the U/V direction and converting a replication of the object with a displacement map into polygonal form." To the uninitiated, it all sounds like a bunch of intimidating techno-speak and to be frank, it very often is. However, when you're watching *Star Trek*, Captain Picard always solves his problems in a little under an hour while in reality, the 3D modeler may have to wait a day and a half for a call back from tech support. I guess that's why they call it science *fiction*. Careful planning and experience will help you cut down the number of unexpected problems that can scuttle your project. But remember, no matter how hard you plan or how much experience you have, there are too many technical variables for any one person to master. Don't buy land from anyone who claims to fully understand everything about 3D computer graphics.

Working in 3D design can be one of the most time-consuming, frustrating and, at the same time, rewarding artistic pursuits. Careful planning and previsualization can often be the difference between a successful project and an unfinished, unsatisfying work experience. You may have a software package that uses different terminology, but don't worry, the concepts remain the same. There is a way of working in 3D whether you are using your $1,500 home PC or a $50,000 workstation.

Common sense dictates that the amount of planning should be roughly proportional to the scope of the project. As you become more experienced working with 3D art, your production plans will become more accurate and simpler to generate. Each artist develops a production process that best fits his or her work habits and personality. In many cases, group dynamics and planning committees dictate an unconventional way of producing a piece driven by unusual client needs or perhaps just by office politics. Flexibility may be your most crucial asset in getting a project through the planning stages and into actual production; therefore, I have distilled the planning process down to a few essential steps. Depending upon time, budget, and how anal-retentive you, your boss, or your client is, you can add as many steps as you like.

The planning stage usually includes these basic steps: determining the scope, defining the subject matter, visualizing the project, estimating time, and planning the production schedule.

STEP 1: DETERMINING THE SCOPE

For your first step, determine the scope of your project — a task easier said than done. As a professional 3D artist, I'm often presented with concepts which seem to be well thought out, yet are impractical to be produced in the given time frame. Don't expect your client to have a clear idea of the extent of the work. The client may have a fairly good idea of the look of the final piece but they will probably not have a good understanding of production requirements. An animated work, for example, will have very different production requirements than a single rendered illustration. Multimedia walkthroughs must also be previsualized in a very different manner than a pre-rendered animation. Part of the job of a 3D artist is to help a client understand the limitations and capabilities of the medium so they can work together to produce concrete results from abstract concepts. Determining the scope of the job based upon budget, time, manpower, delivery medium, realism, length, etc., should be the first joint effort between you and your client. As you read through this chapter you will find many suggestions that will help you with this process.

STEP 2: DEFINING THE SUBJECT MATTER

Before proceeding to the production of artwork, it is crucial to have a strong understanding of the subject matter. Even if you are just producing a simple flythrough, you should start with a written document. It doesn't have to be long, but the ideas and focus should be clear. Start with a brief description of the plot, even if it is something as simple as "a flythrough of a plan for the renovated lobby of a condominium complex." As the artist, you must always consider the potential viewer and the intended message of the piece. In the above example, a client would not go through the time and expense of producing a digital 3D animation if the main objective was simply to show a new design. Floor plans and some sketches would serve that purpose. Most people, especially clients, expect computer animation to be "sexy" and compelling, convincing the viewer that they are looking at a well-thought-out and attractively designed plan. The flythrough of a lobby might be commissioned to emphasize the smooth flow of pedestrian traffic, to display benefits such as handicapped access, or perhaps even to give a run-down building an upscale feel. These points will be the "story" you are trying to tell. Remember that each camera move and subtle ambient effect should help convey your message.

Don't loose sight of the pertinent objectives of your piece throughout the production process. If there are no clear objectives, well, at least you'll know what the trouble is from the start. In short, 3D design, just like any other artistic medium, should have a clear message. Relying on technology and special effects to cover a lack of initial focus will almost always fail.

STEP 3: VISUALIZING THE PROJECT

It's very important to make sure you and your client are on the same page visually. Compile as many reference images as you can at the start of the job, including unrelated images that evoke a certain style or feel that you want to use in your project. The more information you have about your subject matter, the easier the visualization process will go. I often find the inspiration for a project when researching background information on my subject. I've always been able to find at least some small bit of information that helps. For commercial work, a good client will be pleased to see you taking interest in their work and will be more likely to use you again knowing you took the initiative to understand what you were producing.

The next step in visualizing a 3D project is a rough sketch or, in the case of an animation, the storyboard. Use your storyboards as a guide for general composition and flow, just like a live action filmmaker.

Remember that even if you draw the storyboards yourself, there will still be inaccuracies. Proportions, distances, color, and lighting will all be different in the final version. A traditional animator who draws individual frames on plastic cels will have a much tighter correlation between the storyboard and the final output.

STEP 4: ESTIMATING TIME

Every piece of artwork I've ever created has always been under some time constraint. The inherent compromising demanded by hard deadlines is perhaps the greatest difference between commercial and fine art.

Determining the level of technical complexity for the image is one of the most important keys for accurate time estimation. Unfortunately for the novice 3D artist, there is no simple chart or test to determine how complex a model may become. There are, however, a set of parameters you can use as a guideline. Ask your client or boss the following questions to help you define the parameters for your specific job. If nothing else, at least your client or boss will be involved in the process so they understand the complexity of estimating production time for a 3D project.

1. How close will the viewer get to each object?

This will determine the level of detail applied to the model. For example, if I know I'm making a wooden chair that will sit against the wall in the back of my set, I may just produce a rough approximation of the object, knowing the viewer will never see the effort put into a higher level of detail. If the chair is a focal point in the foreground, I may spend a couple of days to create the contours and subtle texture variations of the bent wood. In general, the more detail required, the longer the model will take.

Keep in mind that nothing manmade or shaped by nature is

a perfectly smooth or formed object. If you get close enough to any object you will see subtle imperfections and signs of aging. You can represent a cue ball as a perfect sphere from 2 feet away, but from 2 centimeters away, it looks like the surface of the Moon.

If you are emulating a photograph, you should take into account depth of field which causes objects outside a certain range to blur. Many programs have a "depth of field" feature or an "atmosphere" setting which creates the appropriate effect. If you know you are going to use depth of field or an atmosphere setting, and some parts of the environment will always be shown in soft focus, it is a waste of time to model everything in detail. It is important to note that depth of field and atmospheric settings are special effects that take some experimenting to get right and add significant time to your rendering.

2. How much of the scene will the viewer see?

If you are creating a single image for an illustration, you can fix a camera to a specific point in a set and never worry about what is just beyond view. It's a simple matter to tailor the model to work from a limited perspective and not make any unnecessary objects. Inversely, many computer games place the player in an environment for hours, allowing them to explore the model from numerous points. The viewer's ability to stop and stare at the intricacies of the model from multiple angles requires many more hours of work by the 3D artist.

Where you place the camera also makes a big difference in modeling complexity. For example, the higher up you place your camera in an outdoor scene, the farther the viewer can see. The more they can see, the larger your model becomes. Think of it this way: a camera placed in the valley of a mountain range will show a great deal less than a camera placed on top of the mountain.

3. What kind of lighting will the scene have?

Lighting affects your time estimation in a few different ways. It can serve to limit the field of view as in a night scene with a dim solitary street light, or it can be used to emphasize certain areas of detail like spotlights on a painting in a museum. If the specifications for the job call for a well, evenly lit scene, you will need a lot of detail, and therefore, more time.

The number and types of light sources also affect rendering times. Later chapters go into more detail about lighting and rendering, but it is important to note here that a scene with multiple light sources and special effects may take ten times longer to render than the same scene with one simple light. You need to account for longer render times for complex lighting when planning your project.

4. How realistic should the scene be?

If you ask a client this question, their first answer is frequently an emphatic "photorealistic!," but if you take the time to show them a few different styles, you might find your client/boss would be more pleased with an illustrative style. You could spend countless hours attempting to recreate the subtle shadows and light refractions of the fall foliage as it would appear at 6:00 P.M. on October 25th in northern New Hampshire when your client would be just as happy with a yellow spotlight. Offering your client options up front could save you hours of work.

There is a tendency in the 3D design industry to associate the level of detail with quality, so many novice designers expend a great deal of time and effort adding every detail possible. Of course, this is not necessary since level of detail is not the sole determining factor when judging quality. A well-designed piece will have a much stronger visual impact than a determined attempt to ape reality.

5. How much movement is there?

Think of your model as a stage set with the objects and animations as the players. When creating a set on a traditional stage, a scenic designer knows the audience will only view his work from one side through a rectangular opening. Therefore, he does not concern himself with anything off-stage. When creating a set in a 3D environment, on the other hand, you must concern yourself with more than one view. As you move the camera in your CG space, you change the point of view of the audience and cause different objects to move to the foreground. Objects in the foreground need more detail.

Moving the camera around also exposes different sides of the modeled objects in your environment, requiring detail on more than one surface. If I know I'm moving a camera from one point of a set to another, or perhaps lifting the point of view like in a crane shot, I know I have to create a very detailed and, therefore, time-consuming model that works from many directions.

Movement also applies to animated characters and special effects such as fire and wind. Every six months or so there is another quantum leap in the development of sophisticated character animation tools. You can expect to see a lot more animation incorporated into 3D design as these tools become cheaper and more widespread. Remember, though, the software does not do most of the work. Simply making a character realistically walk across a room and pick up a glass may cost you 50 to 80 hours. Ultimately, there is no simple rule like "1 second of animation equals 10.5 times the amount of work it takes to create a single image," but it is safe to say that animations almost always takes more time than you plan.

There are many more questions you could ask your client before starting a 3D design project, and not all questions are applicable to every project. For instance, a single rendered image for print won't deal with motion or varying levels of detail. However, you might find that asking similar questions like, "Would you like

FORMAT	SIZE *(in pixels)*	FRAME RATE	RESOLUTION
NTSC Video	640 x 480	30fps	72 dpi
PAL Video	768 x 576	30fps	"
35 mm film	2048 x 1366	24fps	"
CD-ROM*	640 x480 (full screen)	~15fps	"
Internet*	32 x 32	~6fps	"
Quicktime VR	2496 x 768	single image	72 dpi or higher
Print	na	single image	double printed lpi at same size

* There are no specific standards for CD-ROM and Internet animations

two points of view?" and "Should I show the same view during different seasons or at different times of day?" can be just as helpful.

Another major factor in accurate time estimation is rendering. Rendering time is based on so many different factors, estimating rendering time is almost like predicting the weather. Very often an animator creates a single frame, renders it at different resolutions, and then extrapolates rendering time by multiplying the test frame by the number of frames needed for the project. Not everyone has that luxury. If you are bidding a small job, chances are you won't be creating scenes before you get a contract. In any event, this method is not always accurate because different frames of an animation may have dramatically different render times.

Even though no method is exact, there are some guidelines to help you estimate rendering times:

- Determine the size and number of frames to be rendered. The above chart covers some of the basic frame rates, aspect ratios, and frame sizes of standard delivery formats.

- Know your hardware and software. The speed of your computer and your rendering software are major factors in determining rendering time. As you become more comfortable with your software package you will be able to estimate rendering times better.

- If you are not familiar with the the idiosyncrasies of your hardware/software package, run a few tests by rendering the same 1 second animation at a few different sizes and frame rates. It is much more accurate to run 1 second of an animation than a single frame. Rendering times may vary dramatically as you move through the model and there will be a delay between each frame. The delay is usually proportional to the file size being rendered.

- Make sure to note when you start each animation. The software will tell you when each file was finished, but not when it was started. A good trick here is to utilize the batch render feature if it is available in your software. A batch renderer enables you to suspend a group of files at the beginning of the rendering process and process them in sequence as a group. This feature is also sometimes referred to as a rendering que. If you can run your render time tests as a batch, you will only have to note the start time of the first render because the time stamp on each completed render will serve as a good approximation for the start time of the next one. While setting up a batch render just to do a test may seem a little obsessive, it will save you from mind-numbing downtime, staring at the screen wondering when the animation will finish so you can start up the next one.

Again, there's no equation to compute rendering time, but you can generally say that the more complex the model, the longer it will take to render.

STEP 5: PLANNING THE PRODUCTION SCHEDULE

Presently, computer artwork has a bad reputation for coming in over budget and behind schedule. There are many frustrated clients who don't understand all the aspects of CGI and therefore don't understand why the work takes so long, nor do they subsequently believe or understand the computer artist when they receive an explanation. Even if the client is happy, poor production planning can spell financial disaster for your company, especially on a big project.

Following are the typical stages of a medium-sized commercial 3D job. I usually like to give the client this breakdown with specific dates as soon as possible so they know how many times we will meet and both parties have a clear idea of what is expected.

Initial Meeting

Get as much pertinent information from the client as possible at this meeting without annoying them. This is also the time to discuss the client's budget and time frame. I usually try to get this information before the meeting just to make sure I don't waste my time.

If you are working for an architect or designer, get your hands on examples of their previous work. If you see that your client is used to receiving fantastically-detailed, beautiful renderings, then you know the level of quality they are expecting. If you see consistently poor work produced by different artists for your client, it should send up a red flare that either your client is very hard to work with or has terrible taste.

Here are some do's and don'ts for the initial meeting to make things go more smoothly no matter who the client is:

- **Do** tell the client about yourself and your company. Tell them the kind of software and hardware you are using, how many people are in your company, and what your experience is. Keep this information short and pertinent.

- **Do** briefly explain the process of 3D design if they have not hired a 3D artist before.

- **Don't** give away too much about how you plan to do the project. Many clients will shop around, using you to educate themselves before they interview other vendors.

- **Don't** give the client a quote off the top of your head. Many clients will press for a quote because they are shopping by price alone. I usually explain that without spending time researching the job and going over the production in detail my quote would be inaccurate.

- **Don't** tell them how easy the job is. Hiring a CG artist can be very uncomfortable for a client who understands little or nothing about the field. You may try to allay their anxiety by assuring them the job will be a snap. However, if you run into any problems or try to charge a decent rate later on, you will have a hard time since you already told the client how easy the job should be. A better way to assuage your client's fears without undermining yourself might be to say something like, "This seems like a straight-forward job. I can give you an accurate estimate and a tight production schedule because I'm fairly confident we won't run into problems."

- **Don't** be condescending. A client hires an outside vendor because they cannot do the work themselves. Many clients will think you are a genius before you walk in the room because of all the industry hype and their own difficulties working with the computer. New clients often have misconceptions about the field. If you make them feel stupid by the way in which you correct them, they will look for another artist to do the job.

Price Quote

Send the client a detailed quote with a schedule before going further. If you give them a fair quote that is well thought out and organized, you can't lose. Even if you don't get this job, the client will look at you as an intelligent professional to be considered for future work.

Here are some do's and don'ts for estimating a 3D job:

- **Do** let the client know the logic used to arrive at the final estimate. The more specific you are breaking down the job, the more comfortable the client will feel during the process.

- **Don't** use too much jargon. Trying to impress the client with your command of technical terms will just confuse and annoy them. If they don't understand your quote, they don't know what they are paying for and they won't be happy.

- **Don't** plan on getting anything for free. If you expect to borrow your friend's computer for rendering and to go to your old school to transfer your files to videotape, you are relying on favors that might not come through. It is better to use established vendors and work the cost into your quote. Using vendors in the industry also helps you build up contacts. You may find that the guy who does your videotape transfers has some work for you.

- **Don't** assume you will learn new software, hardware, or techniques during the job. You may be a fantastic artist whose mother thinks you are brilliant, but if you don't know how to do something that is required for a project, don't assume you're going to pick it up as you go. Set time aside to test. You cannot charge a client for the purchase of software or the time you take to learn it. If the software or hardware is something you think you should know, buy it and accept the expense as part of doing business. Make sure to factor in a certain amount of unbillable time to learn what you are doing.

- **Don't** automatically cut man hours out of a plan because other expenses such as equipment and rent are fixed costs. By far the most expensive part of any 3D project is usually salary. It can account for anywhere between sixty and ninety percent of all the money spent. If the budget is a fixed cost, work backwards and reduce the scope of the project rather than start work and hope for miracles.

- **Don't** underestimate time. Double the time you think it will really take. It will give you a safety margin and a little negotiating room in the price.

First Client Presentation

This is where you present your basic concepts to the client along with a visualization of the final. Some clients will ask to see three different approaches to the same problem. This is a holdover from the olden days of traditional advertising when clients paid for "idea men" to brainstorm and present them with multiple high-concept ad campaigns. Let the client know beforehand how many comps they will see. If they insist on three or more, build the extra work into your quote.

If you are presenting different approaches to the client, make sure the presentation and the color scheme are consistent. If you show dummy models, keep all of the colors neutral. You don't want a client to choose one design over another just because they like blue better than the red you slapped on your best design at the last minute. Remember, just because you can visualize the same design with different lighting and color does not mean your client can do the same. That's why they hired you.

Asset Acquisition

During this phase, you want to gather up every element you will need in the final piece. This includes photographing all the necessary textures and obtaining all the assets you need from the client. Give the client a specific deadline for handing in assets and let them know the job will be late if this deadline is missed.

Modeling and Initial Rendering

The bulk of the work is completed at this stage. All of the technical problems should be hashed out. The composition and animation should also be clearly blocked out and rendered at low resolution. When working with computer models, it's a good idea to design the characters and scene in the early production process and then run a few test animations with cruder, simpler models to work out framing, lighting, and movement.

Second Client Presentation

At this stage many artists show a wireframe or a rough render blocking out the final. If you are showing a wireframe render to a new client, it's a good idea to bring a finished job to show them how a wireframe compares to a final render. It's a lot more effective than hand waving and it gives you a chance to show off another job. The more detail you can fit into this stage of the project, the better. It is possible to skip the final presentation if your models show enough specifics at this stage. I usually find if I can skip the final meeting, I avoid another opportunity for the client to make changes.

The second presentation should be an opportunity to refine the design to meet the client's needs. There should not be major changes during the second presentation. If you literally find yourself "going back to the drawing board" then you know there has been major miscommunication between you and the client. Most of the time you can avoid this problem by sending a short e-mail or fax after every conversation which bullet points the changes and pertinent points discussed.

Animation and Final Render

This stage always takes longer than you plan. Almost every little stupid mistake and seemingly harmless shortcut comes back to haunt you in the light of detailed rendering. It is important to leave extra time in the production plan for rerendering at least half of the final frames.

Remember, nothing ever comes out perfect. No matter which medium they work in, every artist can find fault with their finished work. I usually stop myself when I know I have achieved my objectives, the piece looks great, the client will be happy, and I'm just sick of looking at it.

Final Client Presentation and Delivery of Work

Make sure to deliver the work on the final platform. If you are producing a video animation, your work should be on tape; an illustration should be on boards; etc. It is not a good idea to have the client look at your monitor to view the final piece for a few reasons: it has the appearance of a work in progress which invites annoying changes, the colors on a computer monitor appear very different when viewed on video or in print, and your final presentation will have fewer technical problems if you don't have to worry about running a demo on your production machine.

Some clients will request your source files along with the final render. This occurs all the time in the desktop publishing field where unsophisticated clients give the source files to their secretaries for all future changes. Some desktop publishing programs are inexpensive enough and easy enough to learn that a beginner can make small changes and cut the designer out of the loop after the initial design. 3D design is so much more difficult and expensive that I usually let the client have whatever source files they want.

CHAPTER 3

Modeling

Every well-rounded 3D artist has a variety of skills such as light-ing, texture mapping, modeling, and animation that enables them to work effectively. It could be argued that the single most impor-tant skill of the group is modeling. While it is *possible* to get a job as a 3D artist where you don't need the ability to create an accu-rate 3D model, it would be very difficult to get that job because you couldn't make an attractive portfolio or produce a complete piece of artwork on your own without making models.

3D modeling is simply the ability to sculpt inside the computer. The artist actually moves points around in virtual space to describe the geometry of various shapes. Each software package has a unique combination of modeling features. If you ask ten artists which program has the best set of features, you would probably get six different answers and those answers would change depending on the object you were making. It all boils down to the preferences of the individual artist. There is no one program that can "do it all."

TYPES OF MODELERS

Software programs use many different methods to create 3D objects. Depending on factors such as which hardware the soft-ware is designed to run on, what the retail price of the software is, and what the intended use of the final model is, 3D programs can be designed to create only simple shapes like spheres and cubes, or to create complex organic shapes like plants and animals. Modelers that use only basic shapes are usually designed for novices or artists making simple models for games or for low-end virtual reality environments. The interface for these programs is usually very straightforward so a user can get up and running in a few hours. Modelers used for organic shapes or precise engi-neering are more concerned with providing a wealth of features than with ease of use.

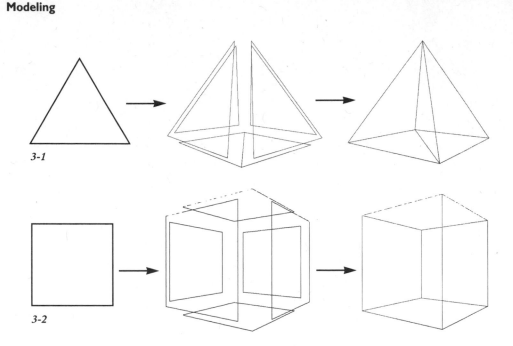

3-1

3-2

*Figures 3-1 and 3-2:
Simple square and
triangular polygons are used
to make a pyramid and a
cube, respectively.*

Almost all modelers use one, or a combination, of three systems to create shapes: polygonal, spline-based, and solid modeling.

POLYGONAL MODELERS

In polygonal modeling, objects are created from simple two-dimensional shapes (polygons) — usually triangles or squares. The polygons are arranged in space to create the surface of three-dimensional objects. In Figure 3-1, six two-dimensional triangles are positioned to form a pyramid. Since the pyramid is made entirely of triangles, it takes two polygons to make up the square base of the pyramid. In Figure 3-2, a cube is created from six square polygons.

Making a pyramid out of triangles and a cube out of squares seem like very obvious, logical geometric equations. It's in the production of more complex objects, like a sphere, that the elegance of the software and clever problem solving by the artist come into play. Creating a sphere out of polygons produces something very similar to Buckminster Fuller's geodesic dome, made popular at the 1939 World's Fair, or the large sphere at Disney World's EPCOT Center (for those of you who aren't familiar with Mr. Fuller's genius).

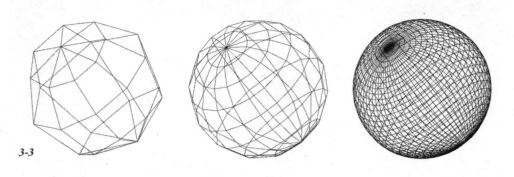

3-3

The three spheres of varying detail in Figure 3-3 were each made from square-shaped polygons. In many cases, the quality of the final rendered image depends on the amount of polygons used to describe the object. As you can see from comparing the spheres in Figure 3-3 to the pyramid and the cube in Figures 3-1 and 3-2, the more complex the object, the greater the number of polygons needed to make it. An object comprised of many polygons is said to be a "heavy" object. It's a good idea to make an object with as few polygons as possible without sacrificing the quality of the final image. Having a smaller "polygon count" will make your model render faster and will make your computer much more responsive.

Figure 3-3:
The same size sphere is rendered at low, medium, and high resolutions.
Figure 3-4:
A sphere displayed in a spline modeling program.

Most low-end and mid-range 3D software programs use polygons to create models because shapes can be made and rendered with less computer processing power than with other modeling methods. 3D computer games requiring fast play and screen redraw on standard PC's also use polygon-based models.

SPLINE-BASED AND NURBS MODELERS

Many high-end and some mid-range 3D packages use splines to create models. Spline-based modeling programs have some advantages over polygonal-based programs. It's generally considered easier to make complex organic shapes using splines than it is using polygons. Spline models usually have smaller file sizes than similar models made with polygons because a surface created with splines is not fully calculated until the image is rendered. Complex spline models can also be rendered in higher detail than polygonal models with the same file size.

3-4

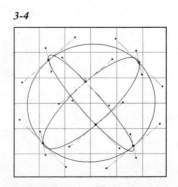

SPLINES AND NURBS

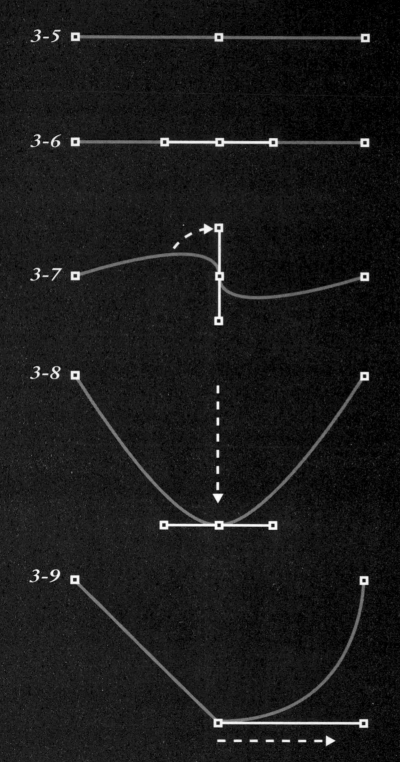

3-5

3-6

3-7

3-8

3-9

Figure 3-5 is a simple line with three points called vertices.

Figure 3-6 shows the same line with a single vertex selected. Note how both the vertex and two more points known as control handles appear.

If the control point is moved as in Figure 3-7 it pulls the spline along with it.

Moving the vertex (Figure 3-8) will also affect the length and shape of the spline.

Figure 3-9 shows the same spline with modifications to the length of the control handles. The handle on the left was pulled on top of the center vertex, creating a straight line between the left and center points. The other control handle was dragged toward the right, creating a rounder arc.

Figures 3-10 and 3-11 show four connected control vertices forming a circle and the manipulation of the shape of that circle by moving just one control handle.

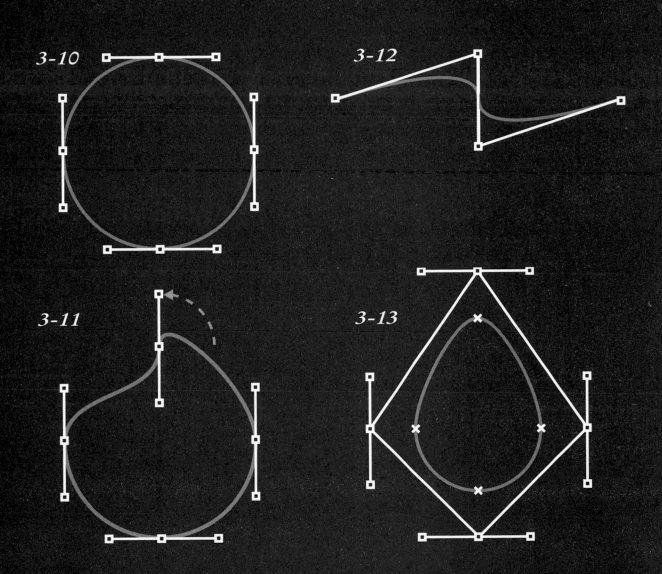

3-10

3-12

3-11

3-13

Figure 3-12 is an illustration of a line made with NURBS (Non-Uniform Rational B-Splines). NURBS are splines that have their control points offset from the actual line. Figure 3-13 shows a NURBS circle with the top control point pulled upward. Working with NURBS or regular splines will produce the same results, it is just a matter of preference for the artist.

Most spline-based programs were originally written for high-end, professional use so they are normally associated with high-end workstations. However, more and more desktop programs are incorporating spline technology to create hybrid and pure spline modelers. Figures 3-5 through 3-13 provide a simplified explanation of the use of spline technology in computer software.

SOLID MODELERS

Solid modeling is a terrific way to produce extremely accurate models while maintaining flexibility during the modeling process. It's most often used by CAD engineers and draftspersons who depend on their computer-generated models for mass production or precision objects.

A solid modeler treats the geometry created in a 3D program as a solid object with volume and weight. In reality, taking a bite out of an apple creates a counterspace (or pit) in one part of the apple; the volume and weight of the apple decrease accordingly. A solid modeler treats geometry in the same way; however, it has the added advantage that the user can move the counterspace around inside the object. Thus an architect can cut a doorway through a wall, move the doorway closer to the window, reduce its size or eliminate it altogether, all without having to recreate the wall each time.

The more common surface-modeling programs, in contrast to solid modelers, represent geometry as only the surface of the shape. Biting into a surface-modeled apple would reveal an empty shell with a piece missing (rather like a hatched egg).

Due to the more natural and accurate method of dealing with geometry, it would seem that solid modeling is always better than surface modeling. That's not necessarily the case. There is a drawback to solid modeling. The CPU makes more calculations in order to determine the entire volume of a complex shape, so rendering and screen redraw are often much slower. Because of their slower speed and generally larger file sizes, many solid-modeling

3-14

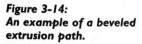

Figure 3-14:
An example of a beveled
extrusion path.

FLAT SHAPES

STRAIGHT EXTRUSION

BEVELED EDGE

INVERTED BEVEL

**CURVED EDGE WITH
LONGER EXTRUSION**

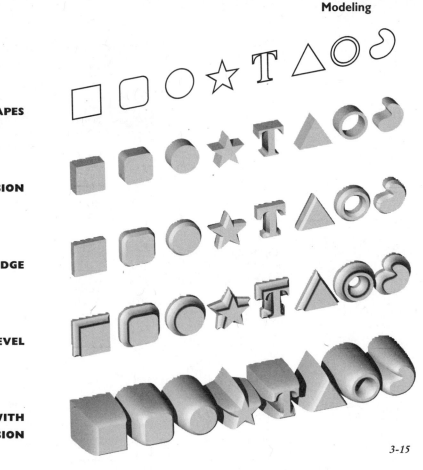

3-15

programs compensate by limiting or omitting their abilities in animation and rendering. I'm sure there are many exceptions to the rule, but as I write this book, Alias/Wavefront, SoftImage, 3D Studio Max, LightWave, ElectricImage, and Studio Pro are all surface modelers. As computers become faster and more powerful over the next few years, solid modeling may become a defacto standard in all high-end programs.

MODELING FUNCTIONS

No matter what kind of 3D program you use — be it a polygonal, spline-based, or solid modeler — you will probably use similar tools and functions to create your artwork. Naturally, each software package has its own strengths and idiosyncrasies, but almost all packages have versions of several basic functions that you find yourself using almost every time you make a model.

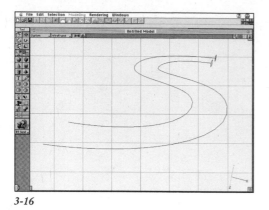

3-16

3-17

EXTRUDE

Extrusion is the most common and perhaps the most useful function you can perform in 3D. It's the process of taking a two-dimensional shape and pulling it out into the third dimension. The extrusion tool works like a virtual pasta maker. If you've ever used a real pasta-making machine (or seen one in use) you know that there is a template with a bunch of holes at the end of the machine. The dough is pushed through these holes and pasta is extruded on the other side. If the holes are round, you get spaghetti; rectangular holes make linguini. In the computer, almost any shape, from a simple line to the floor plan for the Pentagon, can be extruded. Figure 3-15 shows how the extrusion process turns a group of simple shapes into a variety of 3D objects.

EXTRUSION PROFILE

An extrusion profile is the path the surface of the object follows

Figure 3-16:
Strata StudioPro interface showing a set of shapes and spline curves that will be used for a path extrude.
Figure 3-17
The final path-extruded "rails."
Figure 3-18:
Four of the steps used to create a shape using the revolve tool.
Figures 3-19 to 3-22:
Steps showing one way to skin a duck.

3-18

as that object is extended into 3D space. For example, an object going straight back will have a straight line as an extrusion path. If the line is bent slightly, the object will have a beveled edge. Varying the shapes to be extruded with different extrusion paths, you can make an infinite array of distinct objects. It is such a useful tool that I could literally fill all of these pages with remarkably different shapes made just with the extrusion tool.

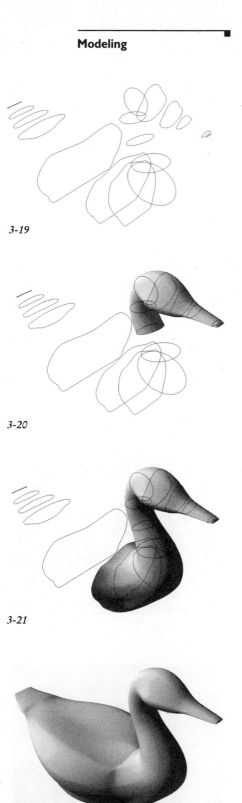

3-19

3-20

3-21

3-22

PATH EXTRUDE

In the same way an artist can customize a shape by changing the extrusion profile, they can create even more complex objects by extruding along a specific path. This function is known as a path extrude. In Figure 3-16 two simple squares are extruded along the same path. The computer works out the complexities of each bend in the tube to create a deceptively elaborate shape which looks like winding train tracks (Figure 3-17).

REVOLVE (LATHE)

The revolve tool is also commonly known as the lathe tool. This tool spins a curve on its axis to produce a symmetrical three-dimensional shape. When using the revolve tool, the artist first draws a 2D line. As that line is swept along an axis, the revolve tool works like a blade on a real lathe, cutting a shape out of 3D space. Figure 3-18 shows the steps used to make a Greek vase using the revolve tool.

SKIN

Working with the skin function is like putting together a pup tent. First you assemble the frame in the outline of the final shape, then you stretch the material over the basic skeleton. In Figure 3-19, I drew the "ribs" which comprise the frame of a duck decoy model. Each of these ribs is a cross section of the duck

3-23

3-24

starting with the tip of the beak and ending with the tail feathers. I then attached the ribs, starting with the beak, to form the surface of the model. It took a good deal of tweaking throughout the process to shape and place the ribs correctly. (For an example of complex skinning, see the tree illustrations in Chapter 8. To see the duck decoy fully rendered with a surface texture, see Chapter 5.)

DEFORM

Deformation is one of the most fun, and simultaneously frustrating, aspects of modeling in 3D. If you are working with a spline-based or hybrid spline/polygonal modeler, you can literally grab the individual points of the geometry and pull them around in 3D space. It's kind of like working with virtual clay. In a few minutes, even a novice can make a blobby, amorphous object out of a simple sphere. The problem with spline deformation is trying to get it to actually look like something, or even harder, look like something real or attractive. It's very easy to get confused about which point you are pushing or pulling and to wind up with a big mess rather than a detailed, accurate model. I'm sorry to say there is no trick to mastering spline modeling other than practice, patience, skill, and talent. Most of the mid- and high-range programs including Alias Power Animator (which is considered the best modeler on the market) use spline deformation a great deal, so it is an extremely useful skill to learn.

Figure 3-23:
A simple sphere with four points pulled out an equal amount using a spline-deformation tool.

Figure 3-24:
The same sphere with a few too many uncontrolled spline deformations.

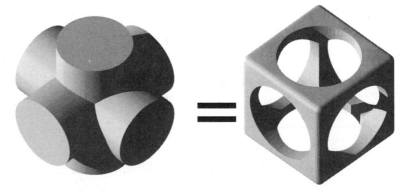

3-25

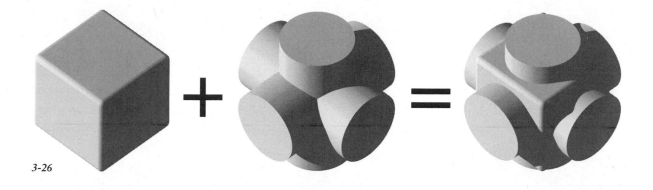

3-26

BOOLEAN

Boolean functions are extremely useful modeling tools which were only available in high-end programs, but are now commonly found in almost every mid-range program, too. A boolean subtraction enables the artist to delete the geometry of one shape or group of shapes from another shape or group of shapes. In Figure 3-25, three cylinders were oriented in the x, y, and z directions and were then grouped. A boolean subtraction was performed deleting the group from a cube to form a distinctive new complex shape. Making this same shape with any method other than boolean subtraction would be a very long and difficult task. With this tool, it took about three minutes.

Figure 3-25:
Boolean subtraction.
Figure 3-26:
Boolean addition.
Figure 3-27:
Transparent shape created by boolean addition of three cylinders and a cube.
Figure 3-28:
Intersecting transparent cylinders and a cube.

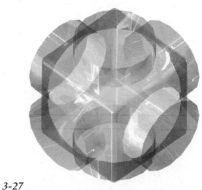

3-27

3-28

I used boolean addition in Figure 3-26 to turn the same group of cylinders and the cube into a single shape. I could have achieved the exact look of boolean addition by allowing the shapes to intersect each other because you can't see what is going on inside the cube. But, there are some cases where you need to make a single boolean surface instead of just intersecting shapes. For example, if the cylinders and the cube are transparent, the affect of an intersecting shape versus a single boolean shape becomes more apparent.

As you can see, Figure 3-27 was created with the boolean function. Figure 3-28 is a render of the same original shapes intersecting. Note the dramatically different reflections generated by the two separate methods. Boolean additions may also be helpful when animating objects because it is easier to work with a single shape than a group of interconnecting objects.

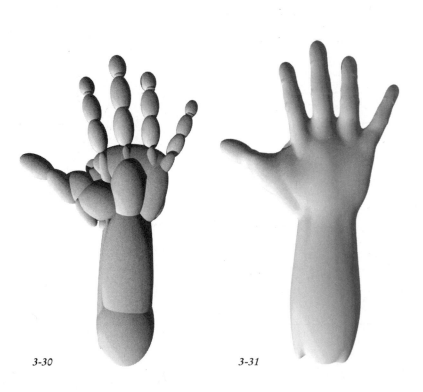

3-29

3-30

3-31

METABALLS

The metaball tool is usually used to develop organic shapes. Metaballs work like mercury. If two blobs of mercury in a dish are brought closer to each other, they start to deform and stretch as their near edges attract. In close proximity, the separate blobs of mercury will fuse to form a single object. In Figure 3-29, I placed two spheres close to each other. When I turned on metaballs, they formed a link. If I increased the attraction factor, the link between the two spheres would become thicker. In Figures 3-30 and 3-31, I made a hand by resizing

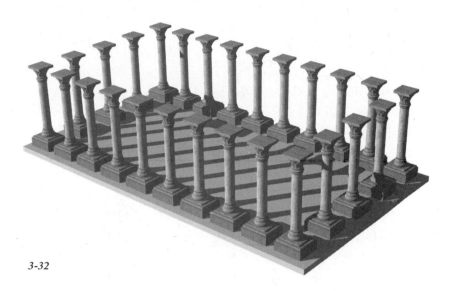

3-32

3-33

3-34

3-35

and carefully placing about 40 spheres near each other, then applying the metaballs tool.

REPLICATE

Creating an exact replica of an object is very difficult for humans, but very simple for a machine. Every commercial 3D program has the ability to replicate (or duplicate) a shape or group of shapes. Replication is the fastest way to make complex models and almost every artist depends heavily upon this simple-to-use feature. In Figure 3-34, a single column (Figure 3-33) was replicated nine times along the x axis to make a row of columns. The first and last columns were then selected, grouped, and replicated along the z axis (Figure 3-35). For the final step, the entire row of 10 columns was grouped and replicated once along the z axis at the appropriate distance (Figure 3-32). Once the model of the column was made, the entire process took about five minutes. You can see how an artist can easily make most of an acropolis or the Temple of Luxor just by repeating a single column.

Figure 3-29:
Two spheres before and after using the metaball tool.

Figures 3-30 and 3-31:
A complex group of spheres in the shape of a hand before and after the application of the metaball tool.

Figures 3-32 to 3-35:
Illustrations showing multiple replications of a single object.

INSTANCES

Replication is a very simple and powerful tool. However, each time the objects are copied, the file size doubles. In the column example, the file size would be 26 times the original if the geometry of the column was copied each time. To cut down on the problem of massive files, most programs will allow the artist to instance an object. When an object is instanced, the computer is told to display a copy of the original object at another point in space. The instance is only a place holder. The computer refers back to the original object for the geometry information so if the original is modified in any way, the same thing will happen to all of the instances. In Figure 3-32, I am showing you one column 26 times.

While instancing will do wonders for file size, it will not help very much when rendering the scene. In order to draw the scene accurately, the computer must treat each instance as if it had its own geometry. A scene that may have taken only a few minutes to make with instancing, may take hours to render. The solution to the render problem is optimization.

MODEL OPTIMIZATION

Every experienced 3D artist has come across the problem of working with large, unwieldy computer files. When a model gets too large, even the fastest computer may slow down to a mind-numbing speed. Working with a large, inefficient file can be a frustrating production nightmare. But what if the specifications call for multiple views of a detailed, complex environment and you don't feel like shelling out $70,000 or so for a high-end workstation? Those of you who have paid attention to the sub-head above know what the answer is: optimize your model. Reducing the number of polygonal surfaces for which the computer must account by replacing complex shapes with their simplified counterparts is one of the most efficient means of creating a smaller model.

In the following example, we are going attempt to place a large number of semi-transparent, highly reflective containers against a flat vertical surface. In layman's terms, we are going to put 100 bottles of beer on the wall.

Figure 3-36 shows a detailed model of a beer bottle. Note the bottle has multiple texture maps and is quite detailed, even to the point of showing some of the carbonated bubbles. This model works well for a foreground object or a scene with just a few objects, but it's impractical to use many of these bottles in a single scene. It would be very easy to replicate the highly-detailed model 99 times, but that would create an unworkable file. If the bottle was copied (not instanced), the polygon count would literally blow up to 100 times the original size. Even if you instanced the bottle, the rendering engine would still have to calculate 100 times the original geometry.

3-36

Figure 3-39 is only a half bottle. This modification was actually quite easy to make. I adjusted the lathe tool to turn only 180 degrees rather than the full 360 degrees. The resulting object has half the polygon count of the original. Of course, there are some limitations to using half a bottle. The viewer can only see the object from a limited point of view and you will not get the same kind of accurate reflection as you get with the original model. This reduced geometry version is very useful if you want to display 10 or 20 bottles from medium range. But there is still much more you can do to optimize the scene.

To reduce the polygon count even further, make a cut-out silhouette of a

Figure 3-36:
Rendering of a complete
model of a bottle.

beer bottle (Figure 3-41). Render out a single bottle from the front view with no distortion. Take the rendered image and bring it into a 2D program like Adobe Photoshop or Illustrator. (Some 3D programs have very good 2D drawing tools which will work fine for this process.) Use the Bézier or spline function to draw a path around the edge of the bottle. (Illustrator has an autotrace function that works quite well for this step.) Save the Bézier curve and import it into your 3D application. Make sure the cut- out has a surface so it is not just an outline. Apply the render of the bottle as a texture map. To avoid a white line around the texture map where the object is not covered, make sure the texture map is slightly bigger than the shape to which it is applied (about 1 percent larger is plenty). These cut-outs of the bottle will have very low polygon counts and can be replicated a great deal without adversely affecting rendering times.

3-37

Polygon count can be cut down even further with transparency maps. Figure 3-43 shows a "billboard" picture of a row of bottles. In 3D design, a billboard is a picture of a three-dimensional object on a two-dimensional plane. The billboard was created by rendering the original detailed bottle along with a mask of the silhouette. The mask of the bottle was applied to a single flat polygon as a transparency map. Next, the picture of the bottle was aligned over the transparency mapped on the billboard. The picture and transparency map were repeated 10 times over the face of the plane. The flat plane was placed on the shelf in front of the wall. With transparency mapping you can make as many bottles as you need without significantly changing the polygon count.

Figures 3-37:
Reduced geometry version
of the bottle shown in
Figure 3-36.

Even though there is very little difference in the look of a transparency-mapped billboard from real geometry when viewed from the front, there is a great deal of difference in the way the computer will render the image. The billboard rendered in about one tenth the time. A two-dimensional billboard, however, has some serious drawbacks. When viewed from an angle, the illusion of 3D can be broken and when viewed from the side, billboards literally disappear. (For more on transparency mapping see Chapter 5).

3-38

Figures 3-38 and 3-39: 10 reduced geometry bottles from front and three-quarter views.

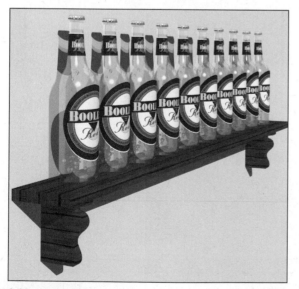

3-39

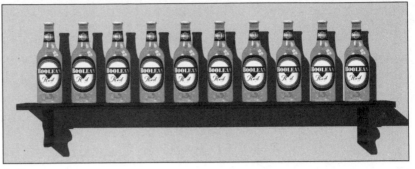

3-40

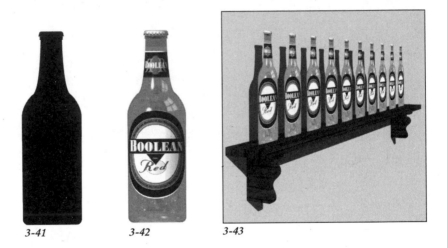

3-41   3-42   3-43

Figure 3-40:
Billboard of ten bottles of beer from the front.

Figures 3-41 to 3-43:
Silhouette and picture map of bottle, three-quarter view of billboard bottles.

The best way to achieve the appearance of 100 identically shaped objects is actually a combination of the methods discussed above. Billboards are an excellent solution if the subject matter is kept in the background. The fully modeled bottle will hold up to extremely close scrutiny while the half-rendered bottle works well in the mid-range. If you place a fully modeled bottle at both ends of each row of billboard bottles, it will hide the flatness of the billboards when viewed from the side. A few well placed 180 degree bottles interspersed with the rows will also add a bit of variation so the objects will not appear too uniform.

There is no rule for how many billboards versus modeled

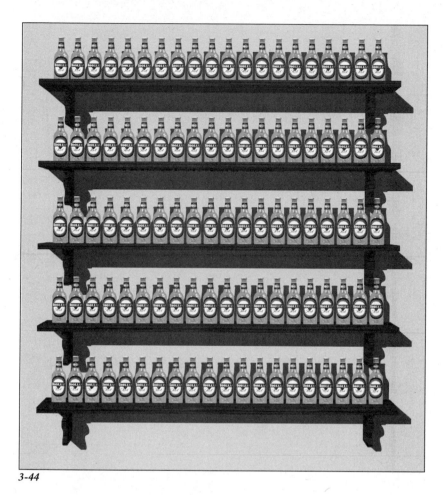

3-44

Figure 3-44:
*One hundred bottles of
beer on the wall.*

objects to use in each scene. There is also no rule stating how
much render time and file size will be saved by using billboards
and reduced polygon models. It depends on the shape and detail
of the original model, the size of the texture maps, and the kind
of software you are using. It's safe to say that if you are planning
on putting 100 bottles of beer on the wall, you should start
thinking about model optimization. Now, if one of those bottles
should happen to fall...work on your animation.

CHAPTER 4

Lighting

Imagine this: You come home from work at about 6:00 P.M. You turn on the living room lamp and set it so it doesn't cast shadows. The room is still a little dark, so you set the ambience to 20 and the room becomes uniformly 20 percent brighter. To create a more romantic mood you change the angle of the sun, tint it red, and then place an invisible blue light source by the couch. Now you're set for the night. Obviously, you would have a harder time doing that in real life than inside a computer. The remarkable thing is most people accept that computer-generated lighting effects have a flexibility not bound by the laws of physics, yet they are perplexed when lighting in the computer does not perform in a totally natural manner An artist must always remember that computer-generated lights and effects are rough simulations of reality. Therefore, a 3D designer must often work in a counterintuitive way to obtain the desired lighting for a scene. As most people know, "counterintuitive" is just computer speak for "really confusing."

In reality, light from a single source may reflect off multiple surfaces, gradually dissipating as it is absorbed as heat and color. In oversimplified terms, a purple object absorbs all light that is not purple and reflects only the purple light in the spectrum. If that purple light comes into contact with a red surface afterward, it divides again throwing off only the reddish/purple part of the spectrum. Matters are complicated more because each surface has varying degrees of reflectivity and texture.

BASIC LIGHTING

There are four basic kinds of lights that can be found in almost any 3D program: ambient, directional, point, and spot. Of course many programs augment these basics with special effects and simulations of specific light sources such as florescent tubing and

ambient light

photographer's fill lights. However, almost any lighting situation can be simulated and just about any lighting problem can be solved with a combination of these four basic lights.

AMBIENT LIGHT

An ambient light is a uniform and directionless light source which means it affects every surface of a model evenly, decreasing the harshness of shadows and brightening light areas by an equal amount. If you set the ambient light to 50 percent of black, a totally black object with no other light shining upon it will be gray. Most artists dislike using significant ambient light because it gives their work a flat, washed-out, unnatural look.

If you are creating a scene with a very simple lighting set up, ambient light may be more of a hindrance than a help. For example, if you want to show a flashlight cutting through the dark in a windowless room, a strong ambient light would destroy the effect of harsh shadows from a single, weak light source. Let's say, however, that you want to show a room on a bright winter day with sunlight streaming through the windows after bouncing off the snow and then reflecting off the white walls and shiny floor. Your most effective lighting solution would be a high ambience with only two or three other light sources.

Ambience is also very useful when a scene just gets too dark. A good example is what I call the "clock radio light phenomenon." The little green numbers on your clock radio are often barely visible in bright daylight. Yet when you wake up in the middle of the night, the entire room has a dim greenish glow caused by the relatively small symbols reading 3:30 A.M. (Usually, I take this opportunity to go into the next room and check on my

directional light

point light

rendering.) If I was trying to recreate this lighting scenario in a 3D program, I would place a green point light with a short falloff in front of the clock and use a dark green ambience to give an overall moody green cast to the scene. The combination of a weak point light and colored ambience will create an environment with subtle shadows and no completely black areas, simulating a dark room to which our eyes have grown accustomed.

In some rare circumstances, you may want to use a strongly colored ambient light. A red light in a photographer's darkroom and a light bluish tint for underwater scenes are both instances where an artist would want an overall colored light to affect an entire scene.

DIRECTIONAL LIGHT

A directional light, sometimes referred to as a global light, generally has no specific point of origin and has a consistent intensity and direction throughout the scene. It is probably the best tool the 3D artist has to simulate sunlight. The sun is so bright and so far away that the light rays hitting the Earth appear to be parallel and uniform in intensity. If we were to view our solar system as an accurate scale model we would see this is clearly not the case, but from the point of view of an artist observing lighting effects on Earth, that does not matter.

spotlight

A directional light has a strong advantage over ambience because it casts shadows and illuminates only the side of an object facing the light, which gives the scene the illusion of depth. Unlike ambience, you can add multiple directional lights to a model.

4-1

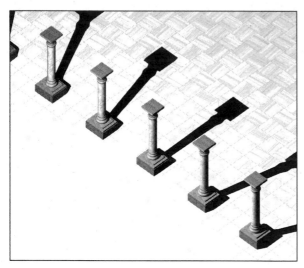

4-2

Figure 4-1:
A line of columns lit by a directional light.

Figure 4-2:
The same columns illuminated by a single point light.

Figure 4-3:
Columns lit by a spotlight with soft edges.

Figure 4-4:
Columns lit by the same spotlight with a hard edge.

POINT LIGHT

A point light emanates from a specific location in three-dimensional space. It has the ability to cast shadows and it is omnidirectional (it shines in all directions from a single point). Unlike ambient and directional lights, point lights can be set to affect a specific area and experience falloff. Point lights are extremely useful when recreating realistic lighting situations. For example, in reality a street lamp can only illuminate a relatively small area of a highway. If an engineer determines that the effective range of a light source is 60 feet, he may place the lamps about 50 feet apart, allowing the lit areas to overlap. This is because a light weakens in intensity as it spreads farther from the source. In 3D design we refer to this effect as falloff. To accurately depict any light source except the sun, an artist must use falloff.

SPOTLIGHT

A spotlight works very much like a point light with the added feature of directional constraints. If you set a spotlight to shine along the z axis with a 15 degree radius, you will create a thin cone of light emanating from the starting point. A spotlight with a 360 degree radius is identical to a point light.

Just like a point light, a spot should have a falloff setting limiting the distance of its influence. Most mid-range to high-end 3D packages will also have a setting to determine the softness of the edge of the spot. A spot with the softness set to zero, pointing directly at a surface creates a perfect circle of light. The same spot with a high softness setting produces a bright spot which gradually dissipates into the darkness.

LINEAR AND EXPONENTIAL FALLOFF

Some software packages give the user a choice of how they want light to decrease in intensity over distance. With linear falloff, the light fades at an equal rate as it spreads from the center point. So a light with a 10 foot linear falloff gets weaker every foot, dissipating completely by the tenth foot. With exponential falloff, an artist can make the light an equal intensity for a distance around the center point and then set the distance where the falloff will start and end. Usually the exponential falloff is represented by two adjustable circles around the light source. Exponential falloff does not follow the laws of physics, but it is useful for representing a large light source, such as the ball of a street lamp, where the entire object appears to be equally intense.

SUNLIGHT AND SHADOWS

Simulating realistic sunlight with shadows is one of the hardest things to do when working in 3D. Computer-generated shadows fre-

4-3

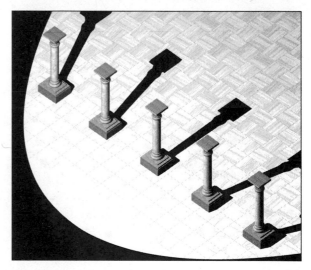

4-4

quently have a very hard edge and lack the subtleties caused by refracted light. These heavily contrasting, hard shadows often give the final rendered image a surreal Dali-esque look. Many programs attempt to alleviate this problem by enabling the user to select "soft shadows" when applying a light source. This function blends the edges of the dark shadows into the background at the expense of shorter render times. While the softer edge helps increase the subtlety of the image, it is not a perfect solution.

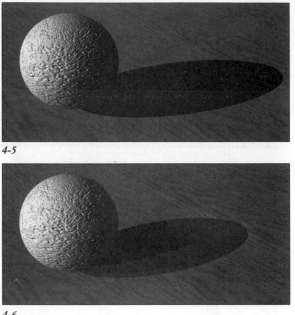

4-5

4-6

A good way to simulate more natural sunlight is to create a cluster of directional lights at slightly different angles rather than use a single source. First place one directional light in the scene at the desired intensity and correct angle. Then decrease the intensity slightly (by maybe 20 percent or so). Place two more lights in the scene offset at about five percent angles from the original light. Make each of the new lights very dim (about 10 percent of full intensity). Finally, place a dim fill light in the scene that points in roughly the opposite direction from the "sun" cluster. Figure 4-5 shows a ball with a single directional light and ambient light. Figure 4-6 uses a cluster of lights for the "sun" with a dim fill light. Note the greater sense of depth and realism in the second image.

GELS

Gels are commonly used by 3D artists, filmmakers, and scenic designers to suggest the shadows and effects of off-camera objects and lights. Surprisingly simple gels can be used to suggest complex model and lighting situations. For example, almost every 3D computer program comes with a venetian blind filter which is just black and white stripes that break up the light. It is also common to use a silhouette of a group of leaves or branches to imitate the speckled light as it filters through a thick forest. There are, of course, almost infinite applications of shadow gels. In Figures 4-7 and 4-8, a transparency map of a cloud and a piece of a wrought iron fence were placed in front of a light source. Note how different the same spotlight looks just by changing the gel.

Gels can be used to add a significant level of realism to a large outdoor scene. The simplest and most efficient lighting solution is to place a strong directional light (or group of lights) in the scene parallel to the angle of where the sun should be. If the sun

Figure 4-5:
Ball on a table lit by a single directional light.

Figure 4-6:
The same ball lit by a cluster of directional lights and a fill light.

Figure 4-7:
Spotlight with a transparency map of a cloud as a gel.

Figure 4-8:
Spotlight with a transparency map of a wrought iron gate as a gel.

is lower in the sky, you may want to give it a yellow or orange tint.

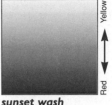

sunset wash gradation

The simple solution of a single directional light combined with some ambience for an outdoor scene often works well if you are showing a single object or a very small area, but it is not effective for a large vista. Light from a setting sun does not always appear totally uniform, especially over a large area. Specifically, the refraction from the atmosphere may cause the light to be a deep red at the horizon and a bright golden yellow at the cloud level. In 3D, this effect can be achieved relatively easily by placing a gradated gel of yellow to red over the directional light.

When using a colored gel, you should use a standard white (uncolored) light as the source. This assures a more accurate representation of the colors in the gel. It also reduces the variables as you run lighting tests. Using only standard lights with gels is very helpful because most programs allow you to save your gels as a separate file so you can reuse them to achieve the same effects in other models.

gradation with added noise

When making a realistic, complex model of a large outdoor space, a gradation gel is usually not enough to simulate realistic lighting. When you view a large landscape, the light is rarely uniform in intensity throughout. Clouds, haze, and various weather conditions break up sunlight into lighter and darker patches. If you look out the window of an airplane, the patterns of light and

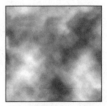

cloud gel

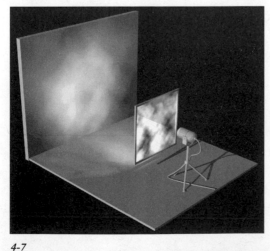

4-7

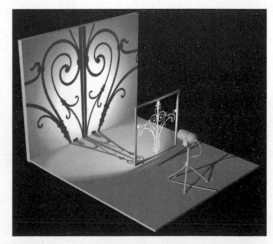

4-8

Figure 4-9:
With exponential falloff, the light has a consistent beam in the center and then dissipates within the parameters set by the user.

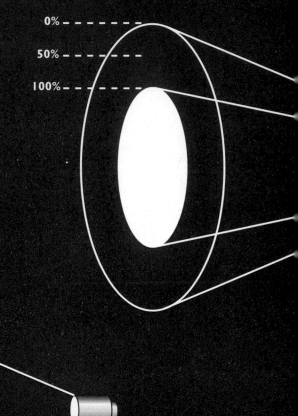

0% – – – – – – –

50% – – – – – –

100% – – – – – –

Figure 4-10:
Note that when there is no falloff setting, the intensity of the light is consistent throughout the spread of the spotlight.

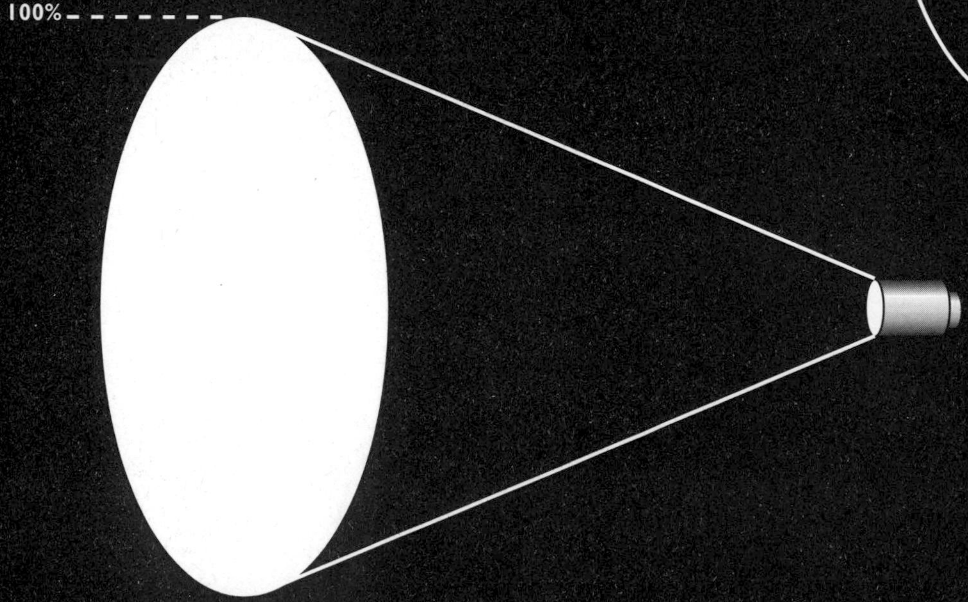

100% – – – – – – – –

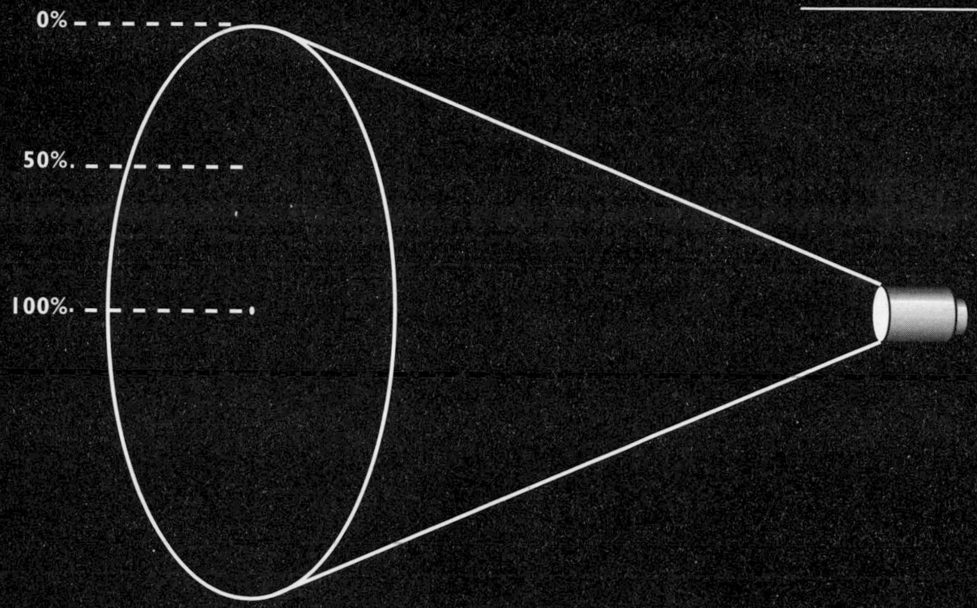

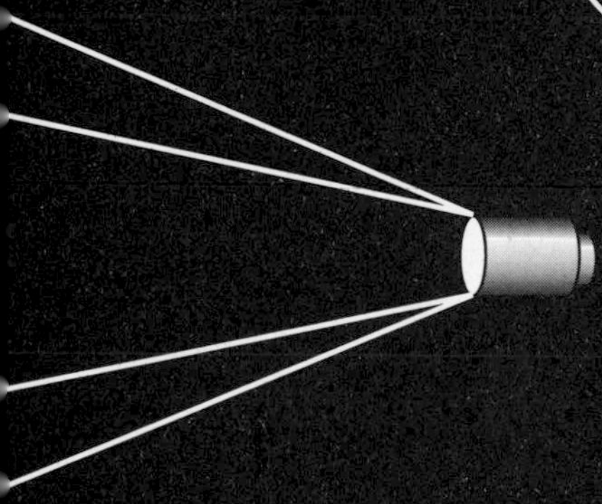

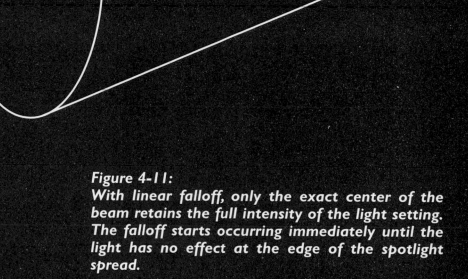

Figure 4-11:
With linear falloff, only the exact center of the beam retains the full intensity of the light setting. The falloff starts occurring immediately until the light has no effect at the edge of the spotlight spread.

Figure 4-12:
From left to right above are the simulated effects of hard edge, exponential falloff, and linear falloff spotlights. Note how much dimmer the linear light appears because it is only at one hundred percent intensity at the exact center.

4-13

Figure 4-13:
An exaggerated lens flare atop a monolith in outer-space.

Figure 4-14:
Outdoor vista with a transparency map used to create clouds and their shadows on the water.

Figure 4-15:
The same scene with a cloud gel added over the directional light.

Figure 4-16:
A view of the model from the top showing the transparency map clouds, the tiled texture of the water, and the land on the bottom of the image.

Figure 4-17:
Volumetric lighting effect of fog coupled with a glow special effect.

dark on the ground are obvious. With CGI it is a good idea to add noise to the gradation or layer a second gel of clouds to make the light uneven. The cloud filter can be a grayscale image so it does not alter the color of the sunset. Note that when you add the cloud gel, the original light may dim noticeably depending upon the density of the gel. To solve this problem, increase the contrast and brightness of the gel so that there are totally white areas which will not reduce the intensity of the light. Don't go overboard lightening the gel though, or you will not be able to see the cloud map at all.

If you have been following the above steps, you now have a gradating colored light with subtle variations in intensity that will blanket your entire model. It makes for a very attractive effect, but it may still lack the necessary detail for a realistic looking scene because the gels over a directional light don't give you a great deal of control over the effects of the gels. The shadows caused by the gel will be very soft and the variations in color will usually appear as subtle blends because they are spread over the entire model.

Using Opacity Maps as Gels

To create the shadow of a specific cloud on just one area of the model, place a transparency map of a cloud on a rectangle that is located perpendicular to the light source and out of the camera's view. Position the transparency map of the clouds precisely so the shadow of the clouds falls on specific parts of the terrain. This technique is also extremely useful when using a tiled texture map for the ground plane because it breaks up the repeating pattern.

Special Effects

Almost every good 3D artist will tell you the same thing about special effects: Use them sparingly! I, too, have been guilty of the "kid in the candy store" syndrome when I've just received a new plug-in or special effects package. Lens flares, volumetric lighting, and glowing objects have become common tools included with every mid- to high-end software package. There are, of course, many more options available depending on the individual program, but these are the basic special effect tools you will use most of the time.

4-14

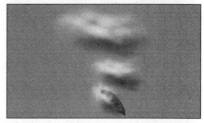

4-15

4-16

4-17

4-18

Figure 4-18:
Very simple model of an empty room illuminated by a directional light and an ambient light.

Figure 4-19:
The same room with two fill lights used to simulate refracted light.

Figure 4-20:
The same model with a volumetric "mist" effect added to the directional light.

LENS FLARES

Lens flares used to be considered an undesirable artifact caused by improperly shading the lens near a bright light source. Since the multiple rings and rays of light were a clear sign that the image was recorded on film through a camera lens, it often broke the illusion of reality for the viewer. There are many exceptions to this case, most notably the famous sunrise over the black monolith in *2001: A Space Odyssey*. Since the 3D artist is often trying to recreate the effects of film and not physical reality, the lens flare becomes a useful visual cue to perpetuate the illusion.

There are two important things to keep in mind when using a lens flare effect. In reality, lens flare generally occurs when the light source is much brighter than the surrounding environment. If you have a high ambience and a lens flare on a relatively weak source, the image will look very artificial. On a more technical note, most software packages treat a lens flare as a kind of post-rendering effect. This means the geometry and the lighting are drawn first, and then the effect is laid over the attached light

4-19

4-20

source. So, the lens flare itself will appear to be in front of every object, even those in the foreground.

VOLUMETRIC LIGHTING

Volumetric lighting is basically light you can see as it moves through space. The physical effect is actually caused by light refracting off tiny particles in the air. The best examples of this effect in real life are light streaming through the window of a dusty attic or the headlights of a car piercing through a foggy night. Using volumetric lighting can create very dramatic effects. In some cases, it drastically alters the mood of the piece.

Technically, most programs allow the user to attach a volumetric effect such as fog, mist, or haze onto a light source, object, or atmosphere, in which case they are referred to as atmospheric effects.

Figure 4-21:
A lamp is an example of a practical light source, as opposed to an off-camera or invisible light, because it is an object in the scene that provides light.

In Figures 4-18 through 4-20, the same scene of light streaming through a window was rendered with and without a "mist" effect attached to the light outside the window. Although this is an extremely simple and easy scene to create, you can see how the dramatic lighting makes for an attractive composition. It is interesting to note that the same scene with the addition of a volumetric effect (Figure 4-20) took about 50 times as long to render as the original (Figure 4-18). That's three hours versus seven-and-one-half straight days! You have to really love the mist effect before you tie up your machine for that long. One reason it took so long is that the program I used required that I turn on the "cast shadow" option so the wall would block out the light, allowing the mist to come through only the window opening. The shadow

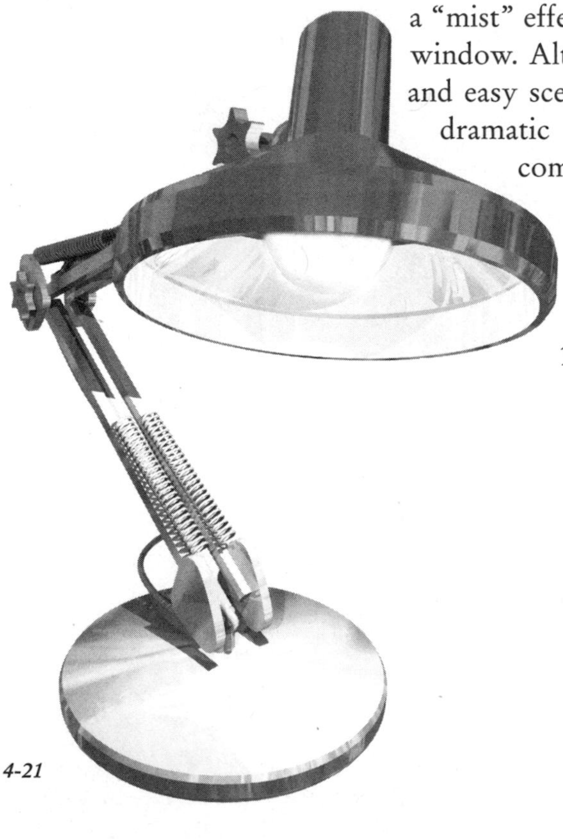

4-21

effect added about another 10 percent onto my render time. Not all software packages will experience such a dramatic performance hit when using volumetric effects, but as a rule they will slow down rendering time significantly. A large factor contributing to slow render times is that, unlike lens flares, volumetric effects are calculated along with the geometry and light render.

When most people think of computer-generated lighting effects they are reminded of slick, Hollywood-style special effects and titling. If you are willing to throw subtlety and nuance out the window, you can create very dramatic volumetric effects like the image in Figure 4-17.

Most programs that include volumetric effects provide a number of parameters such as air density, turbulence, diffuse and specular color, shadow casting, animation, and detail. You can spend many hours trying to come up with the perfect effect. I suggest you carefully study some of the preset examples that come with your software and adjust the closest set of existing parameters to create your own effect. When you are done, save the effect with a name that reflects what it is (like "BlueFog"). Make a small render and keep it in the same directory as your application. Six months from now, you probably won't remember all of the settings, but you can browse through your library of rendered effects to pick the most appropriate one.

VISIBLE LIGHT SOURCES

Visible light sources are perhaps the most useful and common of all lighting effects. When placing a light in a scene, only the light emanating from the source is visible, not the light itself. The actual light is usually represented by an object placed near the light source, set so it does not cast shadows with a halo or glow effect attached. Each program deals with the technical procedures for creating visible light in a different way, but most of them treat visible lights in the same way lens flares are created. They render last, like a post-effect, after the majority of the image is rendered.

I think the most common error an artist makes when creating visible light sources is to model the entire light bulb first, and then set it to glow. A lightbulb is not usually the main subject matter

4-22

4-23

of a scene. It is a simple glowing object and has no shading or shadow. Therefore, it can be represented as a simple sphere or, in some cases, as a flat shape.

SIMULATING REALISTIC LIGHTING

Three-dimensional computer-generated artwork has a tendency to look like, well, it was generated on a computer. Inexperienced artists often blame the computer. It takes a good deal of know-how and experience to control the technology and work within its limitations to produce unique and attractive work that looks like it was produced by an artist and not a machine. The best weapon an artist has against producing plastic-looking work is close observation of reality.

When I teach my class in 3D animation, one of the first assignments is recreating your bedroom. The real environment of your bedroom is so familiar, it is usually taken for granted. When the students place the lights in their three-dimensional models, they usually have the revelation that even though all their lights are in the right place, the shadow, intensity, and color of the light is all wrong.

Most rendering algorithms create very harsh shadows and don't deal with reflected light well. As a matter of fact, they don't deal with reflected light at all. If you place a white ball against a bright red wall in reality, the light bouncing off the wall colors the ball pink. Now try the same thing with a raytrace renderer and 3D software. The ball will remain white.

Software programmers are constantly developing more sophisticated rendering algorithms to attempt to emulate realistic lighting. However, there is a trade-off between rendering time and realistic lighting effects. For example, a render using a radiosity algorithm may take about 50 to 100 times as long as the same scene rendered with a phong algorithm. A phong render will generally handle soft shadows, reflectivity, and transparencies badly, leaving many of the tell-tale signs of computer-generated art. On the other hand, a good radiosity render will be very close to the effect of shooting a scene with traditional film. Unfortunately, radiosity takes so long to render a complex scene that a calender is almost more appropriate than a stopwatch to calculate render times.

There is, of course, a good compromise: raytracing. Basically, raytracing calculates the path of light directly from a surface or light source into the point of view of the camera. Reflectivity and transparent objects are rendered very close to radiosity, while shadows and indirect light will have a harder, less natural feel. Most 3D artists find themselves using raytracing or phong for reasonable render times, however with each new jump in processor speed, radiosity becomes more and more practical. (See Chapter 6.)

An experienced 3D artist will frugally place small light sources around a scene which are separate from visible light sources to create a greater level of realism. Figures 4-23 through 4-27 show the same exact scene rendered 6 times

Figure 4-22:
Cutaway of the set for the lighting examples in Figures 4-23 through 4-27 with models of the practical lights and camera shown for clarity.

Figure 4-23:
Overexposed ambient light washing out details and shadows in the set.

Figure 4-24:
Relatively high ambient setting with the addition of a strong point light in the center of the model.

4-24

Figure 4-25:
The same set using high ambient lighting with the addition of a strong directional light.

Figure 4-26:
A more natural-looking lighting scenario created by keeping a strong directional light and reducing the ambient lighting. A point light was added to the center of the scene to soften shadows and suggest the refraction of sunlight.

4-25

using different standard lighting configurations. Figure 4-22 is a view of the top of the room without the ceiling. It gives you a pretty close approximation of the lighting set-up I've used. There is an overhead light above the couch in the center of the room, a spotlight pointing out of the fireplace, and a small point light near the far window. There is also directional and ambient lighting in this scene. By varying the combination and intensity of these lights I can achieve a variety of moods and visual effects.

Figure 4-23, the first render, uses a very high ambience in combination with a very weak directional light. Notice how the details in the moldings, variations in the wall, and almost all the shadows are missing. The image appears bright, but lacks detail and depth. This is a classic case of overcompensating for the harsh shadows inherent in 3D art.

Figure 4-24 still has a relatively strong ambient light. However, it is used in conjunction with a strong point light in the center of the model. The render still maintains its bright appearance, but the details in the walls and soft shadows from the furniture create a better illusion of three-dimensionality. Note the strong highlights on the couch, which is the object closest to the light source. Without these highlights, a great deal of the effort that went into making this detailed model would have been wasted. Although I believe this render is a vast improvement over the lighting solution of just using high ambience, it's still lacking the subtlety and realism the model deserves. A high ambient light is usually associated with either multiple, deliberately spaced light sources such as the lights at a ball field during a night game or the fluorescent ceiling panels in a bus terminal, or bright sunlit spaces with reflective or bright colored surfaces such as the washed out lighting of a sunny day at the beach. In this case, I created a high ambient light with a single, interior light source. Most observers would know there is something strange and artificial about the scene.

In the next render, Figure 4-25, the ambient light is almost exactly the same as that in Figure 4-24, but the strong center point light has been replaced by an intense directional light shining through the window. The pattern of the panes of glass gives the furniture a great deal of visual interest as well as a touch of realism. This is a good example of using directional lights to simulate sunlight. With no falloff and perfectly parallel light rays, the pattern of light and shadow is projected cleanly across the room. Since the primary light is a single, hard-edged source outside the room, we lose the detail in the angles of the walls and the furniture outside the influence of the directional light.

4-26

Figure 4-27:
A dramatic effect generated by a strong single light source with a gel simulating a fire in the fireplace.

4-27

The fourth render, Figure 4-26, solves some of the lighting problems by reintroducing the overhead point light into the scenario. The overhead light is dimmer than in the second example, but it provides some detail and secondary shadows. Most viewers looking at this image would accept that the shadows and highlights thrown off the point light are partially caused by the natural reflection and diffusion of the sunlight. To make a slightly more realistic scene, the ambience was taken down about 10 percent to imply a later time of day when it would be more appropriate to turn on the overhead light.

In the last render, Figure 4-27, there is only one very strong primary light source along with ambient lighting. A spotlight was placed inside the fireplace with a cloud gel filter in front. The same light then shines through the grating in front of the fireplace creating the effect of a double-gel filter. I had to play a bit with the fireplace screen to obtain believable shadows. The screen had decorative balls at the joints which cast huge spherical shadows on the ceiling. An actual fire in the fireplace would be a large light source that would not cast such a definite shadow, so I turned off the shadow casting option for those objects. The grating itself is actually just a small transparency map on a two-dimensional plane which worked fine for the distance from the camera. But, when its shadow was projected around the room, you could see the jagged stairstepping of the pixels in the map. I had to go in and add a higher-resolution texture map for this render. Using the cloud map gel through another transparency map is a great way to work if you plan on animating. If I was to animate this scene, I could move or morph the gel map to create varying shadows within the framework of the stationary screen. It is important to note that a light with a cloud gel should be made brighter to compensate for the grayish tones of the map.

All of the above images are very frugal with their use of light sources. When lighting a scene, you should think of the RAM and processor of your computer as wattage. Too many lights and you might not have enough power. Instead of blowing a fuse, you will get an equally annoying error message or the scene might not render in an average lifetime.

If you are producing a single image with only one render, you can be much more extravagant with lighting than when you are working on animations or realtime rendered graphics. There is no "best way" to light a scene. Experienced artists still spend hours of trial and error tweaking the lighting parameters to try to achieve their desired results. So, if I am asked the question, "How many lights should be used in a computer model?" there is really no single simple response. However, if I'm in a rush, I'll usually answer, "Five."

CHAPTER 5

Textures

It is easy to make the argument that good texture mapping is the single most important factor determining the difference between mediocre and successful 3D artwork. You could probably make the same case for lighting, modeling, and composition. However, with texture mapping, an artist can take a very simple model with very straightforward lighting and create the illusion of a complex and detailed environment. In its simplest form, texture mapping is applying a veneer of pattern or color onto the surface of a model. With a little practice and a great deal of patience, an artist can use texture mapping to simulate effects like fire, flowing water, and smoke, or to create finely detailed bumps and crevices that would be almost impossible to model. With the use of transparencies in texture mapping, there is literally no limit to the variety of objects an artist can efficiently portray.

Textures can be patterns created from mathematical formulas (procedural textures) or they can be made from a picture imported into a 3D program (image maps). There is a great deal of flexibility with both methods. An artist can achieve dramatically different results by just "tweaking" the application of procedural textures and image maps.

PROCEDURAL TEXTURES

A procedural texture is an image that is generated by a mathematical formula. Fractal geometry has often been referred to as the mathematics of nature because the visualization of certain equations produces images that look like clouds, trees, leaves, veins of marble, and other naturally occurring shapes and textures. There are many programs and plug-ins available which create beautiful two- and three-dimensional fractals for use in modeling.

Procedural textures have the added bonus that fractal formulas can use repeating algorithms to generate images that can be

5-1

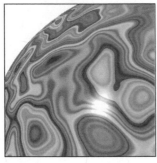

5-2

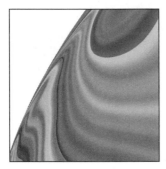

5-3

Figures 5-1 to 5-3:
The same procedural map
viewed at various
magnifications. Note how
the resolution of a
procedural texture holds
up even under extreme
magnification.

viewed at any magnification without losing resolution. When a fractally-generated image is applied to the surface of a 3D model the texture will not break down no matter how close the camera gets, and since procedurals are a mathematical formula, they take up very little disk space compared to a rendered picture. Many artists rely heavily upon procedural methods as a first choice for almost all of their texture mapping because they can be generated within the 3D program, have very little overhead, and do not require a linked texture map.

Many artists who work on high-end programs that run on dedicated UNIX boxes or customized NT machines also rely more heavily on procedural mapping than image maps. This may be due, in part, to the fact that image editing software, 2D drawing tools, and dedicated scanners are relatively expensive and are rarer on high-end workstations than their desktop counterparts. An artist working on a Mac or a PC can easily toggle between image editing programs such as Illustrator, Freehand, Painter, and Photoshop. The images can be imported, modified, and placed as texture maps in a 3D program easily. An artist working on a Silicon Graphics platform, however, can either pay almost twice the price for the same image editing software as a desktop artist, or can set up a second desktop machine to create texture maps.

IMAGE MAP

Image maps are sometimes referred to as texture maps or picture maps depending on the program. An image map is basically a two-dimensional picture that can be applied to 3D geometry. Extensive use of image maps is essential for the creation of photo-realistic work or any piece that requires a high degree of detail.

TILED TEXTURE MAP

Tiling a texture map works just like tiling your bathroom, only you don't have to wait a day for the grout to set. You start with a rectangular texture of a certain size and then repeat it over a given surface. In the case of the bathroom tile, the texture has a seam (the grout line). A very simple seamed texture is shown in Figure 5-31. In this case, two black lines on a white background form a reverse L. When repeated, the L makes a grid pattern.

5-4

5-5

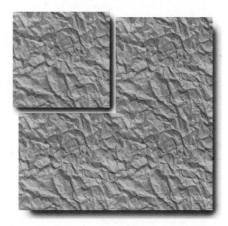

5-6

The simple tiled shape is much more efficient than creating a picture map of an entire grid. The L tile can create an infinitely large picture map in your 3D model while referencing an image that's a fraction of the actual surface area.

When using an L shaped texture, the tiling is immediately apparent, but more often than not, tiled texture maps are designed to appear seamless. A seamless texture is achieved when patterns on the left and right borders, and on the top and bottom of the image, line up.

The image map in Figure 5-4 is a tiled texture of crumpled paper. It is duplicated horizontally in Figure 5-5. It's replicated again in Figure 5-6 with the original tile separated for clarity. This is an excellent example of a seamless texture because the creases and folds appear random and there is no discernible repeating pattern when the texture is replicated.

There is a common pitfall many artists experience when trying to create natural-looking, seamlessly tiled textures. If a texture has too much variation in tone or contrast, your eye can discern a visible pattern as it is tiled. The regular pattern makes the texture look artificial and contrived (just like a wallpaper pattern).

Figures 5-4 to 5-6: Tiled texture map of crumpled paper. Artwork courtesy of Artbeats Software, Inc.

Figures 5-7 to 5-9: Some variations achieved by adjusting the parameters on the same procedural texture.

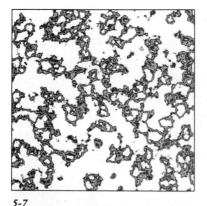

5-7

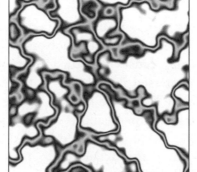

5-8

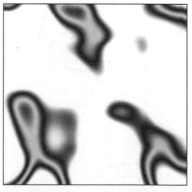

5-9

Figure 5-10:
Brick texture applied to a
cube using cubic mapping.

Figure 5-11:
Brick texture applied to a
cube using planar (or
projection) mapping.

Figure 5-13:
Brick texture applied to a
cube using decal (or label)
mapping.

5-10    5-11

MAPPING TECHNIQUES

The way a texture is placed on the geometry has a very significant impact on the look of the final object. Surprisingly, there
seems to be relative uniformity in the industry in the naming
and utilization of mapping techniques. Higher-end programs
offer more alternatives, but almost all 3D software programs
have a few of the following basic texture mapping methods
available: cylindrical, spherical, cubic, planar, decal, U/V, and
bump mapping.

CYLINDRICAL MAPPING

If your texture map was a soft taco shell, you would be making
a burrito with cylindrical mapping. The texture is mapped in one
direction around the geometry, connecting at two opposite ends,
creating a cylinder. This method of mapping does not work well
with most complex objects or models where accurate mapping of
the top and bottom are crucial.

SPHERICAL MAPPING

Most programs have a spherical mapping feature that pinches the
texture at the top and bottom so it will fit well around a ball. This
usually causes a distortion of the image because the texture is
compressed at the poles . A perfect example of this is an image of
Earth. When laid flat, the Arctic Poles look huge and you won-
der why Greenland is not considered a superpower. When the
same image is wrapped around a globe, the polar regions com-
press to more accurate proportions.

5-12

Figure 5-12:
Spherical map of a world
map on a globe.

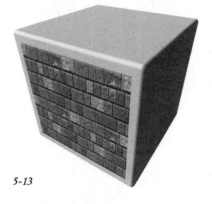

5-13

CUBIC MAPPING

Cubic mapping lays the same texture on all sides of the object in proportion to the dimensions of the side. This is an extremely effective tool for placing precise textures on relatively square objects, or less precise maps on complex objects with many facets. The cubic map resizes the texture to the plane, but it does not distort it like spherical, cylindrical, or planar mapping. I'm often surprised at how many times cubic mapping is appropriate for objects that look nothing like a cube.

PLANAR MAPPING

Do you remember when you were a kid and your dad showed vacation slides on the living room wall? Sometimes the projector wouldn't be straight and some of the image would hit the couch and whatever else was within a 10 foot radius. Well, if you don't share those memories you've missed out on one of the most boring aspects of childhood, as well as an excellent metaphor for the behavior of planar mapping. A planar map, or projection map, as

Figures 5-14 to 5-16: Oops mapping—not all texture maps are appropriate in every situation. From left to right: cubic map with insufficient coverage, spherical map applied to a cube, planar map applied at an off angle.

5-14   5-15   5-16

it is sometimes more accurately referred to, is placed upon the geometry from a single point of view. Instead of wrapping around the model, projection maps stretch and distort so they create an accurate image from the original point of view.

DECAL MAPPING

A decal map works like a planar map that is applied only to a defined area of a model. You would, for example, use a decal map when making a label on a wine bottle. The paper is thin enough so you would not see an edge unless the camera was very close. Using decal mapping, a picture map of an opaque label can be applied to the bottle giving the illusion of two surfaces close together.

U/V MAPPING

U/V mapping was considered a high-end mapping tool until relatively recently. By the time this book comes out, most mid- and high-level programs should have this feature. All other mapping tools treat the geometry as if it was a simple shape. The artist then picks the method which fits best. With U/V mapping, the texture is matched to the coordinates of the geometry so the texture follows the contours of even a complex object. U/V mapping has an added advantage when animating objects. If you animated a character with a planar map, the texture would slide all over the character as it moved. The U/V map would move and deform with the object. With the growing popularity of character animation, U/V mapping is becoming an essential feature for almost every 3D package.

BUMP MAPPING

Bump mapping is one of the most useful methods of creating complex textures and objects out of simple geometry. Almost all programs treat the process of bump mapping the same way. A

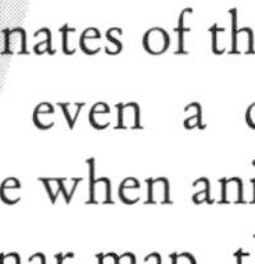

Figures 5-17 and 5-18:
The blurred spot was placed onto flat geometry as a bump map to make an indentation.

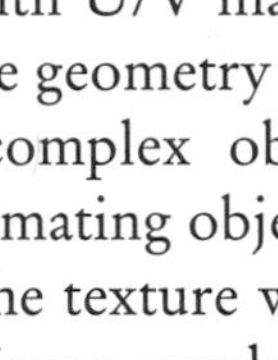

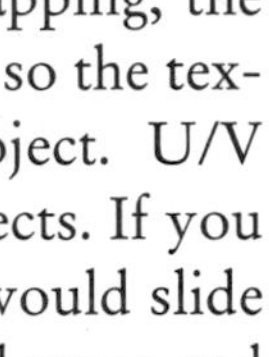

Figure 5-19:
The same image from Figure 5-17 was reversed to create a bump.

5-17   5-18   5-19

grayscale image is placed on the surface geometry. The lighter areas appear to rise from the surface while the darker areas form an indentation. In reality, everything, even chrome bumpers and cue balls, have irregular surfaces. So in theory, every object in a 3D model should have an associated bump map, even if it's very subtle. The problem is bump maps add significant time to the render process, so it is only wise to use bump maps on foreground objects or if the bumpiness of the texture makes a significant contribution to the image. Very often, a 3D artist will save render time by using a photograph of a rough surface, drawing a bumpy surface in Photoshop or other digital imaging software, or by actually rendering out a bump-mapped texture in a 3D program and then applying the picture of the bump map to another model. I have seen many instances where a project

Figures 5-20 and 5-21: The illusion of detail on the column in Figure 5-25 was created by adding the two very simple tiled bump maps in Figure 5-21.

5-20

5-21

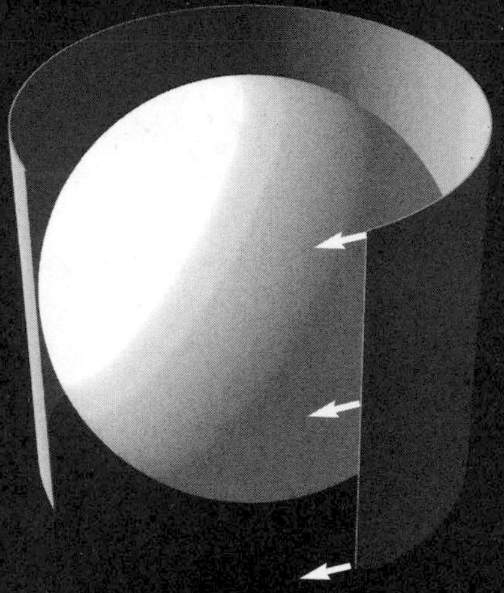

Figure 5-22:
A cylindrical map will wrap around an object in one direction only, stretching the texture across the top and bottom.

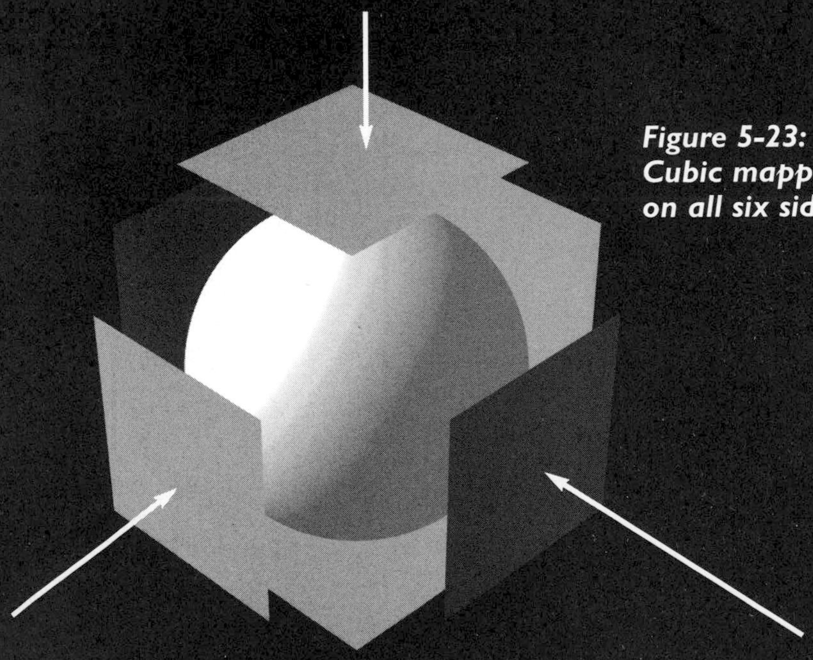

Figure 5-23:
Cubic mapping repeats the texture on all six sides of an object.

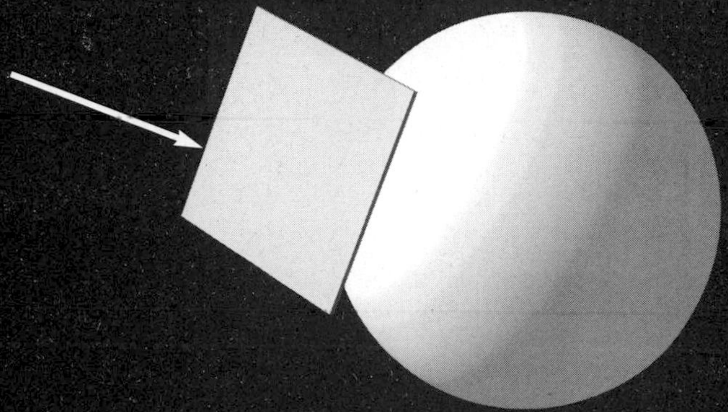

Figure 5-24:
Planar mapping works like a projection of the texture from a single source. If viewed from straight on, it looks flat. If viewed from the side, the texture will be distorted.

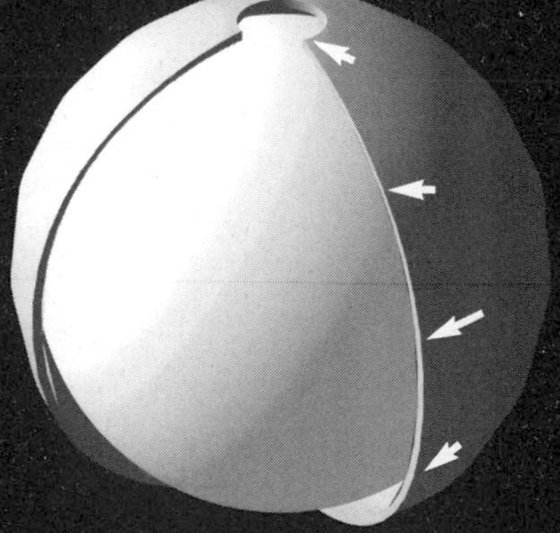

Figure 5-25:
Spherical mapping pinches the texture at the top and bottom so it follows the contours of a round object.

Figure 5-26:
U/V mapping attaches a texture to the specific geometry of an object (in the "U" and "V" directions) so the texture will follow the contours of the model. It is often considered an advanced feature and is not available in some low-end packages.

5-27

5-28

5-29

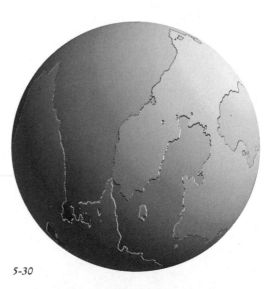

5-30

literally will not render (even on high-end systems) because there are too many bump maps. Nevertheless, it is an extremely useful feature for creating realistic detail.

Figure 5-22 is a very simple example of bump mapping. The flat plane renders out as a concave (Figure 5-23) or convex (Figure 5-24) shape depending upon the grayscale value of the applied image.

Novices are often confused by bump maps because the actual geometry of the model is not deformed. It only appears that way when rendered. To confuse matters more, a bump map does not affect the silhouette of the geometry. Look at the bump-mapped sphere in Figure 5-30.

Figures 5-27 to 5-31:
The same texture was applied to a sphere as (counterclockwise from left) an image map, reflection map, bump map, and transparency map.

Reflectivity ⟶

Index of Refraction ⟶

The above chart shows a transparent cube inside a transparent sphere. The index of refraction increases (left to right) from 10% to 100% in 10% increments. The reflectivity increases (top to bottom) from 10% to 100% in 10% increments. The cube inside the sphere becomes more distorted as refraction is increased while the transparent geometry becomes more visible as reflectivity is increased.

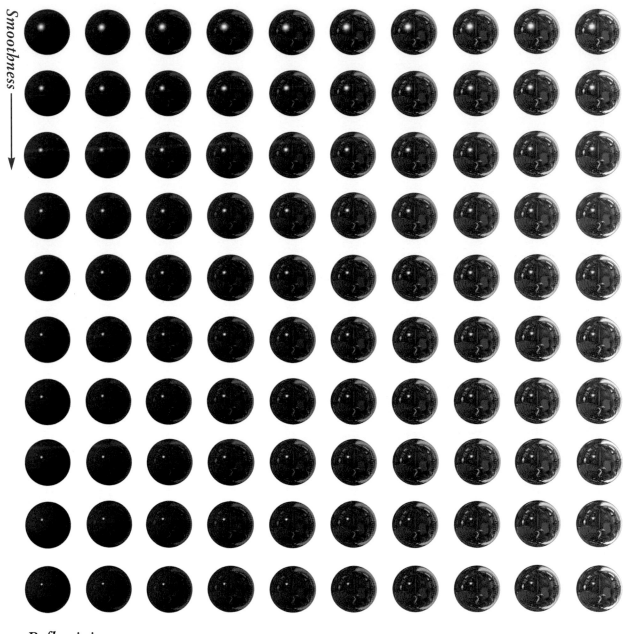

Smoothness ⟶

Reflectivity ⟶

The above chart shows the effects of smoothness and reflectivity on a surface. Reflectivity increases (left to right) from 10% to 100% in 10% increments. Smoothness increases (top to bottom) from 10% to 100% in 10% increments. Note how the highlight decreases as smoothness increases yet this does not affect the reflectivity of the surface.

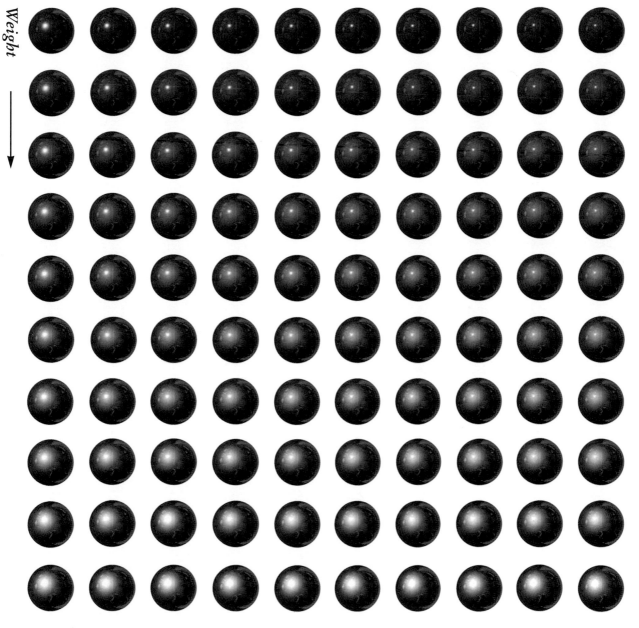

Weight

Smoothness ⟶

The above chart shows how weight percentage affects the smoothness of a surface. Smoothness increases (left to right) from 10% to 100% in 10% increments. Weight increases (top to bottom) from 20% to 200% in 20% increments. As the weight increases, the halo around the highlight spreads, increased smoothness decreases the size of the highlight.

These pages:
Screen shots and final
render of a Spanish Galleon
produced by Chuck Carter
*for **The National***
***Geographic** Website based*
on original sketches by
Richard Schelct.
©1997, National Geographic

Opposite page:
Promotional piece produced
by Chuck Carter.

This page:
Various renderings for a
proposed CD-ROM game.
All images by Chuck Carter.
© Reactor, Inc.

*This page and next:
All images created by Guillermo
Leal Llagun using 3D Studio
Max.*

Opposite page, top left:
Computer illustration and photography by Payne Rowlett.

Top right:
Illustration using 3D Studio Max and PhotoShop courtesy of Dreamworks Interactive.

Bottom:
Image by the author for a proposed CD-ROM game.

This page, top:
Old Hotel Front from Internet and CD-ROM-based title "The Forgotten."
www.forgotten.com. © 1997 Ransom Interactive. Troyan Turner.

This page:
Isometric view and view from inside a tiled set used for a flythrough animation. Images by Bonita Rutigliano Engel.

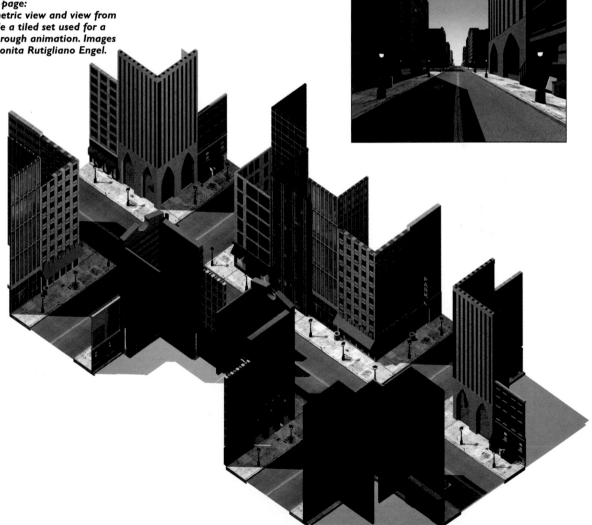

Rendered using the Lightscape Visualization System. Courtesy of and copyright (c) 1994 Ayasamo Architects Inc.

Rendered using the Lightscape Visualization System. Courtesy of and copyright (c) 1994 A.J. Diamond, Donald Schmitt and Company, Toronto, Ont.

Rendered using the Lightscape Visualization System. Courtesy of and copyright (c) 1996 Festival Hall Development Ltd. Creator: M.L. Starr, Toronto, Ont.

Opposite page, top and this page:
Atrium. Courtesy of A. J. Diamond, Donald Schmitt and Company (Toronto, Ontario). © 1994.

Opposite page, bottom, from left to right:
Castle: Courtesy of Agata and Andrzej Wojaczek (Toronto, Ontario). © 1995.
pmnt: Courtesy of A. J. Diamond, Donald Schmitt and Company (Toronto, Ontario). © 1994.
Festival: Courtesy of Festival Hall Development, Ltd. M.L. Starr (Toronto, Ontario). © 1996.
All images rendered with Lightscape™ radiosity renderer.

This page:
Photorealistic images rendered with the Lightscape™ radiosity renderer.

Top:
Courtesy of Design Visualization Partners (Santa Monica, CA). © 1996.

Right:
Courtesy of View by View, Inc. (San Francisco, CA). © 1995.

See if you can notice how the edge of the sphere is still perfectly round even though there is a considerable bump on the surface facing the viewer.

DISPLACEMENT MAPPING

There is another very similar tool called a displacement map that deforms the geometry based upon a grayscale image. Displacement maps can be used to fashion natural-looking terrain and organic shapes that do not require a high degree of accuracy. Most artists find displacement maps a difficult solution for creating small, detailed, or accurate models.

TRANSPARENCY

As you become more experienced in 3D design you will find yourself using more and more transparency maps. Transparency maps are sometimes referred to as opacity maps. Because of the limitations of hardware, software, time and budget, and the general attitude of "anything can be done on the computer," the 3D artist must resort to many different workarounds to simulate elaborate geometry and photorealistic environments. One of the most commonly used and most versatile tools is the

Figures 5-32 to 5-34: A simple L shape was applied to the geometry of a sphere as a transparency map. By varying the coverage, the texture map can create a dome or a complete globe.

5-32

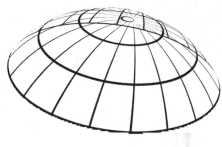

5-33

5-31

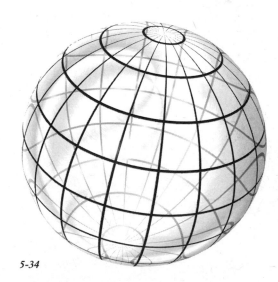

5-34

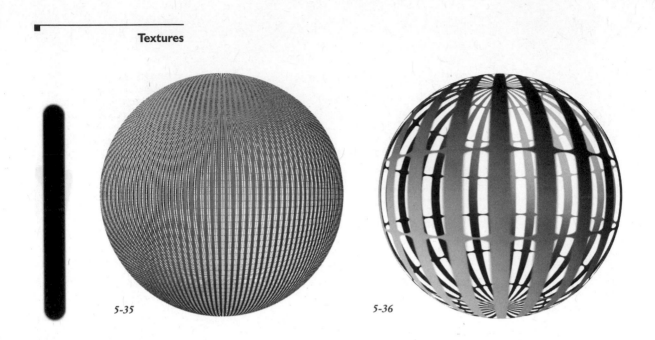

5-35   5-36

Figures 5-35 to 5-38:
*A very simple shape like a
line can be used as a
transparency or a bump to
create rich, complex objects
that require minimal effort
by the artist.*

opacity map. The simple L transparency map in Figure 5-32 was
repeated on a sphere to create the look of a faceted, clear ball
(Figure 5-34). Using the same principle, you can make a variety
of natural and complex shapes.

Figures 5-39 through 5-44 show how complex transparency
mapping is used to create organic shapes. To make a leaf, start
with a simple symmetrical shape, easily made in a drawing program like Illustrator, Freehand, or CoralDraw. Open up the
shape in Photoshop as a grayscale image. Don't anti-alias the
edges because this shape will become your opacity map and you
don't want the edges to be blurry and semitransparent. At this
point, the image is just a black-and-white silhouette which makes
an unconvincing leaf (Figure 5-39).

Next, create a picture map for the leaf. Working only within the
black areas, make a mottled green texture with a drawn in bump
for the veins and the stem of the leaf. This image looks kind of
like a fall leaf after it has been pressed in a phone book for a couple of months (Figure 5-40).

Now open up your 3D program and deform a simple two-
dimensional plane by pulling up the center vertices to create a
simple uneven curve (Figure 5-41). Don't make any attempt to

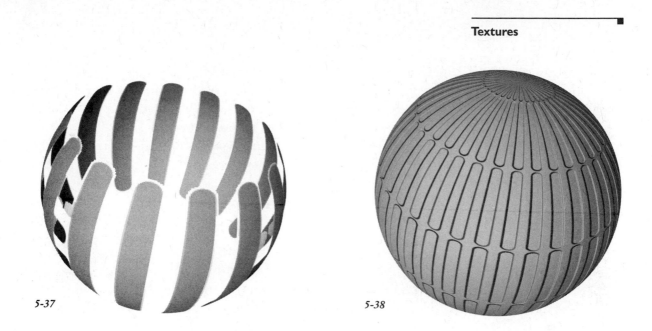

5-37   5-38

mimic the shape of the leaf with geometry; let the texture map do all of the work.

Place the texture on the shape, and see how parts of the leaf bend with the uneven shape to simulate an imperfect, natural object (Figure 5-42). Add the transparency map and set the texture parameters to 100 percent clear. Watch the leaf take shape (Figure 5-43).

At this point, inspect the leaf from many different angles, maybe even try a couple of test renders. Since the shape is just a curved two-dimensional plane you want to look for angles where the leaf seems to disappear. These are areas where you are not seeing enough of the top or bottom of the curved plane. Go back into the modeler and adjust the vertices until the problem is corrected.

Once you are happy with the leaf shape, place it against a contrasting background and see how well the opacity map and the shadows are working. If your texture map and opacity map are not lined up well, you will see an obvious line around the image when you view it against a white or black background. If the transparency map is not working right, the shadow cast will not be a good silhouette of the image. Naturally, shadow casting must be on for the test to work.

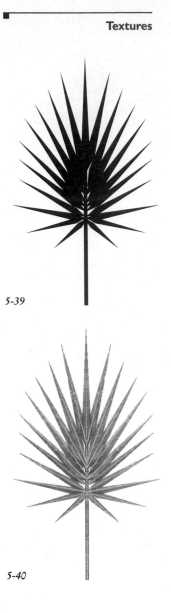

5-39

For the final image (used in Figure 5-46), I took the single leaf, replicated it a few times, then placed the shapes so the leaves pointed out from a central area. I was deliberately loose with the way I placed the instances of the leaves and I resized a few of them down on the top. Figure 5-45 shows the geometry of the plant without the use of transparencies. In Figure 5-46, the opacity maps are used. You can see that the shadows of the leaves contribute to the sense of dimensionality as much as the geometry and the textures.

You should also note that I left the texture with an overall even tone, resisting the temptation to make dramatic light and dark areas to create the illusion of dimension. If I had drawn strong shadows on the individual leaves, it would look wrong when I moved the leaf into different areas of light.

There are a number of excellent plug-ins and programs that generate organic shapes such as trees and smaller plants. Using transparency maps with limited geometry is usually a more efficient method which gives the artist greater control over the final result.

OPTIMIZATION

One basic principal holds true for every aspect of 3D design: Work efficiently. A model with lots of complex shaders and imported pictures can get out of hand very fast causing problems with file sizes and rendering times. I'm sorry to say that there is no rule for the amount of textures that should be applied to a given size model. It would certainly make everyone's life

5-40

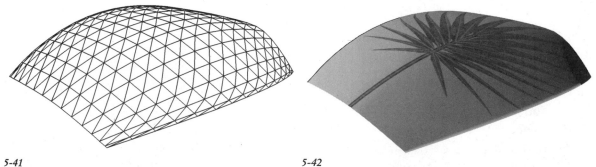

5-41

5-42

easier if there was a rule like "for every 1/2 megabyte of geometry make sure you use no more than 2 megabytes of textures." If you want, you can make up arbitrary standards, but the best way to work is through careful planning and common sense.

Even if you are only doing a simple model with a couple of applied shaders on a state of the art system, it's a good idea to get in the habit of optimizing your texture maps. If you are producing a tiled map, see how small you can make the tile before it starts to visually break down. With practice you'll be able to spot problems in the tile before it is applied to the model.

The most important factor in determining the size of the texture is how close the viewer will get to the object. In reality, objects get grayer and more desaturated as they fall off in the distance. When something is far enough away, the only thing the observer can see is color. A simple flat color will take almost no time to create and very little effort on the part of the artist to implement. Most objects at extreme distances can be mapped with just color, especially if you are using haze or an atmospheric effect.

Another simple trick is to import a small image of tiled noise. This texture can be applied to rough objects with a color overlay. For example, a haystack in the distance can be a simple dome with a yellowish noise texture. You can even apply the noise as a planar texture from the top view so it stretches around the dome to match the grain of hay. The same noise could be applied to distant ground with a tan color attached.

Figures 5-39 to 5-44: Illustrations of the steps used to make a billboard leaf. Counter-clockwise from top left: the silhouette of a flattened leaf; picture map created by drawing inside the silhouette; a two-dimensional plane with a subtle, uneven curve; the picture map applied to the geometry; the combination of picture and the transparency map generated from the original silhouette; the leaf with its cast shadow creates a convincing illusion of a complex 3D object.

5-43

5-44

5-45

For objects closer to the camera, but still in the background, consider converting the picture maps from 24-bit to 8-bit color. An 8-bit image is usually about four times as small as its 24-bit counterpart. If viewers get too close, they will see the ugly, jagged-edged squares indicative of low-resolution texture mapping. But from a distance, an 8-bit image may actually appear a little better. The reduction of colors often gives the picture a higher contrast which makes it "pop" better on screen. Of course this is all a matter of personal preference. In most cases, you will find there is no discernible difference in quality between low- and high-resolution textures in the distance.

Mid-range is perhaps the hardest area to optimize, especially in an animation with a moving camera, because what is mid-ground one second may become foreground the next. However, there are still a few tricks you can use for objects in the middle range, between background and foreground. For mid-ground texture mapping, create a few different versions of the texture in an image editing program like Photoshop. Let them vary in size by, let's say, 20 percent. Try the smallest texture on the object. If that looks good, cut it down again until you see pixilation or texture blurring. Some high-end programs actually automatically swap out geometry and texture as the viewer approaches distant objects. If you are using a desktop program, you can do essentially the same thing by keeping different resolutions of the same texture which you manually swap in and out as the camera moves through the scene. Although this sounds like a big pain, a few extra hours creating low-resolution textures may save weeks in render times.

A client of mine introduced me to one of the best tricks for optimizing textures. They were making a dynamic flythrough of a

5-46

pinball machine. The camera followed closely behind the pinball as it careened off bumpers, bells, and chrome slides. When they started running rendering tests, each frame was taking over a half hour to render. A quick calculation told them the final animation would take a few weeks on their fastest machine. After running a few tests, they discovered that the reflective surfaces were the culprit, slowing rendering down to a crawl. Therein lies the dilemma: You can't make a very convincing pinball machine without a lot of chrome surfaces and a shiny steel ball, but you can't get the job done in time if it takes you weeks to render all those shiny surfaces.

My client's solution was to render a single frame of the pinball machine without the ball. The chrome texture of the ball was then replaced with the nonreflective spherical map of the rendered machine, giving the appearance of 100 percent reflectivity. They used the same method on some of the other highly reflective areas. The camera moves so fast and frenetically through the scene, the viewer doesn't notice that the reflections don't change.

Figure 5-45:
A plant made out of billboard leaves with the transparency map turned off.

Figure 5-46:
The same geometry with transparency maps.

Needless to say, my clever client cut down on render times significantly and was able to finish the job on time.

The same technique can be used in many different situations. To humanize an environment, an architect will often place pictures on a wall when showing comps to a client. To make the hanging pictures in a comp look more realistic and detailed, you can take a two-dimensional plane, make it 100 percent transparent and highly reflective, then place it over every picture in the scene to simulate protective glass. In reality, it's actually very difficult to look at a picture with protective glass and *not* see a reflection of the surroundings. Placing the ghosted reflection of the room on the picture map before the image is imported into the 3D program solves the problem easily. Although the effect is subtle, it adds a great deal of realism to the scene. The pictures in Figures 5-47 and 5-48 show this technique at work. They took exactly the same amount of rendering time, however, Figure 5-48 has a much better feeling of being in a real space.

Textures are not always straightforward tiles or spheres. Complex geometry very often calls for some strange-looking solutions. In the following example, I made the model of a duck decoy using a skin tool. The only practical way to map a texture onto this figure was through trial and error. To start, I rendered

Figures 5-47 to 5-48: Renderings of an almost identical scene. The texture map inside the picture frame in Figure 5-48 was altered to include a ghosted picture of an interior and a blurred hotspot. The render time for both images was identical, but the image in Figure 5-48 appears to include reflective surfaces and additional light sources.

5-47

5-48

an orthographic side view of the duck. I brought the rendered image into Photoshop and crudely blocked out the general area of the eyes, bill, and feathers. I took the crude image and mapped it onto the duck. I tried U/V and cubic mapping, and finally chose a projection map as the easiest solution. After a couple of more rounds of repositioning the wings and other elements, I added the detail. The resulting map looks more like abstract art than a flattened duck (Figure 5-50). I could have used a 3D paint program which allows the artist to "draw" directly on a model rather than apply imported images. Three-dimensional paint programs may cut down on some of the trial and error when positioning the individual elements; however, they take a little bit of getting used to so you may find yourself inadvertently painting a duck's derriere instead of his beak.

Good textures can go a long way to enhance the beauty and realism of your model. There are many methods an artist can use to create complex texture maps like the image applied to the decoy. I have found there is no real shortcut, and the best results usually stem from trial, error, and patience. All of the effort is worth it because a skilled 3D designer can create the illusion of complex objects and rich environments through mastering the art of textures.

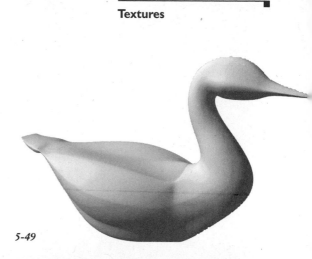

5-49

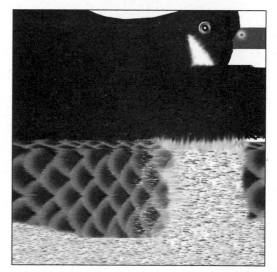

5-50

5-51

Figures 5-49 to 5-51: Model of a duck decoy and a complex texture map combined to create the final image.

97

CHAPTER 6

Rendering

The final stage of almost all 3D work is rendering the image. Just as an artist renders a painting, the computer completes a drawing of a wire frame model with textures, light, and shadow. There are many different forms of rendering, all of which are based upon mathematical algorithms. The same exact scene may look very different depending on whether the artist chooses radiosity, raytracing, scanline, or phong renderers. To make matters a little more confusing, the same rendering method in different software packages may have dramatically different results. It is through deliberate experimentation and practice that each individual artist learns which rendering method best suits his or her tastes and needs. Nevertheless, this chapter should help you get a jump start on understanding the process.

Without a doubt, rendering will be the greatest challenge to the patience of any budding 3D artist. Friends and family often chuckle at me when I tell them how I leave my computers to render a job over the weekend or even a long vacation. Large studios will often set up networked render farms or purchase exorbitantly expensive multiprocessor computers with maxed-out RAM and huge disk arrays just for the purpose of rendering 3D animations. Even with all that amazing equipment, most artists still complain about the time it takes to render their work. Invariably, there seems to be a trade-off between the speed of the render and the quality of the final rendered image.

So far the general solution has been to throw raw horsepower at the problem of render times. A computer optimized for 3D design will often have about 128 megabytes of RAM, a specialized graphics board, 4 gigabytes of hard drive space, and the fastest processor (or multiple processors) available. Most of this raw power will be used for rendering and screen redraw. I've seen many instances where an artist completes an entire model and

6-1

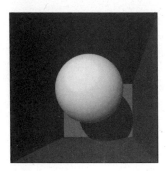

6-2

Figure 6-1:
Radiosity render of a sphere inside a cube which shows the diffuse shadows generated by just a single light source.

Figure 6-2:
The same model and lighting as in Figure 6-1 rendered using raytracing.

then can't render it without switching to a more powerful machine. If you are a freelancer, without access to more powerful computers, you might have to start from scratch, reducing the polygon count or rendering only parts of the model.

It sounds kind of scary, doesn't it? Well, it is. Every 3D artist has some horror story about the job the client wants to see "first thing in the morning" that just wouldn't render out at 4:00 A.M. I'm deliberately pointing out some of the problems that can be encountered when the artist doesn't plan well or has simply overestimated the capabilities of his hardware. To a beginning artist, an unrenderable model may seem like a disaster of biblical proportions. To a seasoned professional, it's just another opportunity to come up with a clever workaround and then brag to your friends.

RADIOSITY

In most artists' opinions, radiosity is the most photorealistic of all renderers. Radiosity treats each surface in the model as a potential light source, allowing light to bounce off and change as it comes into contact with the geometry. Radiosity simulates photorealism so well because of the sophisticated manner in which it handles light.

If you place a white ping-pong ball in a red box and shine a white light upon it, the ball takes on a pinkish glow. This is due to the fact that a red object will only reflect red light. The pink light on the ball is caused only by bounced light. Just like reality, the lighter the surface color, the more light bounces around the model. Figure 6-1 is a radiosity render of a ball in a colored box with a single light source. Figure 6-2 shows the same file rendered with raytracing. Because each surface is treated as a possible light source with the radiosity render, the shadows are softer and there is more detail in the darker areas.

Radiosity is the most accurate and, many would say, the most attractive rendering algorithm available. There are many different programs on the market with this feature. Depending on the model, hardware, and software, radiosity can take any-

6-3

6-4

where from two times to hundreds of times as long as other rendering methods.

RAYTRACING

By most artists' standards, raytracing is the next best thing to radiosity renderers. Raytracing creates an imaginary ray between the object and the camera lens, calculating light only between that object and the viewer. It does not calculate light bouncing between objects. Raytracing is an excellent method for showing reflective, refractive, and transparent objects. For example, water has a certain index of refraction, that is, a numerical value assigned to a transparent substance to gauge how much light bends when passing through it. If the water is in a clear glass, the glass will have higher reflectivity than the water but a lower index of refraction. Place a straw in that glass, then put the glass on a shiny table, and you will begin to appreciate the complexity made possible by raytrace rendering.

The largest single drawback to raytracing is that it does not handle light as well as radiosity which determines how each individual surface is affected by the environment.

Figure 6-3:
Raytrace image of a glass of water. The shaders of glass, water, and ice only differ in their refraction, reflection, and bump settings.

Figure 6-4:
The same image produced with a scanline renderer.

6-5

6-6

SCANLINE RENDERING

Scanline rendering is an excellent alternative to raytracing. It renders an image by calculating a series of horizontal lines. Scanline rendering is often much faster than raytracing and can produce a very similar result, though it usually does not handle transparency, refraction, and reflection as well. Scanline renderers vary in quality. In some cases the difference in quality is indiscernible from the more time-intensive algorithms, radiosity and raytracing. Scanline rendering is often used for animations where clarity of image is very important, but the subtler qualities of radiosity and raytracing are unnecessary.

GOURAUD

The Gouraud renderer is extremely fast. It renders objects smoothly, but shows complex textures only as rudimentary colors and patterns. Gouraud is a terrific renderer for quick comps and dummy animations because it usually has render times of just a few seconds per frame. However, reflection, transparency, and most atmospheric effects won't register with Gouraud rendering.

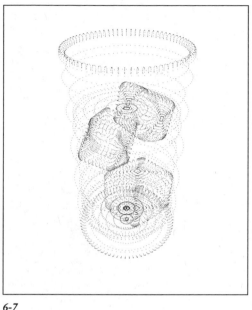

6-7

Many desktop 3D applications now take advantage of innovative software libraries which enable them to use Gouraud (or a very similar rendering method) for real-time display. Open GL (Open Graphics Library), developed by Silicon Graphics, Inc. is by far the most common library used for 3D. Other popular software libraries include Heidi, which is used with 3D Studio Max, and QuickDraw 3D, which is used with most Macintosh software. Most of the industry is currently standardizing to Open GL.

PHONG

A man named Phong Biu-Tuong developed a renderer which uses the properties of diffusion, shininess, and specularity to draw an object. He called it the Phong renderer. There are many different iterations of Phong rendering. Some have shadows, reflectivity, and transparency while others use only the basic elements of Phong rendering to produce images that are similar to Gouraud with more accurate highlights and textures.

BLINN

Blinn shading is similar to Phong except it uses diffusion, specularity, eccentricity, and refractive index to render an image. The end results of Blinn shading are similar to Phong, however, they will not have the strong, shiny highlights that are achievable with Phong. Blinn is not as common as the other rendering techniques, but it is very useful for rendering mat-textured, detailed objects.

Figures 6-5 to 6-7: Gouraud, wireframe, and point clould renderings of the glass from Figures 6-3 and 6-4.

WIREFRAME

Most of the time, only the artist sees a wireframe render. It's generally used in the working environment because the screen redraw is incredibly fast. I've found wireframe renderings of animations very useful for two important reasons: They render extremely fast and, when I'm showing a comp to a client, it's obvious the comp's a work in progress. Even though I'll often have the time to use a more complex and rich rendering method, I'll use wireframe because, sometimes, it's more difficult to explain to the client that their final animation will look exactly the same as what they are seeing, only it will have better reflective surfaces and a higher transparency recursion. Anyway, most clients think wireframe renders look cool and when they see them they feel like they are part of the process.

POINT CLOUD

The image in Figure 6-7 is the first time I ever saved a point cloud render. Up until now, I only used point cloud rendering while working on a model because it's probably the fastest way to view geometry. Point clouds are primarily used to draw geometry when the artist is looking for a very fast screen redraw. If an artist is working with a complex familiar model he will often toggle up

Figure 6-8:
Correct size raytrace render of a sphinx using anti-aliasing on the edges.

Figure 6-9:
The sphinx enlarged by a factor of 10 to show the jagged non-anti-aliased edges.

Figure 6-10:
The enlarged sphinx image using anti-aliasing.

Figure 6-11:
Correct size, non-anti-aliased image of a sphinx.

6-8

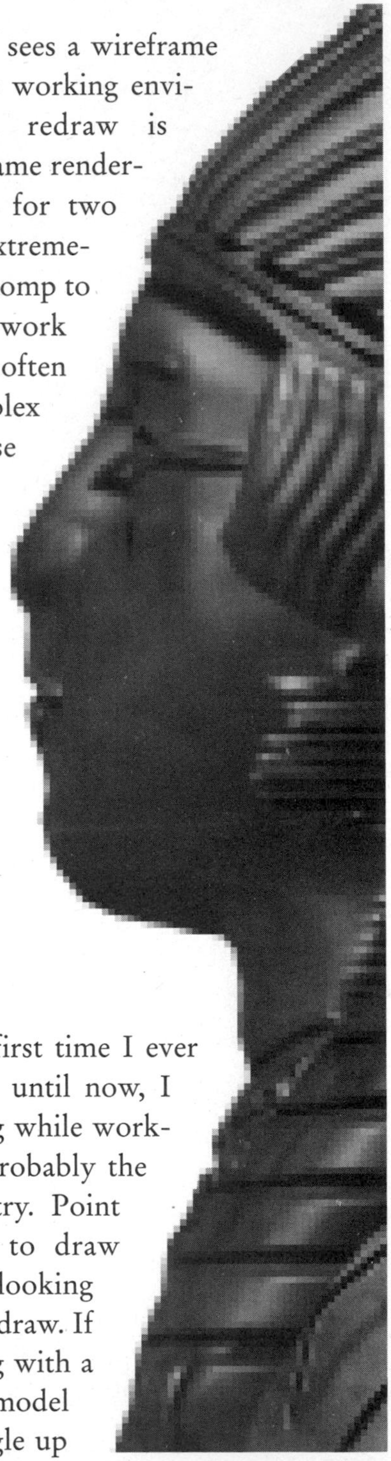

6-9

and back between point cloud and more detailed renderers to get a combination of fast redraw and detail. In
some cases, it's actually easier to select and work
with elements in a model when they are drawn
as a point cloud.

RENDER SETTINGS AND SPECIAL EFFECTS

ANTI-ALIASING

Anti-aliasing is simply the process of
smoothing out a bit-mapped image
by blending the hard edges. Unlike
vector-based graphics which can
be resized to any dimension
and still maintain a smooth
edge, bit-mapped images
have finite resolutions.

The grayscale images in the
black-and-white section of this
book have 300 dots per inch. If
they are blown up like the two
sphinx in Figures 6-9 and 6-10,
the images will show obvious
pixilation. The sphinx in
Figures 6-8 and 6-9 were rendered with anti-aliasing. Figure
6-8 appears to have a smooth edge
because it is printed at the proper resolution.
In Figure 6-9, the face of the sphinx is enlarged
10 times to show how the smooth edge is actually simulated by the gray pixels interpolated
between the white background and the dark
image. The sphinx in Figures 6-9 and 6-
10 is printed at the same resolution.
The file size is identical. However, I
did not use anti-aliasing so the edge is
not smooth. Artists refer to this
effect as "the jaggies,"
"stair-stepping," "saw
tooth," or "blocki-
ness." Note that the

6-11

6-10

"jaggie" sphinx does not look *that* bad when printed small enough.

Anti-aliasing is often essential when rendering an animation. If animated objects are not anti-aliased, their hard edge moves in a jumpy fashion causing an annoying flicker. Most artists agree that anti-aliasing looks much better for both still illustrations and animations. The only drawback is anti-aliasing adds significantly to render times.

OVERSAMPLING

Each rendering method is capable of rendering varying degrees of detail from extremely rough to ultra high resolution. Some software just has low, medium, and high settings; others are more specific. Think of the rendered image as a mosaic. A mason (your CPU) would use the largest size tiles on a low-resolution image. A medium-resolution image uses tiles that are half the area so that four of them fit into the same space as a single large tile. The mason (your CPU) must then do four times the work to fill the same area. With each higher setting the work quadruples until eventually your mason quits and you go out and buy yourself a new mason with dual processors and 256 megs of RAM. Increasing the oversampling is just like reducing the size of the tile in the mosiac. The image becomes more detailed and accurate, but takes longer to produce. If you are producing a high-resolution illustration, most programs will have some method of oversampling to produce extremely fine quality illustrations.

6-12

Figure 6-12:
Depth of field effect
applied to a raytace render.

OCTREE

The octree height is a relatively esoteric setting that is actually extremely important in determining the quality and time of a render. Octree is a method of dividing three-dimensional space into more easily processed chunks. With a larger octree height, the CPU is less taxed and the render goes faster, however, some of the finer detail in textures and shading may be lost. Decreasing the octree size can dramatically improve the rendering of finer detail, but it will also increase render times. Adjusting the octree height is most useful when rendering items with fine type or subtle textures that are important to the piece.

DEPTH OF FIELD

All camera lenses have a limited depth of field, that is the distance in which objects are in focus when viewed through the lens. Our eye also has a limited depth of field, refocusing as we look at

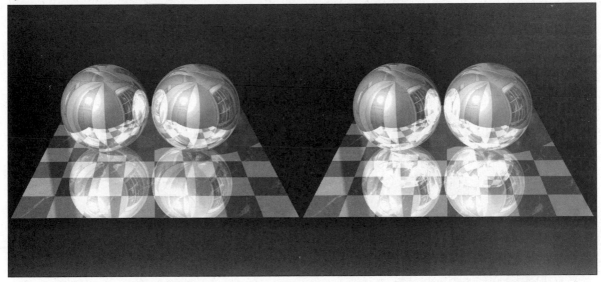

6-13

objects at different distances. Our eye refocuses so fast that it is virtually imperceptible. So depth of field settings in 3D software are meant to emulate photographic effects and not reality.

Depth of field was used on the image of the replicated townhouse in Figure 6-12. The focus was set to be sharp from about 5 to 25 feet. If the focus was set to infinity, the blur would have been reversed. Note how depth of field also reduces the contrast of the image farther from the focal range.

MOTION BLUR

Flap your hand quickly in front of your face. Although there's a strong probability you have five fingers, you will find it pretty

Figure 6-13:
The two spheres on the left were renderd using one level of reflectivity recursion. The spheres on the right have two levels of reflectivity recursion. Note the extra brightness and reflected images in the spheres and the floor of the image on the right.

hard to count them while flapping because they are blurred by the motion. Motion blur is captured on film when an object moves so quickly that its image is captured at different points along a single frame. The faster the object, the greater the blur. Faster shutter speeds reduce the rate of blur.

Most software that has a motion blur feature will enable the user to adjust the amount of blur with a shutter speed control.

TRANSPARENCY AND REFLECTIVITY RECURSION

To speed up render times, every 3D program that I'm aware of sets limits on the number of times the camera can see through transparent objects. If transparent recursion was set to five, the sixth object would appear opaque.

Reflectivity recursion determines the number of times an object is reflected. This is usually set to one because higher settings significantly hamper render times.

Figure 6-13 is an illustration of the most hackneyed subject in all of 3D design: chrome spheres on a checkered floor. The spheres on the left were rendered with the reflectivity recursion set to one; the spheres on the right were rendered with the exact same setting, except reflectivity was set to two. If you look closely, you can see the extra reflection in the tiled floor and at the point where the two spheres are closest to each other.

SUBDIVISION

Most programs give the artist the capability of changing the render subdivision to speed up rendering times. An oversimplified explanation is that the program chops the image into smaller units so the CPU does not have to process as much information at once. For smaller models, changing the rendering subdivision parameter will have negligible results. Larger, more unwieldy models can benefit a great deal by reducing the subdivision.

SHADOW MAPPING

This function is very useful if you are making a flythrough or rendering multiple versions of the same model. Shadow mapping calculates the effects of light and geometry for the first frame of an animation and saves that information in a separate file. The shadow map is not a picture channel. It is information that can be applied to subsequent frames even if the camera moves to a completely different angle. Shadow mapping can result in significant savings in render times, but it doesn't work on objects and lights that are animated. So, if a bird was flying overhead in a shadow-mapped scene, it would not cast a shadow.

RENDERING PROBLEMS AND SOLUTIONS

As I mentioned, rendering can be a huge headache that precipitates sleepless nights and the desire to quit your job and join the circus. The following are some of the pitfalls and workarounds that commonly occur when working in 3D.

Problem : "Out of memory"

❑ **Solution 1**: Set up a render queue

> Your computer allocates a certain amount of RAM to run the system and 3D software. When you start rendering while still working on your original model, the program will have one set of data open for the working model and a duplicate set for your render. Set up a suspended render or a render queue, quit the program, restart the computer to clear the RAM, and then open only the rendering version of the model.

❑ **Solution 2:** Reallocate memory

> IRIX, Windows, and Mac OS all have a method of observing memory usage. With your 3D program running, see how much RAM is being used by both the system and the 3D application. If all of the available RAM is used up, you may have to resort to virtual memory to render your file. Remember, virtual memory uses the hard drive as simulated RAM (about 10 megabytes of space for every 1 meg of virtual RAM) so you will need ample hard drive space to make a significant difference. If you have enough room on your hard drive, try increasing the swap space, too.

❏ **Solution 3:** Reduce texture sizes

The file may not render because it is loading too many megabytes of textures. You may have to rethink your utilization of texture maps. Make a duplicate copy of the file and then delete or disassociate the largest textures from the geometry. Try a test render. If you still get an "out of memory" message, try deleting more textures and rerender. If the image starts to render fine with fewer textures, make smaller versions of the textures with the same file names as the originals. Swap the smaller textures with their larger versions in the referenced directory and reopen the file. The smaller version will be automatically imported. If your 3D program does not reference outside images, just swap the textures inside the program.

❏ **Solution 4:** Optimize geometry

Hide half of the objects in the model and do a render. If that works, render only the objects that were hidden the first time. If both sides render fine, then the model is too big or unwieldy for your computer. If you are using a polygonal modeler, you can optimize the geometry by reducing the number of segments in a revolve (lathe) and resmoothing polygon mesh objects (in some programs the tool is called polygon reduction). Try to replace far away objects with primitive shapes like simple cubes where it will not adversely affect the detail of the model. If the model size is still too large, remake some of the individual objects more efficiently.

❏ **Solution 5:** Compositing

Some high-end programs enable the user to render objects at specified distances from the camera. The user could render the scene three times with one version from 0 to 10 feet, another from 10 feet to 30 feet, and the last from 30 feet to infinity. Each render can include an alpha channel background so the render will seam perfectly when compositing.

Problem : "Bad file format"

❑ **Solution 1:** Check referenced textures

Most programs reference outside picture maps to build their shaders (sometimes referred to as materials or texture maps). This keeps the file size relatively small because it only contains the data for the geometry, lighting, and texture settings without incorporating the TIFF or PICT files. In the course of a project, those image maps could have changed format or been moved to a new folder. Try reimporting the textures into the existing shaders. Also, check the paths to make sure that all files are in the correct directories.

❑ **Solution 2:** Test for bad data

The "bad file format" message may actually be caused by problems in the geometry. Select half of the objects in the model and "hide" them so they do not render. If the visible objects render okay, then reverse the hidden and visible objects and do another render. If these objects do not render, keep subdividing the elements until you have found the object with the bad data. Unless the object with the bad data took a few days to make, it is best to delete it and recreate that part of the model from scratch.

❑ **Solution 3:** Make a new file

Sometimes it's not the geometry or the textures that are causing problems, it's the file itself. Using the "save as" function won't do the trick. You'll just wind up with the same bad file with a different name. Use the "select all" command to grab all of the geometry in the file with the attached textures. Open up a new file and paste everything into it, then try rerendering.

Some artists who are very knowledgeable about programming and computers will go into the code and revise their files. Unless you know what you are doing, you'll find playing with code very frustrating.

Problem : "Dark areas render blurry or blocky"

❑ **Solution 1:** Change lighting

Occasionally, an area of a model may be too dark for the texture to render properly. Instead of subtle detail in the shadow areas, large blocks of muted color appear. Either increase the ambient light or place a small light source that does not cast shadows in the problem area. If this makes the image too light, you can increase the contrast in post-production. Sometimes it helps to make the small light source placed in the problem area a color and shade similar to the textures, giving the illusion of reflected light caused by bouncing off the surrounding geometry.

❑ **Solution 2:** Modify the shader

Try adding a subtle iridescent map (or "glow map," or "change the brightness," etc. depending upon the program) to the shader. A slight "glow" of even 5 percent to 10 percent will be virtually imperceptible in the bright areas, yet there will be a noticeable improvement in the detail of the shadow areas. If subtle changes in the brightness of the texture are not enough, create a glow map so only the dark areas are modified, then boost the value to around 20 percent. Increasing the iridescence map too much will flatten out the geometry, so don't go overboard.

Increasing the contrast of the texture map may also help to bring out detail in shaded areas.

❑ **Solution 3:** Switch rendering algorithms

A raytraced render often appears a little brighter than a scanline render due to raytracing's ability to better handle reflective surfaces. If the textures in the dark areas of your model have some reflective surfaces, there should be a noticeable difference. If you are already using raytracing and are producing a single illustration, try using a radiosity renderer. Not all programs are equipped with radiosity, but if your software has it, this renderer does the best job of drawing subtle shades and details in the shadows.

Problem : "Black squares and triangles render that are invisible in the model window"

❏ **Solution 1:** Increase transparency recursion

A transparency (or opacity) map that is being viewed through other transparent objects may appear black if the transparency recursion is not high enough. To test if this is the problem, increase the transparency recursion to its maximum value and then rerender the problem frame. If it renders okay, reduce the transparency recursion to a more reasonable setting.

❏ **Solution 2:** Check vertices

Complex objects, especially polygon meshes and imported DXF files, often generate what I like to call wild vertices. There are one or maybe two vertices on an object that get corrupt and read as if they are in an entirely different part of the model. The dark triangle generated in the render is actually just one or two polygons sticking out of an object. Sometimes, if you use a "fit views to all" command and then view the model with Gouraud shading you will see the polygon jutting from the object. Usually, it's better to toss the problem object and remake it rather than try to repair the geometry.

❏ **Solution 3:** Check for duplicate geometry

Sometimes an artist inadvertently duplicates large segments of a file. When looking through the modeling window, the extra geometry is not visible because it takes up the exact same space as the original geometry. The duplicate geometry very often produces some funky results, especially if the object uses transparencies. To test for the problem, select one of the objects that is not rendering well and move it to the side. If you see double, well, then you have your work cut out for you. Many programs provide hierarchical structures of the file which makes finding and weeding out duplicate objects much easier. Even if your piece is rendering fine with duplicate geometry, you should go through and clean up the file. Excess geometry slows render times, requires more RAM, and increases your wireframe file size, all of which are bad things.

Problem : "Inexplicably slow renders"

Not to be confused with just plain old really slow renders, this is a problem where one minute things are rendering just fine and then after only a couple of changes, the render goes from normal to glacial speeds. There are a few common settings that may cause this kind of problem.

❏ **Solution 1:** Check special effects

Special effects, like depth of field, that rely on the power of the CPU can be real killers. Turn off any atmospheric effects such as fog, haze, motion blur, and depth of field, and any particle effects such as hair, fire, fountains, etc., then rerender the frame. If the frame renders five or ten times faster, readjust the quality and detail of the special effects. In many cases, effects interact with each other to significantly hamper rendering. For example, if an atmospheric fog effect and a particle smoke effect are both set to cast shadows, the processor may try to calculate the shadow of smoke on fog. This may work, but it will take a really long time.

❏ **Solution 2:** Reallocate RAM

You may be running your render without enough RAM allocated to the software. You may not get an "out of memory" message because the program is taking advantage of a swap disk to complete the render. Since a swap disk is much slower than real RAM you may experience serious delays, especially with an animation where each frame is saved and then a new one is started up. Try restarting the computer and rendering again. Many 3D programs do not "release" the memory after a render so eventually, no matter how much RAM you have in your computer, you will start reverting to swap space.

If you have already optimized your file, restarted your machine, and reallocated RAM, the only solution may be to buy more memory for your system.

❏ **Solution 3:** Check bump and displacement maps

Bump and displacement maps can add very realistic and complex detail to a model without significantly changing the file size. However, when rendering, each bump takes as much time as if it were made from geometry. Try turning off all bump and displacement maps and rerendering. If render times speed up significantly, you found the problem. You can "fake" a bumpy surface by opening a new file and rendering a flat surface with the bump map shader applied. Then take the rendered bump map and apply it as a flat texture in the problem model. You will get a very similar effect to having applied a real bump map without the hit in render time.

A displacement map can often be converted into a polygon mesh. Many programs have a "convert to polygon" function. The user can usually control the amount of detail in the mesh to make the simplest object possible that doesn't look too jagged.

Software manuals, tech support, online help, and colleagues are all good resources to turn to for software-specific render problems not covered here. The idiosyncrasies of each software package often stump even the most grizzled 3D veteran when trying to solve render problems. So remember to run test renders after each complex operation to nip potential problems in the bud.

CHAPTER 7

Interior Space

When Shakespeare said, "All the world is a stage," I don't think he was referring to the world of 3D design. But like DaVinci and his corkscrew helicopters, Shakespeare was actually a little more prophetic than he might have guessed. When creating an environment in the computer you should think more like a scenic designer than a programmer. Yes, you are still concerned with polygon count, texture size, render times, hardware limitations, and an array of technical issues that would baffle the minds of most neurosurgeons, but it is a common trap to get so embroiled in the technical aspects, like the correct setting for the rendering subdivision and the animation of fractally-generated volumetric clouds, that you lose sight of the fundamentals of design established through literally hundreds of years. These next few chapters will help you apply many of the conventions of traditional set design to the digital world.

Interior environments are perhaps the most common and, in some ways, the simplest sets used in 3D design. A manmade structure, especially a small room, has a distinct advantage over exteriors in that the artist has a defined limit to the geometry of the model – the inside wall. If the room is simple enough, the entire shell of the model can be created with just a few polygons.

In the following pages, I show the step-by-step construction of a simple interior space. Naturally, manmade structures vary a great deal and there is no one right way to build an interior set. This chapter is only meant to give you some basic techniques for planning and constructing a model.

Figures 7-1 through 7-5 show very simple floor plans. They are not workable "real world" plans. If I applied this layout to a physically constructed object, it would probably be a disaster, but for creating a 3D animation for entertainment purposes, it will

7-1

7-2

7-3

*Figures 7-1 to 7-5:
Two-dimensional floor plan
images which will be used
to create a 3D model.*

*Figure 7-6:
Two-dimensional forms
which will be used for windows, doors, and details for
the 3D model.*

do just fine. Remember that the laws of physics do not apply in computer-generated space. Objects can occupy the same space at the same time; spheres are perfectly round; light sources are points in space without dimension; and, you don't need to pour a foundation to hold up a building.

Notice that I put a few thicker spots in the walls in this floor plan. These squares indicate a load-bearing part of the structure. They are just there for aesthetic reasons as they help break up the plain walls and generate some interesting shadows. The walls here also have a thickness. If I was producing a very large animation where I worked with this model for many days, I would delete much of the outside wall that the viewer never sees. This cuts down on the polygon count giving me faster screen redraw and render times. Since I only used this for a few simple black-and-white renders, it was not worth the time to fully optimize the model.

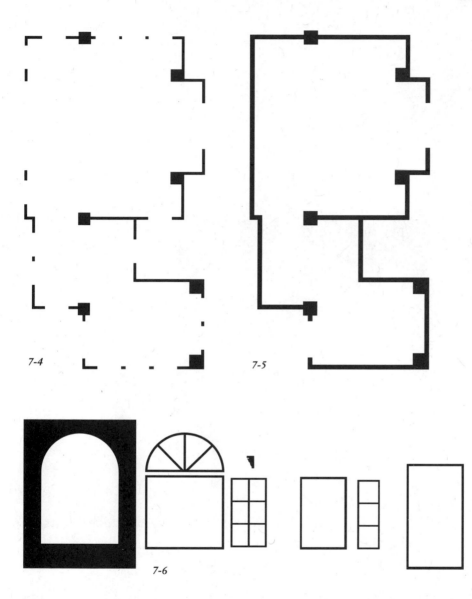

7-4   7-5

7-6

Along with the floor plan, I made a few silhouetted shapes that
will be used to add detail to the set such as decorative molding,
arches, window frames, and hardware (Figure 7-6). I made these
shapes at the same time as the floor plan for expediency. I won't
actually need them until I put the final touches on the model.

You can use any drawing program that has a direct import into
your 3D software. If you use 3D software with very good 2D
drawing tools such as AutoCAD or Alias, you are one step

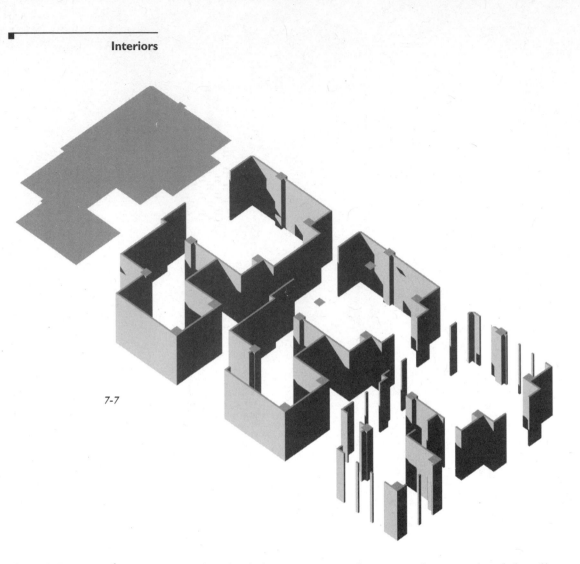

7-7

Figure 7-7:
Extruded shapes made from
Figures 7-1 to 7-5.

Figure 7-8:
The extruded shapes were
resized and aligned to form
the basic shape of a
structure.

Figure 7-9:
The detail items made from
the flat shapes in Figure 7-
6.

ahead of the game. For this example, I used Adobe Illustrator imported into Strata StudioPro. The same basic techniques should hold true for whatever software configuration you choose.

After I made the basic floor plan, I duplicated the entire shape in the 2D program and cut out spaces in the wall for doorways (Figure 7-3). In this example, I had one opening on the upper right wall and one on the lower left. I also cut out a very large space on the upper left wall. I'm going to have some interesting architectural detail in that area so I reserved the space and will produce that section last. It is very important to think ahead like this when you are starting your model. Thoughtful planning will make the model size and your workload much smaller.

For the next step I duplicated the second floor plan that has the doorways cut out. In the same manner that I created the doorway, I cut out window spaces. I made sure to use the same size opening for all of the windows so I can use instances when I place frames and glass on the windows. In reality, an architect does a very similar thing by specifying standard window sizes to utilize prefabricated window units.

7-8

Once I cut out enough window spaces, I saved the fourth floor plan (Figure 7-4). To make the modeling a little easier, I also created simple rectangles with a counterspace which will serve as door and window frames. It is

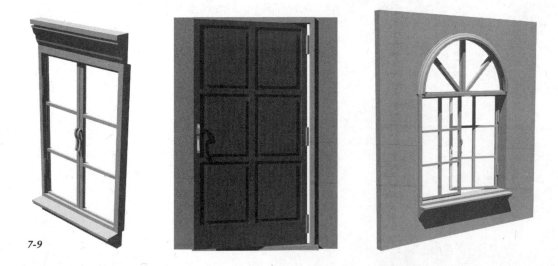

7-9

7-10

7-11

7-12

7-13

7-14

important to note that I made the outside edges of the window frame slightly larger than the window openings. The inside of the frame is slightly smaller than the opening. When I construct my model I will let the frame overlap the opening on both sides. This gives me a little leeway so if I am off by a small fraction, the viewer will not notice.

Once I determined the window size, I made a flat shape that will serve as the frame for the individual glass panes. Depending upon the kind of construction you are making, this could be an unnecessary step. As we discussed in Chapter 5 on texture mapping, window panes can be effectively simulated with a very simple texture map. In this case, I am going to let the viewer get very close to some of the windows, so I want there to be some depth to the geometry.

The last step I did in my drawing program was create the floor. This was simply done by taking the first floor plan with no openings cut out, duplicating it, and deleting the counterspace (Figure 7-1). This is kind of an unnecessary step since I could use a single polygon flat plane for the floor and ceiling. The floor shape might be about 12 to 16 polygons, but it is worth the extra weight for the convenience of having the floor the same shape as the walls.

Next I opened all of my shapes in my 3D program. Because I spent a little time in setup, this stage of the project went surprisingly fast. From the top view I selected each floor plan and extruded them upward. Note that I left the floor as a flat plane. There is no need for this shape to be three-dimensional.

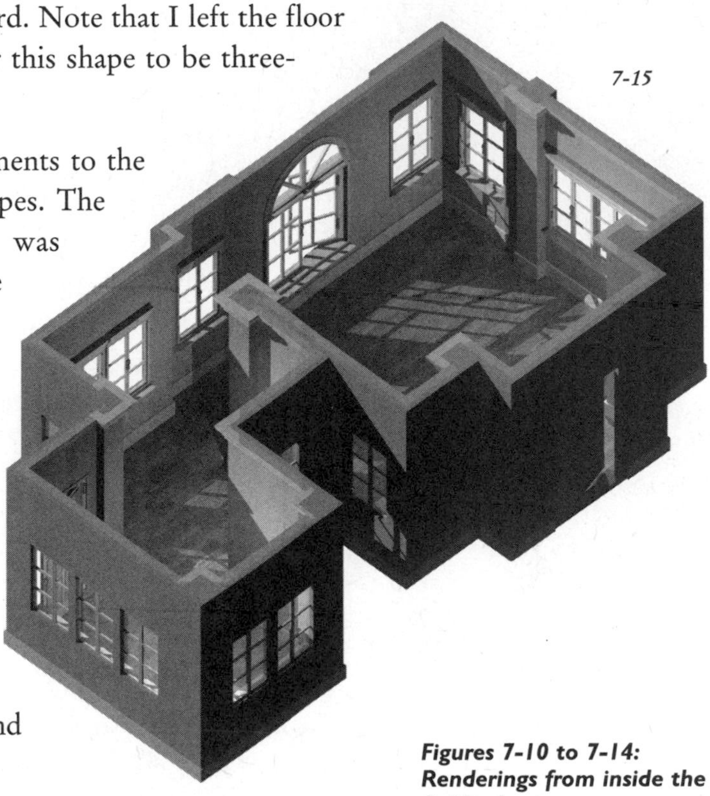

7-15

From the side view, I made adjustments to the height of each of my extruded shapes. The shape with the window cut out was adjusted to be slightly taller than the window frame. The floor plan with no holes cut out was adjusted to serve as the area between the windows and the ceiling. The floor plan with just the doors cut out was sized to equal the difference in height between the door and the window. This process sounds complicated, but it took me less than five minutes. It's made easier if you use the door and window frames as your guide.

Figures 7-10 to 7-14: Renderings from inside the finished set.

Figure 7-15: Isometric view of the finished model.

Figure 7-16: 360 degree QuicktimeVR render from the inside of the model.

From the top view I aligned objects, then dragged each piece of the floor plan to the appropriate height. Next, I selected the floor and aligned it to the bottom of the structure. You can see that all of my windows are uniform in height, and the walls are in perfect alignment. Using this method I can produce very complex structures with multiple hallways and

7-16

7-17

Figure 7-17:
Interior office space with
detailed foreground objects
and complex shadows.

chambers very quickly. This method is particularly effective for flythroughs or prerendered games where the model will be shown from many points of view. The alternative of creating each wall separately and dragging it into place could add many hours onto a project and would result in a less efficient model.

You will notice that I haven't placed a ceiling on the model yet. I usually place the ceiling on last, or at least hide it from view until the end, so I can "reach in" and adjust individual interior elements more easily.

The next few steps apply to any method you use to create an interior space. Remember that at the same time I made the floor plans, I created a group of simple shapes for the doors and windows. Each of the shapes was extruded and composited in a similar manner. The frames were lined up with the inside of the windows, etc.

The only time-consuming aspect of the entire model was placing the decorative molding around the top of the wall. I duplicated the simple cross section of the molding and extruded one of the shapes. That same shape was then instanced throughout the model for the window ledges, decorative window frames, and the tops of the walls. To get a perfectly metered corner, I took the copy of the flat shape and lathed it 180 degrees while keeping the lathe segments to two. I instanced the corner molding shape and wrapped it around all of the convex corners. For the concave corners, I simply let the instanced straight molding strips intersect each other. The decorative molding around the curved window was made with another 180 degree lathe of the flat molding shape, only this time I used 18 segments to create a smooth curve.

The decorative molding around the top of the walls certainly adds a more realistic, detailed look to the model. However, it took me over an hour to position all of the top molding in the 3D program, making this the most time-consuming part of the process. The solution to this time problem can be found in the way I handled the bottom molding. While working in my drawing program, I created a version of the floor plan with the windows cut out that has slightly thicker walls. I extruded that floor plan to the height of the molding and aligned it to the other sections of wall. I could have gotten a little fancier by extruding the shape along a short, curved path to create curved or ridged molding, but I didn't feel it was worth the extra geometry.

Notice that the model I made for this example is missing the kind of care and detail that would distinguish it as a professional quality piece. Textures, furniture, visible lighting, and human touches are needed to make the environment complete.

Along with the considerable advantages of producing interior sets this way come a few disadvantages. There is some unnecessary geometry, especially in the outside walls which are only visible when looking through the windows at certain angles. It also limits the camera movement to the confines inside the set. In some ways, lighting is simplified because the directional light is boxed out and all light sources other than light streaming through the windows have to be placed inside the set.

To create the most efficient model, it is best to only make the objects that appear on camera and only include detail where it will be shown. An experience I had many years ago when I was putting together a display for a client illustrates what I'm saying. This was a job using real physical props at a time so long ago that I thought computers were just for geeks with punchcards. Anyway, we were renting a prop of a full-size rickshaw. The designer who rented the piece before us needed a red rickshaw, so he had placed the prop on the stage and only painted the parts that faced the audience. When I complained, "What am I going to do with a rickshaw that is $5/8$ red and $3/8$ black?" the prop house suggested that I turn the item as it would face my audience and then paint only the part the audience would see. Well, I had them paint the entire thing one color to be safe, but I did learn valuable lessons: Professionals only do what is absolutely necessary; and, before you rent a rickshaw, give it a thorough once-over.

CONCEPTUALIZING INTERIOR SPACES

Many artists prefer to sketch a scene in detail before starting their 3D model. In some cases, the 3D artist is the second link in the chain of visualizing an idea and most of the shots will be planned in detail by someone who is less familiar with 3D design than the 3D artist. The sketch artist plays with perspective and proportion to create the most visually interesting composition. This is, of course, the artist's prerogative. When these ideas are realized in 3D, however, the composition may look dramatically different. When a 3D artist literally interprets a drawing into a CAD-accurate piece, it very often loses the life and vitality of the original sketch. I believe it is the miscommunication between traditional artists and technically adept, yet literal-minded, CAD artists that has fostered the false notion that computer art is a soulless medium. Fortunately, there are a few ways of working that may help alleviate some of these problems.

Most high-end programs enable the artist to import a bit-mapped picture as a tissue overlay. The artist can then place a camera in the model from the same perspective as the sketch, and as the model is constructed there will be a constant in-context reference. You will find as you work that it's almost impossible to match hand-drawn work with actual geometry. If you are building backgrounds for entertainment, it's okay to distort the geometry a bit to match the feel of the sketch. If you are an architect, well, you have a different set of priorities.

The tissue overlay can be very useful, but it's not always the most efficient solution. The tissue itself slows down screen redraw and it's very difficult to match the correct angle, lens, and point of view of the original artwork. Also, just because a model matches up with an image from a certain angle does not mean it will work from a slightly different perspective. For example, a box floating in the air that does not cast shadows will look the same as a larger box in the distance sitting on the ground plane. As a test, try this method with a photograph and you will see how difficult the process is.

I prefer to work with much looser drawings and to flesh out the details by constructing an interim model on the computer. I find it is best to start off "sketching in 3D" with simple shapes in place of complex objects. Block out the scene by using facsimiles of the final shapes. For example, a table can be represented in a comp by a cube with four cylinders as legs. When placed in the scene it gives you a very accurate idea of how big the piece should be and how it affects the lighting and the overall composition. It is easy to alter and move around, and it renders very quickly. Sometimes I'll slap a dummy shader on the object that is close in color and texture to my final objective. Once the table has been sized, shoved around and manipulated into the desired proportions, the comp serves as a template for a more ornate final. It sounds like a very simple idea, but most 3D artists do not work in this manner. We should think of ourselves as painters: First make the bold strokes, then concentrate on areas of detail.

SMALL INTERIOR SPACES

The same factors that make interiors simpler to create than exteriors may also cause them to be a bit artificial and even a little boring. The point of view is cut off by an artificial barrier: A wall. You can create oversized cathedrals and endless factory floors by repeating dozens of columns, arches, and machinery, but eventually you will be faced with creating a smaller, more intimate space where walls and the relationship of common objects dictate the success of your composition.

It is here, in the replication of more common day-to-day surroundings, that 3D art is often lacking. I am amazed at the dedication and attention to detail some of my fellow 3D artists put into their work. A wall which most of the world sees as a simple plane is portrayed with cracks in the plaster, slight discolorations from sun and dirt, and even the unevenness of the paint job. The problems arise when a technically adept person constructs a scene with the realistic detail of a photographic image and the accuracy of an engineering schematic without the perspective of an artist.

Traditionally an artist pulls the center focus of a piece into the foreground adding detail and highlights to the areas where he wishes to draw the viewer's eye. Mid-ground objects enhance the meaning of the subject matter through their relationship with the focal object and their position in space. Background objects set the mood, place, and sense of depth. Think of an Italian Renaissance portrait. The figure in the foreground is the main subject; the details, such as jewelry and fine clothing, tell the viewer about the subject's social status. There may be objects in the room that symbolize the subject's daily life and family history. Through an open window the viewer can see the Italian countryside, perhaps showing land holdings and the particular region from which the subject comes.

In a religious painting, every element has a symbolic meaning. The symbolism decreased in secular works and later, with "modern" art, the composition became more important. I digress into this oversimplification of interior composition because the fundamentals are often lost in 3D digital art.

Even if all the geometry and lighting in a room are accurately portrayed in proportion without any fantastic elements, inte-

Figures 7-18 to 7-20:
A simple geometric shape and complex image map used to make a hexagonal column.

Figure 7-21:
The illusion of a large interior space created by instancing a single object.

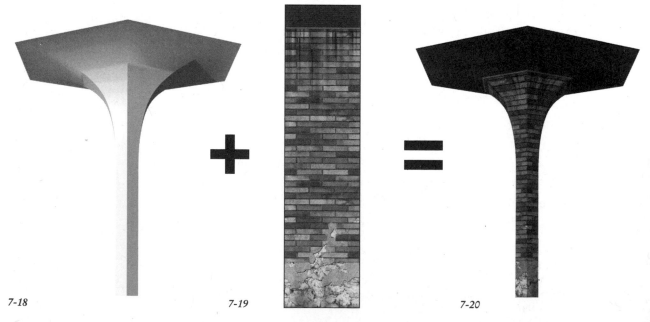

7-18   7-19   7-20

rior spaces still often have a surreal, stage-set appearance. Very often the stage-set appearance is due to a lack of focus. A scenic designer, especially when working with a small set, usually expects the actor to be the focus of the audience's attention. Without a central focus, careful renderings of realistic interiors may look, at best, like a shot from a real estate brochure. The same does not hold true for monumental architecture or fantasy-inspired spaces where the focus is on the unusual nature of the surroundings. Naturally, these are not hard and fast rules. There are many significant exceptions, but these rules of set design have worked for the last thousand years or so.

LARGE INTERIOR SPACES

When I first started working as a 3D designer, I decided to make a large cathedral as a demo piece. I figured cathedrals are impressive, huge spaces that most people travel all the way to Europe to see. I started out by modeling one arched stained glass window set into a stucco wall that was supported by an ornate marble column. I instanced that shape and repeated it in the out-

7-21

7-22

Figure 7-22:
A single organic shape coupled with dramatic lighting creates the illusion of a cavernous interior space.

line of a cross. By the time I added the buttressed roof, center basilica, candelabras, and rows of pews, it took about two days to render one frame. At that rate, I would have been an old man before my demo reel was done. I had to start from scratch to optimize the geometry for faster render times and my boss was already getting a little edgy. My solution was to delete the pews and replace them with high-backed wooden chairs at about ten times the scale of the pews. I took out all but two of the candelabras and increased their scale by a factor of ten. I also simplified the lighting scheme to accommodate fewer light sources. The cathedral became an intimate chapel and the long flythrough was sped up to reflect the smaller area. The piece still looks very nice, and up until the writing of this book, only I knew that the little chapel was originally supposed to rival St. Peter's. By changing the relationship of familiar objects to the rest of the set I was able to dramatically alter the perceived scale. The physical size of the model does not matter; it's the proportions of the objects that are the key.

In this case I was able to render faster by removing large chunks of geometry that are associated with a grand, public space. The tiny chapel looked right with only three or four chairs. In most instances, a monumental space does not have to be a larger file than a single small room.

Figure 7-21 shows how repetition of geometry and simple lighting techniques can be used to create large interior spaces. I started with a simple curve connecting a horizontal and a vertical line. It took me less than a minute to draw in a 3D program. Next, I used a revolve tool and created a 360 degree lathe with five segments. I deliberately used a polygonal modeler so the finished shape would be a hexagon from the top view.

The only fine detail I put into the model was in the texture map in Figure 7-19. I used a combination of royalty-free textures from a CD-ROM. The only mildly time-consuming task was making the bricks look like they were broken up at the bottom. I could have achieved the same effect by layering masked textures on the geometry in my 3D program, but that would have been more time consuming and would have afforded me less control.

My next step was to simply place the texture on the geometry at 100 percent vertical and horizontal proportions. This was all the modeling I needed to make the entire environment. I replicated instances of the hexagonal columns and allowed them to butt each other, so from the top view the columns made a honey-comb effect.

The lighting scenario was equally simple. I had a strong white light near the camera and three identical lights with a flame gel in the mid-ground. The mid-ground lights all had a short falloff so they did not make the entire scene too yellow.

The ground plane is made up of two polygons on top of each other. I made the top texture look like the surface of water by making it highly reflective and transparent with a high index of refraction. I also used a cloud filter as a bump map. The shader on the bottom polygon is just a dark tiled stock texture at a fairly low resolution. The bottom texture did not have to be very detailed because it is viewed through the distortion of the water. The most striking thing about this model is not the texture mapping, it is the pleasing composition created by the repetition of the column shape. There is a definite feeling of space achieved without complex geometry or a great deal of time producing the model. The same effect can be achieved with stalactites in a cave, trees in a forest, or rock formations in a desert. Repetition of simple elements can create the illusion of a large detailed space.

There are a few things you should keep in mind when creating large-scale environments. These are not absolutes, but in general they should help.

• *Texture Scale* - By changing the scale of a texture, an artist can create the illusion of a large space. Things like the size of a red brick or the grain in a piece of wood are known textures that will prompt the viewer to see the model in a different scale.

• *Camera Angle* - The height of the camera gives the viewer a visual cue as to his or her relationship to the scale of the model. Most film directors position the camera about a foot below eye level. Try to emulate this relative camera position in your model. If your animation calls for the camera to move freely about the space at many different heights and angles, try to start with an establishing shot that puts the camera a little below eye level.

• *Frame of Reference* - Place known or recognizable objects in a scene. A chair, desk or, of course, a person will establish the scale of your piece very quickly. When the viewer sees a familiar object such as a human figure, he or she will subconsciously adjust the scale of the unfamiliar objects in the scene.

• *Atmospheric Effects* - One of the surest signs that a piece is created on the computer is that everything is in perfect focus, even objects that are extremely far away. If your program enables you to set air density, use it. Objects far away will get blurrier and grayer just like real life. If you are simulating traditional film and your scene has foreground and far background objects, use depth of field. Fog, mist, haze, and volumetric light are all effects which give depth to a scene. Special effects take a terrible toll on render times, so use them sparingly; however, it is important to remember that atmospheric effects that we normally associate with outdoors are applicable to monumental interior spaces too.

• *Weight and Structure* - Pay careful attention to the supporting frames of a large interior environment, especially when recreating older structures. Your 3D model defies the laws of gravity and stands straight inside the computer without any infrastructure at all. However, the viewer expects to see a network of beams and supports made of heavy building materials. Pay attention to things like the thickness of walls, diameter of pillars, size of beams, and even the thickness of window glass. Remember that most viewers have never been inside a building without adequate support that would crumble under its own weight. If your animation puts them inside one, they will know something is wrong.

• *Lighting* - If an interior space uses artificial lighting, pay careful attention to the falloff of each source. In many public spaces, like train stations and domed stadiums, there are literally thousands of light sources. However, there is no need to panic. The general effect of all of these light sources is to create an overall ambient light that can be simulated by simply adjusting the ambient setting. The look of hundreds of light sources can be created with iridescent dots in the texture maps. You can then increase realism by adding a few spotlights to create more complex shadows. Inversely, you don't want to oversimplify with too few light sources. Just think how artificial it would look if the Astrodome was lit by a single really, really bright bulb.

CHAPTER 8

Exterior Space

One of the most daunting tasks for any 3D artist is creating believable outdoor environments. The complexity of nature and the myriad of organic shapes needed to accurately portray the average suburban backyard would bring most 3D artists and their workstations to their knees. There are some excellent programs on the market that generate fractal trees and terrain. As these tools become more sophisticated, the individual artist is getting more control over the look of the fractal environment. In many cases though, the artist is asked to recreate a specific look and composition. The only viable alternative is to learn to model nature. That is actually just about as hard as it sounds. This chapter deals with some of the common conventions and practical knowledge that most experienced 3D artists will apply to this type of model.

One of my favorite TV shows of all time was *The Joy of Painting* with Bob Ross. Each week Bob would stand in front of the camera with a blank canvas and in 22 minutes (give or take a few minutes to talk to the audience), he completed an entire landscape in oils. I used to marvel at the way he put what seemed to be half a tube of green paint on one side of a pallet knife and an equal amount of white on the other side, then gently applied it to portions of the canvas to make an entire pine forest. Well, I don't think these paintings will become part of the Louvre's permanent collection, but it was a pleasure to see Mr. Ross create complex natural environments with such ease and enthusiasm.

There is a very important lesson here for every 3D artist: You don't have to see the trees for the forest. You should approach outdoor landscapes like a painter and not an engineer. A good painter knows that a totally accurate depiction of nature is impossible. As he works the canvas, the painter makes thousands of little decisions. Direction of the brush stroke, thickness of

Figure 8-1:
The ribs that will be skinned to form the trunk of a tree.

Figure 8-2:
The resulting skinned tree trunk.

Figure 8-3:
Model of a tree branch made with the same skinning method as the trunk.

Figure 8-4:
The single branch was instanced and resized two times, then positioned around the trunk to form the bulk of the geometry for the final tree.

Figure 8-5:
The tree with a texture map of bark.

Figures 8-6 and 8-7:
Wireframe renders of the tree showing the criss-crossing billboards of the leaves.

Figure 8-8:
Texture map of the leaves on the tree.

Figure 8-9:
The completed render of the tree.

Figure 8-10:
An example of a hair particle render.

paint, and size of brush are all elements that help create an artist's unique vision. What an artist chooses to leave out is just as important as the things he or she includes. Even when creating photorealistic backgrounds, it is not necessary to include every leaf.

TREES

When I first started working in 3D I set up a small project for myself. I wanted to recreate a Japanese garden. In my ignorance, I didn't know that this was one of the hardest things to achieve given the state of the medium. While the project proved to be a very long, frustrating experience (it took every single night and weekend for about eight months), it did get me my first job in 3D. And the project had a side benefit: I am no longer afraid of modeling trees.

Like a painter, I vary the detail of my trees depending on how close the viewer gets to each object. The tree in Figure 8-9 is best viewed mid-range. I started my model with the trunk of the tree. With the 2D drawing tool I drew a cross section of the base of the tree where it will intersect the ground plane (Figure 8-1). You will notice that I made a few lumps and extra circular shapes for the beginnings of roots to give the tree a little character. I then copied the shape a few times making it about 10 percent smaller with each replication. I also smoothed out some of the bumps and added some

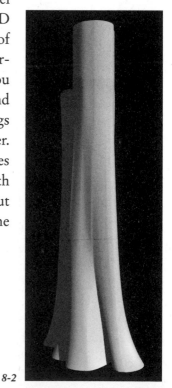

8-1

8-2

others to work as the base for a branch. I modified a single shape and replicated it rather than making a new shape for each cross section because I intended to use them as ribs for a skin tool. In most programs, you'll want to make sure you have the same number and order of points in the curve that make up each rib. The skin tool will try to match up the points between ribs. If there are different numbers of points going in different directions between ribs, the resulting skin may have twists or tears. I find the easiest way to do this is to start with the same shape for each rib (Figure 8-2).

I made the branches in a similar way, but I deliberately did not add as much detail. Note that I used a vertical oval as the rib at the base of the branch. This way, when I butted the branch up next to the tree trunk, there would not be as jarring an angle. All of the branches on the tree (Figure 8-4) are the same shape (Figure 8-3) replicated, resized, and turned around the up axis. I

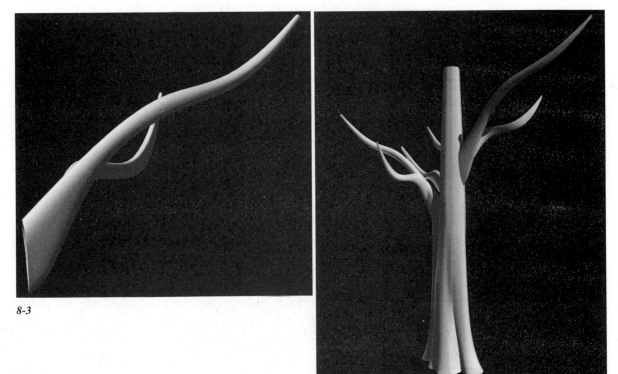

8-3

8-4

8-5

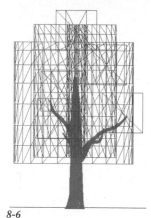

8-6

let the geometry of the branches intersect the trunk a bit because frankly, it was a lot easier than butting things up exactly. I applied the same rough tiled texture to the branches and the leaves to give the model a more unified, less pristine look.

If I was doing a close-up of a tree, I would make groups of leaves in a similar fashion to the plant in Chapter 5, but for the mid-range view tree, I made one, slightly curved giant billboard of all of the leaves on the tree and then replicated it on its up axis just like the branches. As you can see in Figure 8-8, the billboard picture of the leaves looks pretty sparse. This is because I planned to make the object transparent and replicate it two or three times. The overall look will be of a much denser tree. To make the tree a little less even and more wild looking, I made a smaller bunch of leaves, replicated it twice on its axis and placed it randomly around the tree. This is a great way to cover up mistakes and annoying pieces of geometry that make the model look fake. In the top view (Figure 8-7), you can see the layouts of the smaller billboards very clearly.

The final rendered tree looks pretty good, though it's far from a photorealistic representation. However, it will hold up in the background as part of a forest or in a scene where the camera is moving and not focusing on this particular tree. If the tree was an essential foreground element in an animation or illustration, I would still approach the model in a similar manner, skinning the trunk and branches. I would use a much larger, more elaborate photographic texture map for the bark with an accompanying bump map. The ribs that comprise the skin would have more control points and curves to give the bark more ridges. The branches would also contain more geometry and higher-level texture maps. I don't think there is an artist out there who would be nuts enough to make every leaf on a tree, but that could be done for some branches if they will be extremely close to the camera.

8-7

8-8

8-9

If this tree was in the background, I would reduce the geometry by replacing the trunk and branches with simple cylinders and use less billboards to make up the leaves. I would also reduce the size of the texture map making up the leaves. If the tree only took up a very small portion of the frame and it was very far in the distance, I would use one billboard for the entire tree.

There is, of course, more than one way to make a tree. Each 3D artist has their own method of working and their own tricks to save time and reduce file size. Another popular method which I will not go into in depth is creating a simplified skeleton of the trunk and branches, then using a smoothing tool to round out and join the shapes. The leaves can be generated through particle effects attached to the branches in the same way particles are used to generate hair and fur. If the artist spends enough

8-10

time testing the particle parameters, it is possible to generate a fairly convincing tree. However, you should expect to take quite a hit in rendering time if you rely on the CPU to generate an entire tree. The image in Figure 8-10 that looks like the offspring of "Cousin It" and a Koosh® ball is just a simple sphere with a particle hair effect.

NATURAL SHAPES

There is more to simulating natural environments than just making trees and leaves. While a photographer or a painter can easily capture the infinate number of shapes ocurring in nature with the click of a button or a few well-placed brush strokes, a 3D artist can spend weeks, even months, attempting to create the same setting. Two of the hardest things for a 3D artist to produce are natural-looking grass and ground. Many artists default to using tiled textures; however, tiled textures give you a very manicured look and nature is anything but uniform. Using a tiled texture of grass, for example, will make your greens look more like a golf course than an untamed field. When creating an outdoor setting, remember to visually break up any regular patterns caused by tiled texture maps or instanced objects and hide all parallel lines and hard-edged objects. This will give you the more haphazard look you need to emulate nature.

THE OUTDOOR SET

I am often asked by students and other 3D artists how to set up a model for an outdoor environment. The first question I usually ask them is "Where will the camera be?" I'm not answering a question with a question just to be annoying. Camera placement and movement are the strongest factors determining the layout of your model. The following general model layouts all involve the use of billboard backgrounds. Similar, more detailed sets can be made using real geometry. In most cases, especially when there is complex geometry and shaders, billboarding faraway objects will save huge amounts of render time and will make the work flow much easier.

Figure 8-11:
Overhead wireframe render of a 360 degree set used for a QuicktimeVR walk-through.

Figures 8-12 and 8-13:
A fully rendered image of the top view of the same set, and an isometric view which clearly shows the layout of the building, facades, and trees.

Figure 8-14
A 360-degree panoramic render inside the set for use with QuicktimeVR. Note how the parallel lines have been distorted so they will appear straight when wrapped inside a cylinder.

CYCLORAMA

A cyclorama is a 360-degree image that wraps around the viewer. If you've ever been to Disney World and stood in the middle of one of those 360-degree theaters that flies you through the wilds of Canada or a military parade in Red Square, then you have experienced the real thing. What most visitors to Disney World don't think about as they get that slightly nauseous feeling, dipping and diving through the Canadian Rockies, is that they are watching eight separate movies on eight flat screens. When the images move in unison, the effect is so convincing that it's possible to lose your balance as the camera tilts.

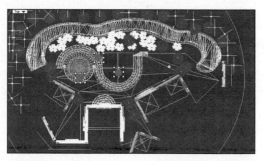

8-11

In virtual environments, a cyclorama is best used when the camera stays in the center area of the model and takes many different views of the scene. An interactive piece such as a CD-ROM game or a "virtual tour" is a perfect use for a cyclorama. In these instances, it is actually easier to create a set that works no matter which way the camera is pointing than it is to readjust the set each time the keyframes are changed.

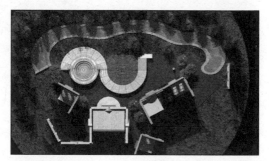

8-12

Using photography for the background of a cyclorama creates a unique challenge. Seeing a seam in the background where one photograph butts the next

8-13

BASIC 3D SETS

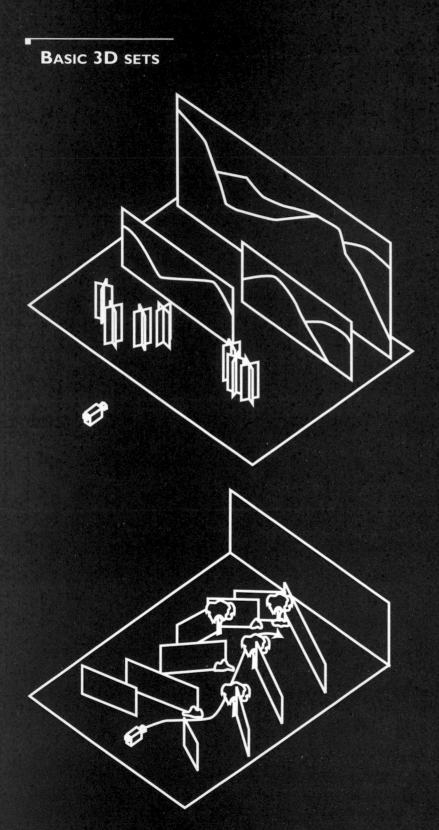

Figure 8-15:
A simple flat set, ideal for still lifes or situations where the camera stays in a fixed position. The billboard background planes are set at various distances to enhance the illusion of depth.

Figure 8-16:
In this set designed for a moving camera, the flat billboards are placed at roughly 45 degree angles to the path of the camera. Careful attention was paid to placing 3D objects at the edge of the billboards to mask the hard edges of the 2D planes.

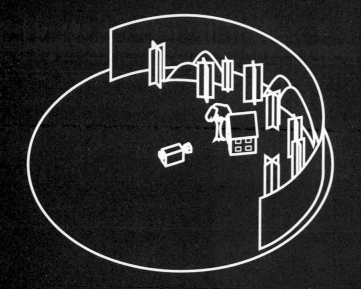

Figure 8-17:
A 180-degree set,
perfect for panning
shots or multiple
points of view.
This set uses a
combination of 3D
geometry in the
foreground which can
be viewed from any
angle, and curved 2D
billboards in the mid-
and background.

Figure 8-18:
A 360-degree set is
ideal for interactive
applications where
the user can view the
model from any direc-
tion. The illusion of a
vast open space does
not break down from
any angle as long as
the camera stays in
the center area of the
model.

8-19

Figure 8-19:
A simple set with a curved billboard background and three-dimensional geometry of trees in the foreground.

Figure 8-20:
View of the same set from the front. This render uses a fog effect to help create the illusion of depth.

breaks the illusion. If you've ever gone on vacation and popped a series of pictures of a large vista with each shot pointing at a slightly different angle, you'll notice that no matter how steady you held the camera, the photos never quite line up. Don't beat yourself up; it's not your fault. You can blame it on the camera lens. A normal camera lens distorts light as it is recorded onto film. The wider the angle of the lens, the greater the distortion. This distortion at the edge of your photographs prevents you from lining the pictures up perfectly. The same problem holds true when making a virtual cyclorama from photographs. There is an excellent tool which, as I'm writing this book, is only available on the Macintosh platform: Quicktime VR. The software has a "stitching" tool which seamlessly blends the images together. The tool also compensates for the distortion caused by wrapping an image around the inside of a cylinder.

Some 3D programs have the ability to render a Quicktime VR panorama from any point in the model. The artist can then take the seamed 360-degree image and place it on the inside of a cylinder surrounding another model. It seems like a pretty long way to go when almost every program has the ability to place an image as a set background for a model, but there is a distinct advantage to using a cyclorama: When the camera moves, there will be a parallax effect between the image on the cyclorama and the background. This is the effect you get when you are traveling at night and the trees seem to speed by you while the moon follows along with the car. Objects farther away appear to move with the viewer. So, a single cylinder cyclorama or a few different cylinders nested inside each other can create an incredible feeling of depth with a moving camera.

SINGLE PERSPECTIVE SETS

Single perspective sets are, by far, the most common setups for an outdoor model. They also most closely approximate a typical photographer's set. With a single perspective set, the camera is only pointed in one direction and does not pivot or move a great deal. Figure 8-19 uses a billboard image as a backdrop with modeled objects occupying the foreground and mid-ground. I prefer to use a billboard as a backdrop rather than just apply the image to the background render settings because it gives me a great deal more control over the precise placement of the image. Also, when I'm viewing the unrendered, working model, I can get a very clear idea of the images that will be seen.

Figure 8-20 uses instances of the same tree trunk to simulate a forest. The model was constructed with the camera in place so I could toggle up and back between the camera view and working view to include only the necessary shapes. Note how the trees get taller as they recede from the camera. This accommodates the wider field of vision as objects get farther from the viewer. I kept the trees shorter in the foreground to show all the variations in the trunk caused by the varying shaped ribs. If the trees were twice as tall, they would have half the detail with the same number of ribs. The branches themselves are simple cylinders with two-dimensional leaves. All of these are just instances of the same branch.

8-20

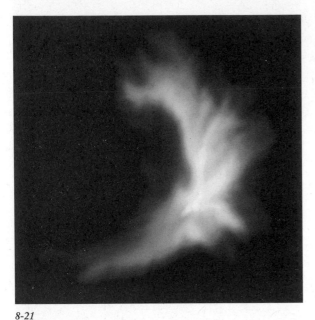

8-21

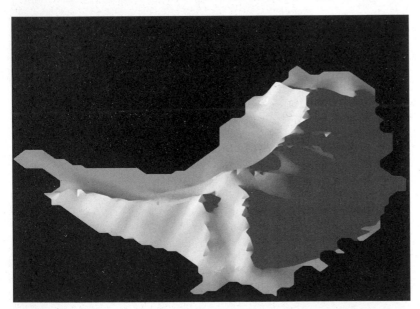

8-22

This is a very simple model. It was done as a rush job and it did not require a great deal of modeling or render time. The trick here was to work like a photographer, only placing objects within the locked-down frame of the camera. If you are doing a single frame illustration or you are not moving the camera in an animation, it is always best to create a set for a single perspective.

WALKTHROUGHS AND FLYTHROUGHS

The simplest and most common forms of computer animation are walkthroughs and flythroughs. In these types of animations, everything can remain locked in place while the camera moves along a set path through the model. A walkthrough animation looks like someone walked through your set with a hand-held camera. The vantage point is around eye level and the movement is fairly steady. A flythrough can be made at any speed or from any vantage point. X-wing fighters buzzing through the trenches of the Death Star at the end of *Star Wars* is a premier example of a flythrough.

Walkthroughs and flythroughs are among the most effective forms of computer animation because there can be a great deal of movement and change between frames with only one object (the camera) moving.

The same kind of movement would be exceedingly difficult with cel animation because the background would have to be redrawn for each frame. In traditional film a walkthrough is very expensive requiring steadycams or dollys, booms, and other expensive, mobile systems. So with the computer you get a big bang for your buck just by moving the camera.

It is more efficient to use billboards for walkthroughs and fly-

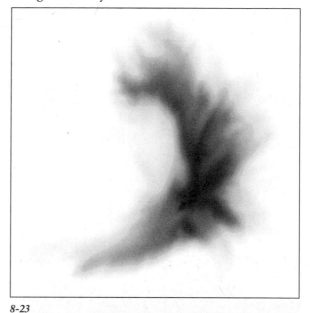

throughs, but when there is a significant change in the viewer's perspective, the illusion created by the billboard tends to break down. A well-planned set for a walkthrough or flythrough will usually use a combination of billboard images and modeled geometry. When you view a two-dimensional billboard from the side, it disappears, so the shot and the billboards should be planned carefully. In Figure 8-16, the billboard images are transparencies at an approximately 45-degree angle from the camera. Interspersed with the billboards are trees, grass, and rocks made of 3D geometry. Special care is taken at the edges of the billboard images and the points where they intersect the groundplane. These are the areas most likely to break the illusion by showing a hard edge.

8-23

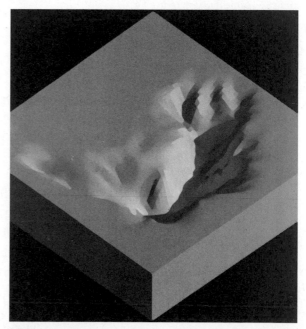

If you've ever seen a war movie you may have noticed how marines in the jungle don't just wear camouflage uniforms. They often put leafy branches into the netting of their helmets and the folds of their uniforms. This is not so enemy soldiers will mistake them for bushes or trees when standing out in the open. The branches are meant to break the familiar silhouette of a soldier because it is easier for the human eye to pick out a smooth, artificial, shape like a soldier's helmet against a natural background, than it is to single out one odd-shaped object from another.

8-24

8-25

It is the silhouette and the shape of an object which registers first in our brain. When we place a picture of an object in a natural scene, it is the hard edge, the artificial shape of the picture, that is most detrimental to creating a believable image.

Figures 8-21 and 8-22:
Grayscale image and polygon mesh of a hill generated by using the grayscale image as a displacement map.

Figures 8-23 and 8-24:
The reverse of the grayscale image shown in Figure 8-21 and the resulting inverted "valley" generated with a polygon mesh.

Figure 8-25:
A view from inside the same valley.

Figures 8-26 and 8-27:
A varied terrain created by positioning multiple copies of varying sizes of the same hill on a flat surface shown from inside the set and from an isometric view.

TERRAIN

I think one of the most fun things to make in 3D art is terrain. It's just about the closest anyone can get to playing God. Just as with texture mapping and modeling natural objects, there are procedural (or fractal) algorithms to create some very impressive virtual terrain. Many fractal terrain generators produce spectacular and sublime effects by adjusting a few preset parameters. These fractal landscapes often have an otherworldly feel. They look like alien landscapes because the subtleties of natural environments such as vegetation and erosion are very difficult to generate through algorithms on a desktop computer.

The only major drawback to purely fractally-created environments is control. Most artists find it almost impossible to create landscapes that meet their exact specifications and proportions by adjusting mathematical formulas. Fractal terrains can be very pretty, but just like in nature, you often have to deal with what you can get.

Most programs work in a similar fashion to create specific terrains. Using a digital paint program such as Photoshop, the artist makes a grayscale relief map of the terrain where lighter values represent mountains or hills. Black becomes the lowest point of the model and is represented by a flat plane or no geometry at all. White areas will be the highest point of the model. Most software can generate a kind of displacement map based upon the grayscale image. A displacement map works like a bump map except it actually changes the geometry of the object to which it is applied. The artist can adjust the detail of the terrain by increasing the resolution of the grayscale and adding more variations in light and dark. In spline-based modeling programs, the flat geometry with displacement maps can be converted into a polygon mesh.

8-26

Figures 8-21 through 8-27 show how to use imported grayscale maps to generate modeled terrain. In Figure 8-22, an island was created by importing an image which is lighter in the

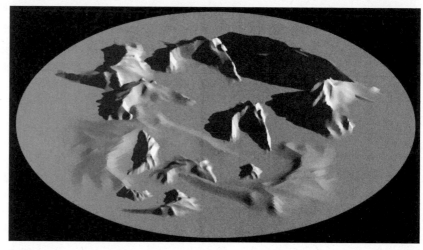

8-27

center and black on the edges (Figure 8-21). The resulting polygon mesh is a hill or island. Compare the polygon mesh to the grayscale image it is based on. You can see the higher ridges correspond to the light areas of the map.

Figure 8-23 reverses the grayscale map used to create the island. The darker area in the center forms an indentation in the geometry created by the white edges of the map, creating the valley in Figure 8-24. Figure 8-25 is a view from inside the valley model. In this illustration the camera is very close to the model and you can actually see the triangular planes which make up the polygon mesh.

If you are planning to allow the viewer to get this close to the model, it's a good idea to create a higher-density polygon mesh and then "smooth" the surface before rendering. Another word for smoothing is "tesilation." A model that is tesilated will round off the corners of the polygons when it is rendered. Note that increasing the density of the mesh and smoothing can add considerable weight to the model and time to the rendering process.

Figure 8-26 is a render of multiple instances of the same hill at different sizes and angles. Even from the aerial view it is pretty hard to tell that you are looking at the same object many times. Instancing natural objects like trees, rocks, and terrain is the best solution for creating complex environments. The viewer will usually be drawn to the silhouette of the shape and not pick up on the similarities of instanced organic shapes.

CHAPTER 9

Perspective and Trompe L'Oeil

Traditional set designers and effects artists know how to create magic using light, paint, plywood, and cloth. A good designer can create dramatic effects like thunderstorms, fires, and fog without actually releasing forces of nature inside a theater. In the same way, a 3D artist can create fantastic illusions by learning to think more like a traditional set designers.

It is possible to accurately recreate entire real environments in the computer. In some cases, creating a detailed, accurate model takes precedence over the strain on the CPU, the tremendous production time, and very slow render times. If the computer model will be used as the basis for a real structure or object, as a floor plan, or for a scientific simulation, you won't want to skimp on accuracy. However, most of the time you should try to think like a traditional set designer. This is because a set designer is used to creating a convincing illusion with practical limitations such as the size of the theater, the line of sight of the audience, controlled lighting and restricted production budgets. CGI can create anything an artist can imagine, but practical considerations like finishing the job make it nescassary to set limits on things like the amount of lights, geometry, and cameras.

FORCED PERSPECTIVE

In the first example, I've used an old set designers' convention called forced perspective. Have you ever been in a fun house hallway that appears to be very long yet is actually a short space with smaller and smaller doorways? Then you have been tricked by forced perspective. As objects get farther away from the camera they become smaller and less intense in color and parallel lines seem to converge on the horizon. When set designers must create a large room or outdoor scene, they almost always force the perspective by decreasing the size of known objects in the background. A known object can be something like a doorway or a chair. If a designer places a full-

9-1

9-2

Figure 9-1:
Rendered image of a pier
extending to the horizon.

Figure 9-2:
Rendered image of a much
shorter pier using forced
perspective.

sized doorway front stage and a three-quarter-sized doorway of equal proportions farther back on the stage, the audience perceives the stage to be larger than it actually is. Even when a designer has a huge backstage area, he will very often use forced perspective because it is less expensive and time consuming than building an entire set. This kind of thinking relates directly to designing 3D environments. Figure 9-1 is a rendering of a pier with 30 street lamps with a horizon line. Figure 9-2 uses forced perspective to achieve a very similar result. The forced perspective render uses only 20 street lamps and the dock is about half as long as in the original model. If you look closely at both images, you will notice that the pier in Figure 9-2 does not come as close to the horizon line as the pier in Figure 9-1, but that difference is negligible especially if there is no basis for comparison.

The forced perspective image was achieved by decreasing the size of the lamps by 5 percent with each replication. The distance between each lamp was decreased by 10 percent as they got farther away from the camera. Similar steps were followed to generate the poles on the railing. The model of the pier is in the shape of a trapezoid which comes close to converging at the far end. The railing also converges in the distance.

Figures 9-3 and 9-4 clearly show the differences between the two models. The forced perspective model takes a little bit more time and thought to make, but it will generate significant savings in file size and render times. Even with a model as simple as the one shown in Figure 9-2, the 33 percent reduction in geometry and shorter distances decreased render times by about half.

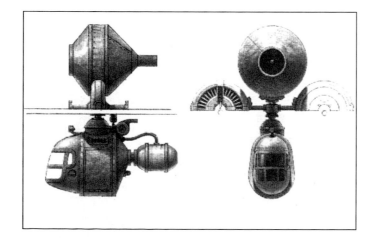

*Clockwise from above:
Rendering of the village
environment from Riven; early
sketches of the cable car by
Robyn Miller; final render of
the cable car in its berth; pilot's
eye views of an environment
from within the cable car.
Following page: Observatory.
All images from the CD-ROM
game Riven.
© 1997 Cyan, Inc.*

This page and preceding page: Foundation Imaging, Inc. composited traditionally drawn cel animation with CG models to create these stunning images for the made-for-video film "Batman vs. Subzero."
© Warner Bros.

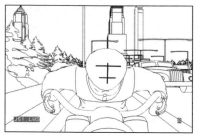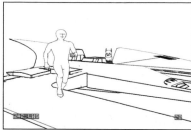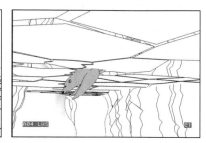

This page:

Stills illustrating some of the process involved with compositing hand drawn and computer-generated art; top images are wireframe renders with drawn characters blocked out; green screen frames show the two-dimensional elements only; bottom frames are fully composited images.
© *Warner Bros.*

All images created by Foundation Imaging, Inc.

The illusion of forced perspective will not be broken if the camera moves from side to side or pans along this model. If viewed from a distance the illusion will still be intact. The effect will, however, be lost if the camera moves down the pier or the model is seen from the back or side view. While forced perspective can save time and energy when making still images or an environment with fixed camera positions, it is not a great solution for virtual reality where the user does not have a restricted point of view.

The same principles of forced perspective can be applied to lighting and atmospheric effects to create the illusion of distance. Lights can be dimmed as they recede from the camera to simulate natural falloff. Textures can be grayed out on objects that are in the background to simulate the dissipation of light in the atmosphere, an effect known as atmospheric perspective.

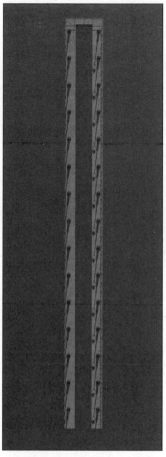

9-3 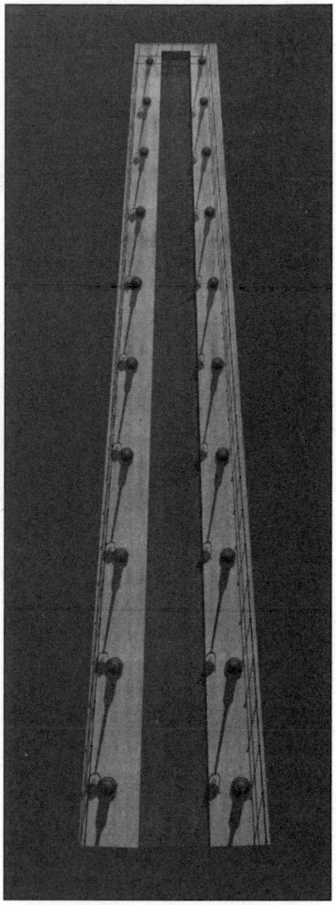   9-4

Figure 9-3:
Top view of the image of the pier shown in Figure 9-1.

Figure 9-4:
Top view of the image of the shortened pier using forced perspective shown in Figure 9-2.

If you are making a detailed animation or illustration and you have plotted out your camera movements or composition beforehand, using forced perspective to decrease geometry can be the difference between a successfully completed or a failed render.

TILED SETS

When set designers must show movement from one place to another they are faced with a myriad of challenges. The audience in a traditional theater cannot move, therefore the set must move for the audience. Tiling the background and moving it past the viewer is an old trick that has been around since at least the days of Vaudeville when the set designers would put a background on a scroll and roll it between two drums. Moving the set, not the camera, is also a very useful device when working in computer graphics. If you are planning a very long camera movement or flythrough, it may seem

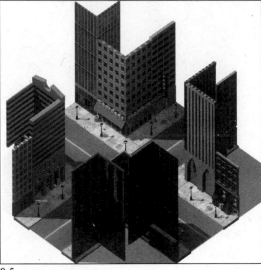

9-5

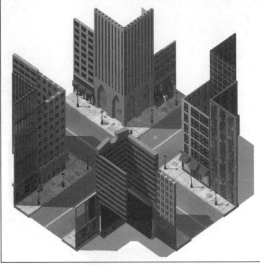

9-6

*Figures 9-5 to 9-8:
Isometric renders of the
intersection set from four
different points of view.*

*Figure 9-9:
Isometric view of a street
made from two copies of
the intersection set butted
against each other.*

logical to build an elaborate set and then move the camera through the model. But, this necessitates building a very large, complex set. Instead, use a "tiled set."

Figures 9-5 through 9-9 show a set for a scene of a car driving through New York City. The entire set is simply a model of an intersection of two perpendicular streets. The model includes facades for the four corner buildings in the intersection and a few buildings that face only one street. No forced perspective was used because the camera will move through almost every part of the model. The clever part about this model is it can be tiled just like a texture map or a parquet floor. The entire model can be instanced and rotated at either 90, 180, or 270 degrees. The rotated instance can be butted up against the original to create a full city block. Since each of the buildings is distinct, there are 16 different combinations of city blocks available by placing various sides of the intersection next to each other. Yes, if you look closely you will probably be able to spot the same building going by, but that can be fixed with motion blur and varying camera angles.

The real elegance of this tiled model comes into play when you start your animation. The camera, lighting setup, and automobile can be left in a fixed place making it very easy to have a single simple, fixed lighting solution or to perhaps animate characters in the car, and the set can move past the camera. Once the intersection is out of range, it can be deleted from the model keeping the file size comparatively small.

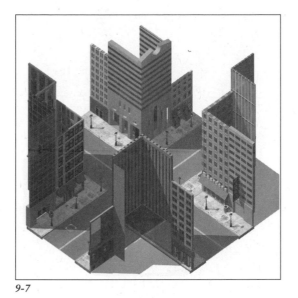

9-7

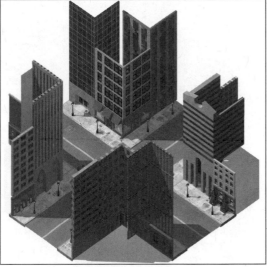

9-8

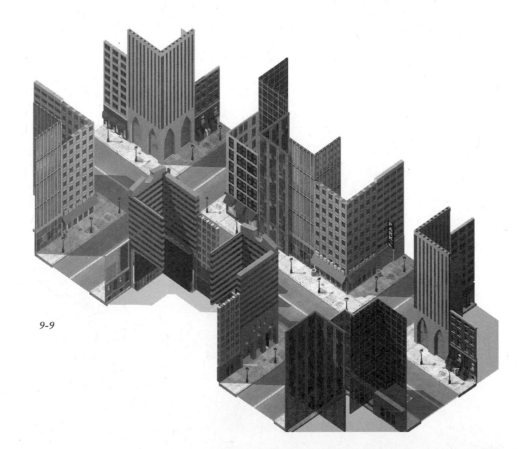

9-9

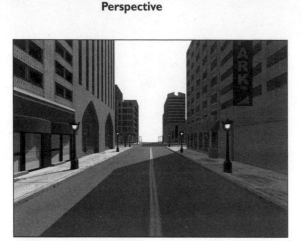

9-10

9-11

**Figures 9-10,9-11,9-13,9-14:
Four views from inside the
intersection set looking
down the street.**

**Figure 9-12:
View down the street
created by placing three
interection sets next to
each other.**

**Figure 9-15:
Classical trompe l'oeil
painted by Paolo Veronese
for a Palladio-designed villa
in northern Italy.**

Figures 9-5 through 9-8 show four isometric renderings of the intersection set from different views. Figure 9-9 shows one of the
possible combinations making a city block. Figures 9-10 through
9-13 show different views of the single intersection from inside the
set. Figure 9-12 is a view looking down a street made by using the
same intersection three times.

When working with large 3D sets it is very difficult to determine the
level of detail necessary to create a convincing piece. Even if you use
forced perspective, simulated atmospheric effects, and tiled sets you
will probably still need to sacrifice some detail to keep the file size
small enough to manipulate easily.

9-12

9-13   9-14

TROMPE L'OEIL

You can make a very detailed model and still keep your file size manageable using the principles of trompe l'oeil. In English, the French "trompe l'oeil" means "to fool the eye." It is a very old technique which was extremely popular during the Renaissance when artists learned to master the techniques of perspective drawing. The painting in Figure 9-15, from a Palladio villa in northern Italy, is an elaborate example of trompe l'oeil. The railings, doorway, and people were all painted on the wall to create the illusion of depth and architectural detail. This painting is part of an ornate villa where trompe l'oeil was used for its delightful effect rather than to save on architectural details as a cost-cutting measure. A 3D computer artist usually uses trompe l'oeil for practical purposes like cutting down modeling and render times, and speeding up the production process.

The very detailed city block in Figure 9-17 was modeled using only simple, primitive shapes (Figure 9-16). The facades of all of the build-ings were created using trompe l'oeil textures. This example is a bit of an exaggeration since even the foreground objects are not modeled with any detail, but the finished model is attractive nonetheless.

SIMULATED MOTION BLUR AND SIMULATED DEPTH OF FIELD

Motion blur and depth of field are special effects that add a great deal of realism to an animation or illustration;

9-15

9-16

however, they also add significant time to a render. Both effects can triple or quadruple render times on even a simple illustration or animation. Most programs first start rendering these effects after completing the calculations for light and geometry. Simulating motion blur or depth of field is a great solution to the rendering problem. These two effects work particularly well when coupled with the trompe l'oeil technique of emulating depth with a texture map.

Most software imitates motion blur by rendering a ghosted version of the subject trailing the original image. If the artist adds more motion blur, the software will generate a few more ghosted versions of the original. Rather than going through this process for each frame of an animation, it is

9-17

easier to create the same effect once in Photoshop and then apply the blurred texture to the model. The effect of motion-blurred textures breaks down at the edges of the actual geometry because it still has sharp edges. This is why "faking" motion blur and depth of field work so well with trompe l'oeil images where depth and complex geometry are simulated on a single surface.

When working with simulated depth of field and motion blur, trompe l'oeil, simulated atmospheric perspective, and forced perspective, an artist must be very conscious of the line of sight of the viewer. A traditional set designer will make sure his or her work can be viewed from every seat in the house without the illusion breaking down. All of the effects in this chapter require extra planning by the artist to make sure there are no serious visual compromises when the audience views the final piece. However, the time invested in planning will be well spent when the final piece is rendered with the illusion of depth, volume, and realism.

Figure: 9-16:
The set of a city block rendered without texture maps to show the simple geometric shapes used to make the entire model.

Figure 9-17:
The same set with texture maps.

Figure 9-18:
Photograph of a building which can be used as a tiled texture to simulate depth and detail on a flat object. Image from the Artbeats CD-ROM "City Surfaces," courtesy of ARTBEATS Software, Inc., Myrtle Creek, OR.

Figure 9-19:
The same image as in Figure 9-18 tiled twice with a simulated motion blur.

9-18

9-19

Robyn Miller:
Cyan, Inc.

It would not be an exaggeration to say that Robyn Miller and his brother Rand revolutionized the multimedia industry when their company released the CD-ROM Myst *in 1993. Their company, Cyan, Inc., located in rural Washington State, already had a string of attractive and well-conceived CD-ROM titles, but it was* Myst *that spawned a huge popular and cult following, and went on to become the best-selling adventure game of all time. With Macintosh computers and StrataVision, they created convincing and beautiful worlds which enveloped the user in a surrealistic experience. Literally hundreds of imitators tried to duplicate their success, but to this date none have come close. At the time of this interview, Cyan has released* Riven *(pronounced like "given"), the much-anticipated sequel which reenters the world of* Myst *with even more incredible groundbreaking imagery.*

Author: Creatively, was there a conscious choice to capture the same feel as when you started Riven?

Robyn Miller: In some ways we wanted to capture the same deal as was present in *Myst*. For example, we wanted *Riven* to contain a bit of the mood that was so prevalent in *Myst*. There was also an interface in *Myst* that made navigation fairly easy and painless; it was important that we maintain this interface for *Riven*. But one of the most exciting things about working on a project like *Riven* was that we had freedom to create a world that expressed a different mood, a different feel. Visually, *Riven* is in many ways different from *Myst*. Where *Myst* was more

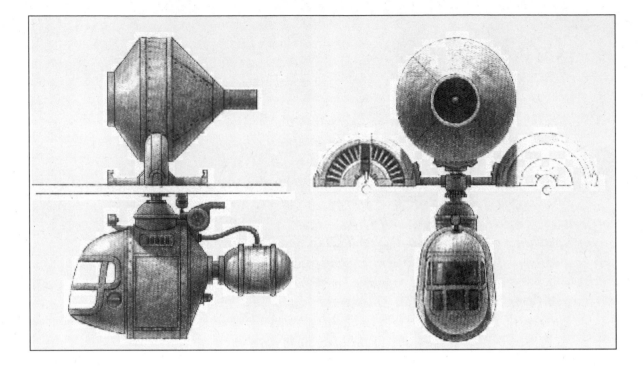

Sketches for the Mag car for the CD-ROM game Riven.

dependent on traditional, Western architectural forms, *Riven* is a place that is much more unfamiliar, much more foreign. The last thing we wanted to do was create a carbon copy of *Myst*.

PW: *How many different environments were planned and realized?*

RM: It's almost impossible to count the number of environments that we planned. In *Riven*, one environment merges into the next one. I'm not sure how we would divide them up. We did not cut back to a lower amount of environments than initially planned. If anything, we increased the number of environments.

PW: *What kind of hardware and software options did you consider?*

RM: We wanted to continue working on Macintoshes, but, for the

3D work, we knew that would be impossible because of the power limitations. After exploring every possible Macintosh and PC 3D software available, we decided to make the switch to SGI's. Of course, this was a platform we knew absolutely nothing about, so finding the correct software was difficult. It boiled down to taking each of the major 3D software packages back to our offices and testing them out for prolonged periods. We finally decided on SoftImage. It was able to handle the most data (and we knew we'd be throwing a lot at it), and its animation capabilities were, for our purposes, superior to the other software we tried.

PW: *What kind of reference materials did you use?*

RM: We have stacks and stacks of books in our art department, and we rely on them heavily during both the design and production phases of our work. We most heavily referenced books relating to African, Arabic, and Celtic designs. But, I can't say we didn't spend a good deal of time looking through books on the making of *Star Wars*. Seriously, these *Star Wars* books offer a lot of indirect inspiration because the films (or at least a couple of them) were designed in such a visually superior fashion.

PW: *Were there any actual locations or objects shot for reference?*

RM: Throughout the design and production of *Riven* we compiled quite a library of textures. These are photos, taken by our *Riven* team, of thousands of textures: from woods, to adobe, to rock, to rusted metals.

These textures were mostly used by the artists at Cyan to apply to objects in 3D space. At one point during production, three of us made a trip to Santa Fe, New Mexico, specifically to capture adobe textures. The Santa Fe trip was, for us, the jackpot. We went there and spent the entire time holding our cameras a foot away or so from walls, doors, fences, and even a horse...clicking, clicking, clicking. The locals must have thought we were nuts.

PW: *Was there an effort to adapt a specific artistic style to the effort?*

RM: We wanted the visual style of *Riven* to be consistent. We wanted it to make sense with itself; we wanted it to relate to itself and be believable. But instead of choosing an established styling, we tried to stretch ourselves and invent a look that we had not seen before. We tried to create something original. For an artist to create something completely original is impossible; there really isn't such a thing as something that is completely original, but it's very possible and sometimes very powerful to combine existing elements into a new whole. This is what an artist does: Ingest the world around him or her and regurgitate it, putting it back together into something that is familiar, yet unfamiliar; normal, yet magical. I can cite examples of resources that proved to be an inspiration for us, but really, those resources inspired us in very superficial ways. We've been "ingesting" since we were born, and what comes out now is the sum of our entire lives. If I were to say that stylistically we drew from African art, I may as well say that stylistically we drew from Dr. Seuss or Sesame Street (yes, I'm that young).

PW: *What were the original estimates for the size of the production crew and the time schedule?*

RM: "Estimates" seems too formal a word. Perhaps we should call them "wild guesses." The truth is, we grossly underestimated. At one, very early point (for a few days), we thought we could do the entire project with two artists. Then (for a few weeks), we thought we could do it with three artists. There ended up being about thirteen Cyan artists that have worked on the project, in addition to numerous programmers, video crews, costume designers, actors, etc.... I look at the credit list and it's difficult to believe how many talented people have come together to work on it, especially when I remember the size of the team on *Myst*: two artists, two programmers, and a sound designer.

We originally thought that we might get it done in two years, but that quickly jumped up to about three years. We finished it in three and a half years, so I think we did pretty well.

PW: *How was the work divided?*

For a project of this nature, we had a lot of people on the team, but still, because there was so much for us to do, everyone wore a lot of hats. None of our artists, for example, were stuck painting texture maps the entire project. No one spent all their time doing lighting. A lot of big effects houses are extremely specialized, but, for this project, we had the luxury of diversity.

PW: *How did you account for production limitations when designing environments?*

RM: Because we're so involved in the production, it's easier for us to know what is and what is not possible. When we're actually sitting around brainstorming, trying to piece

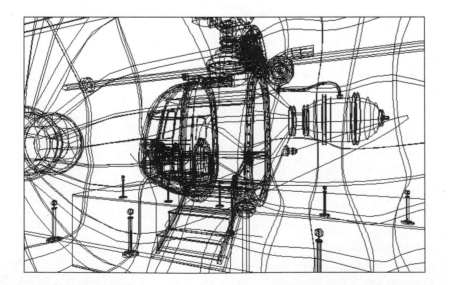

Wireframe render of Mag car and surrounding environment.

together this world, we aren't usually thinking about the potential production limitations; I think that this would tend to hinder creative energy. But we often look over the designs from the past week or the past day, and reevaluate with more of a practical mindset. This doesn't mean that we don't push ourselves in the direction of challenges; there are, many times, elements we design not having any idea how we will practically accomplish them. But, at least, we have a fair idea of how to keep our costs relatively low. And we don't often find ourselves traveling down a road which is absolutely impossible to take to completion.

PW: Did you consider animated characters rather than compositing live action?

RM: If we did, it was only during a momentary lack of reason. Computer-animated people (humans) just don't cut it. Why make computer-animated people when real people do a much better job, are much easier to work with, and are much less expensive than CG people? Perhaps there will be animated humans (some day) that are so believable that they are indistinguishable from the real thing. But why go to all the trouble when actors already do the job so well? Humans are, arguably, the most expressive animals on the planet; trying to recreate the myriad of emotions that a human can so

View from the surreal funicular ride in Riven.

subtly express seems to be a waste of efforts and resources.

CG character animation is much better suited to animals that don't really exist. In fact, it is probably the most ideal way to create new creatures and animals as characters. We did a bit of this in *Riven*. I could see us doing a lot more of it in the future.

This is one of the most exciting aspects of 3D animations; giving life to creatures that are not human.

Having so belligerently said all of that, I would also add that I do think that CG is still appropriate for those cases when humans are heavily involved in a CG shot. For example, CG is probably the best way to go if you want to show some guy falling out of an airplane, or being stomped on by a parade of elephants. We should have done more of this in *Riven*, and we will probably do more in the DVD version of *Riven*.

PW: *Were there any scenes that were scrapped once they were visualized in 3D?*

RM: We scrapped some of our work; mostly in the beginning of the project, when Richard VanderWende (director of the sequel) and I were still establishing the visual rules and look of the place. We have high-resolution stills if you'd like them.

PW: *Were there any happy accidents?*

RM: "Happy Accidents" is our middle name. We often encounter them no matter what we are doing. There's a short solo during Gehn's Theme. I played it while testing the recording software and thought I had completely screwed up. By chance, I listened to it; it's the nicest solo I think I've ever done. Though, I'm not sure I can claim credit for it; it was random.

But, as many happy accidents as we have, we have about 20 unhappy accidents...."Unhappy Accidents" is our first name.

PW: *File management — how did Cyan keep track of production, backup, etc...?*

RM: You mean we were supposed to keep track of these things? Actually, backups were automatic and regular. But keeping track of all of what's been done and what still needs to be done is insane, especially when you consider that, on a nonlinear project like *Riven*, we never get the chance to just sit down and review the entire thing from start to finish. We don't get to watch dailies, or even weeklies, as is typically done in the movie industry during production. Instead, when we want to make sure we've got everything correct, we have to walk through the entire world, flipping every switch, setting up every possible combination of states. In some areas there are as many as 32 states. The production is a week away from signing out and still we are finding backgrounds that are incorrect, or animations that don't match the states of a particular background. We will not find all of these mistakes. Some of them will be discovered by our audiences after release. This is the single most frustrating aspect of creating a world like *Riven*; there is just no possible way to completely review it. Even when I walk through it (which I've done many times) and test it. I'm probably only seeing a tenth of the possible imagery, because of the particular way I tend to play. I watch someone else play and suddenly they do things that I would have never imagined anyone doing! It's maddening. Imagine an author only being able to review half a book which he or she is about to release. He may know the story he wrote the first time through, but he can never really check to see all the changes that the editor may have made. This is the nature of nonlinear media.

PW: *Did you ever consider any other mediums other than 3D to create this product?*

RM: For *Myst*, we considered more traditional media for a while: paintings. But for *Riven*, we never seriously considered anything but 3D.

PW: *Was the realization of any of the environments dramatically different than any of the sketches?*

RM: Because of the size of our team, it was not usually necessary

to create especially articulate sketches. Most of our sketches were very rough, so the environments were necessarily dramatically different from them. But, by the time we would actually begin production on a specific environment, it would usually end up being something that was not far off from the way Richard and I had envisioned it.

PW: *How was the mood visually changed between environments?*

RM: A change of mood and atmosphere, from one environment to another, was extremely important to us. It's our way of injecting drama into the environment. We don't think of our environments strictly as just a place; we think of them as an extension of the story, we think of the environment as staging. The lagoon is a good example of that. The player finds themselves on a set of steep, stone stairs, wedged between two semivertical stone walls. These walls are in complete shadow, so the immediate surroundings are rather dark, though down at the base of the stairs, a glint of light can barely be seen. As the player continues down the stairs, the glint of light grows into an obvious parting of the stone cliffs through which can barely be seen a brightly lit lagoon, inhabited by two large creatures which are turning themselves on a rock. As the player continues down, the dark rock walls part, curtain-like, until finally the player emerges from them and can fully see all of the contrasting, and very brightly lit, little lagoon. Most people will probably never notice this transition, and they shouldn't. But, hopefully, it will make everyone's first view of these creatures more effective.

PW: *Describe how you used lighting to refine the images.*

RM: The same way that a cinematographer would. We use lighting, color, contrast, etc. to make our world more meaningful.

PW: *Did the piece visually achieve the original goals?*

RM: I believe we achieved our goals almost as much as is possible. But I don't believe it's possible to be 100 percent there when you're dealing with budgets and schedules (which are both extremely necessary on a project with more than one person working on it). If we made 80 percent or 90 percent then I'm thrilled. We achieved more on this project than we've ever achieved before, and even if it fails in the market, I will have felt like we were successful.

PW: *How different was the final from the original concept?*

RM: *Riven* was an evolving world. We were still designing, and making changes (some of them, major) to the design well into the production. I believe this has to do with the difficult nature of a nonlinear medium and it's a feature which I don't enjoy. It's exciting, but it's exasperating and expensive.

PW: *In retrospect, what would you change?*

RM: You learn many things throughout the course of each project. One thing I would change would be our process, especially in the area of designs. I think we could have saved production time by creating a sort of working prototype of the finished product before we even began. There is no real reason not to make a version of the entire game that works, but contains placement sounds and storyboard-type drawings instead of finished assets. With something like this, we could have even tested our designs more thoroughly up front (by play-testing this prototype), made changes in the design very easily, and, most importantly, cut out the time that the design phase overlapped into the production phase.

PW: Would you do it again and will there be a sequel?

RM: If there's a sequel, I can't imagine what it would be and I can't imagine being involved with it. In my mind, the *Myst/Riven* story is over and I'm extremely anxious to get on to other things. We designed *Myst* with a sequel in mind. We designed *Riven* to be the end of the story.

PW: Would you consider working in any other medium?

RM: I can't imagine myself just doing interactive for my entire life. There are other areas that I am interested in exploring: perhaps those that are more suited to storytelling than the interactive medium.

PW: What is next for Cyan?

RM: Vacations. And I can't wait!

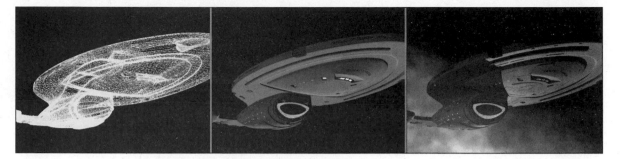

Ron Thornton:
Foundation Imaging

In 1992, Ron Thornton and his partner Paul Beigle-Bryant formed their production company, Foundation Imaging. Their break-through concept, to create cinematic-quality, computer-generated effects on desktop computers, profoundly changed the television and special effects industry. Foundation Imaging made the production of the science fiction drama Babylon 5 *a reality by showing the studios that the "anything is possible" world of CG effects could be brought to the small screen on time with a limited budget. In 1993, they received an Emmy for "Outstanding Achievement in Special Effects" for their work on* Babylon 5. *Since then, there has been an explosion of science fiction and fantasy television shows and feature films which all owe a debt of gratitude to the pioneering work of Ron Thornton and Paul Beigle-Bryant.*

Foundation Imaging has moved on to create their own production, Hypernauts, *special effects for the syndicated series* Star Trek: Voyager, *and special effects for Hollywood films such as* Contact *starring Jodie Foster and* The Jackel *with Bruce Willis and Richard Gere, while still utilizing relatively inexpensive desktop computers and LightWave software. While being masters of technology, their focus and dedication to art will assure that Foundation Imaging will continue to make a significant mark on their industry for years to come.*

Author: What kind of background did you have before you got into 3D computer graphics?

Ron Thornton: Well, before I got into "3D" I had had quite a few years of experience with traditional visual effects, you know, modelmaking, camera work, lighting, animation, and various disciplines within the field.

PW: *Did you do a lot of stop motion work?*

RT: I didn't do a lot of stop motion work. I did some motion control programming, which was a help because it uses similar techniques to 3D in terms of keyframing, and the way in which you create moves is very similar.

PW: *And your partner was also doing something similar?*

RT: No, actually my partner, Paul, was a vice president of a bank, but he was involved in the computer networking side of it. We work really well together as a team. I mean, I'm pretty much the content side of things and Paul looks after the hardware and makes sure the place runs properly.

PW: *Did you form Foundation Imaging to do the effects for Babylon 5?*

RT: Yes, absolutely. It was initially started to do the effects for *Babylon 5*, but part and parcel of it was that we had an agreement with the producers to make an investment in ourselves by giving them a reduced rate that we were keeping the equipment and creating a company of our own.

PW: *So, it was in conjunction with the television producers...*

RT: Yes, and that was the only way I would do it because otherwise it's not worth it...at least not for the money that they were paying. It was a very cheaply-produced show.

PW: *It was a breakthrough in the way you used LightWave and the VideoToaster for broadcast production. Tell me how the sequence of events worked.*

RT: Well, I'd worked in Canada on *Captain Power and the Soldiers of the Future* and one of the modelmakers on the team had an Amiga computer. His brother had written this very strange piece of software that took video and had...I'm trying to find a way to describe it...things called Mandela, I think, and what you could perform in front of a bluescreen and move your hand to a certain position and trigger things in the computer. So, you could set up these icons all around yourself and play tunes with it and stuff. It was a very strange, very weird program, but it was very interesting, very graphics orientated, and it was the first time I'd ever seen anything like that.

When I came back from Canada, I told my next door neighbor, Paul, about this. I said that we should go and have a look at these machines and there was just about to be an Amiga expo so we went down there and Paul was amazingly impressed. He had never seen anything like it and, you know, he'd seen an awful lot of computers in his time, but this was a first true multitasking operating system. The thing had great video capabilities. Unfortunately, it never grew as much as it should have. I mean it was an amazing computer...it was very, very smart.

So anyway, we bought one Amiga each and bought a couple of the early 3D programs, and most of them were horrible. They were atrocious. They were really difficult to use. In fact, I think the first one that Paul bought was written by the gentleman who now programs LightWave, Alan Hastings. It was called VideoScape 3D and, oh boy, it was tough. It was very text-based. It was very difficult to use. We eventually found one piece of software that we could play with but the rendering just wasn't there. There was no way of displaying 16 million colors; it was all in 4,096 color. So what I've mainly used it for was previsualizing shots. I'd do wireframe animations...

Earth battleship from the television series **Babylon 5.**

PW: *Kind of like an animatics?*

RT: Exactly. I'd make a wireframe model and then I'd do an animation of it and then dump that to videotape. And that would be good for a producer to see what sort of shot I was planning with miniatures. It went on that way for awhile and then the Video-

Still from **Babylon 5.**

Toaster came along. The guys at Newtek had created this very cool card which could do fades and wipes and mixes and was basically a video mixer board. It came bundled with a lot of stuff and one of the programs was the early version of LightWave. It was a full 24-bit 3D package that wasn't difficult to use. So I immediately bought one of these and started experimenting. It was only about a month and a half after that that I realized that this could really work. I started working with Todd Rundgren in Northern California on a rock video. At the same time I was working, in my time off, on coming up with a way to do science fiction television shows using computer graphics, just because nobody could really do that at the time. We did this test for *Babylon 5* because apparently there was interest in it. I'd been following it for a long time because the producers had approached me to do images for it some five years earlier.

PW: *So what year was this?*

RT: It was late 1991. We did about a minute-long test doing shots that you couldn't possibly do with motion control with full cosmic zooms from miles away and stuff, and showing really close detail of an object. That was shown with the next pitch of the show when, as always, the executives would ask, "Okay, well this is all well and good, you're going to do this show about a space station. How are you going to do the effects? How are you going to afford it?" Well this time we had a tape and we could put it in and say we're going to do it like this. The show was up and running in a matter of a couple of months after that.

PW: So the first few shows were done with not just yourself and Paul and two Amigas. I assume you hired your staff right away.

RT: Oh no, at the time, Paul and I had a hole drilled through the wall networking our Amigas together that way. Paul was constantly looking for solutions about how to deal with this. So, I was designing and building the ships way, way before they had greenlighted the project because I wanted to make absolutely sure that we could do it. So by the time they eventually did, we were ready to roll and all we needed was the first check and we moved into the facility and bought the machines. We literally had all of our ducks in a row so we could just throw the switch as soon as money arrived.

Wireframe render of a robot from the television series Hypernauts.

PW: Do you still use any Amigas?

RT: I have one. Unfortunately, I've lent it to someone at the moment. There is one program that's on it that is absolutely indispensible and it's one of the best things ever. It's D-Paint. And it's just so good. It's a little 2D animation package and when you use it with just 16 or 32 or 64 colors, it's just amazing what you can do. You can paint stuff in real time and just do all sorts of neat tricks which are very, very handy. In fact, most of the texture maps of *Babylon 5* were done in D-Paint.

PW: Creatively, do you have a general philosophy of design at Foundation Imaging or do you take each project as it comes?

RT: You kind of have to take each project as it comes because if you apply some of the rules that you used before in a new show, you'll end up with a similar look. But sometimes there is crossover. You know, there are unavoidable situations where you have that, but mostly it's up to whoever you're dealing with as a client. Each show has a certain look and a certain style. For example, *Star Trek* will very, very rarely bank or tumble the camera because all the way through their history they've had very, very smooth, steady shots. Some of the battle scenes that we used to do in *Babylon 5* where the camera was going all over the place and shaking and shuddering, we don't do that with *Star Trek* because it doesn't fit in with their universe. So, to answer your question: Yes, there are differences between each show.

PW: Did you follow some sort of Star Trek *bible telling you the specific ways the models should look beyond the camera movements?*

Wireframe and character renders for the **Hypernaut** *series.*

RT: No, there is no such animal. There is no bible, but it's all based on the experience of the supervisors with Dan Curry being the senior supervisor in place. He's the Effects Producer on *Star Trek* and all the less-experienced supervisors all go to him with questions or what have you. I mean Ron Moore obviously has been around for awhile so he knows a lot of the *Star Trek* rules, but Dan ultimately knows what they've been through.

We've been pretty lucky actually. We've been able to do some pretty unique stuff this last year and we're getting more and more of it in the show. And you know they're realizing that some of these more bizarre moves bring real production value to the show.

PW: I was also going to ask you about the 3D character that you created, the virtual alien. Is that a first for Star Trek?

RT: Well, yes and no. Our very first *Voyager* that we did, we just did a few shots of a synthetic worm creature and that was kind of our introduction to the show. So it's kind of interesting that we started the season with a creature and ended the season with a creature, but it [the virtual alien], certainly to me, was the most characterized of anything we'd done. I mean previously it had been monsters really, but the character we did in this had to display intelligence and be nasty. It was great fun to do.

PW: *You're using LightWave for all the production on this job?*

RT: Yes, LightWave, AfterEffects, and PhotoShop are pretty much the main programs that we use.

PW: *Have you ever considered using SoftImage, Alias, or some of the other UNIX-based programs, too?*

RT: No. The problem with that is the per-seat (unit) cost is enormous. What you have to do is think about how much a PC workstation costs and how much a Silicon Graphics workstation costs and how much the software costs on top of that and I can't buy as many workstations, therefore I can't get as many animators in. And when it comes down to it, it's a tool. It doesn't matter what computer you're using or what software you're using so long as the artist is there who knows how to utilize it.

PW: *About how many animators do you have working at Foundation Imaging now?*

RT: We've got 20 animators working right now.

PW: *How about the whole corporation?*

RT: The whole corporation including Paul and myself is 27.

PW: *So you are very heavily into the animator and I guess a few programmers and systems people?*

RT: Yes. The thing is that I'm not interested in overhead. I mean if we got so huge that we needed coordinators to run stuff, then we may end up having more what you call management I suppose, but I really don't believe in that because I think it distances you from the work and it makes it very

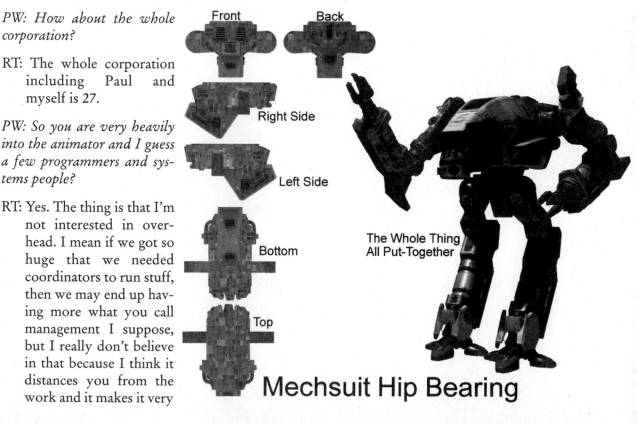

Front

Back

Right Side

Left Side

Bottom

Top

The Whole Thing
All Put-Together

Mechsuit Hip Bearing

difficult. I prefer for the place to be a little bit more personable. After all, it's not an office job. We're working with artists and you have to have a certain flow of communication. Artists don't respond well to being locked in cubby holes.

PW: When you're hiring an animator, what combination of skills do you look for?

RT: The main thing that I look for is a sense of visual drama, that somebody knows composition, pacing, editorial, and that they understand natural motion and lighting. I prefer that to somebody who has a knowledge of software. When it comes down to it, I'm looking for filmmakers who want to make the transition because when it comes down to it we're filmmakers, and we're just using different tools. I can teach a filmmaker of 15 years how to use a computer in a few weeks. I can't teach a computer programmer how to be a filmmaker in that time.

PW: I wanted to ask you about the Hypernauts *project. Was that both your idea and your production? Did you actually go to the studios with the entire project?*

RT: Yes, it was very much that. I mean Foundation Imaging kind of differs from some effects houses in that we're not really an effects house. We're a film company and it just so happens that a lot of our films are only five seconds long. For example, we're doing a whole presentation at the moment for Phillips Labs for the military to do spaceborne, reusable ship designs. Basically, it's to convince them to invest money in some of these possible military space applications.

PW: And you'll be doing this in-house at Foundation Imaging?

RT: Yes, we're doing everything there, start to finish, so the whole bit. We cast it, got actors, writers, everything. We're working at the moment on several other possibilities that will involve us just completely producing a show. To us, that's the best way to go. Being a service business is not particularly thrilling, nor is it very profitable. The best way to be is to be your own content provider, and as we've already done one show, you have a certain amount of track record so it becomes a little easier to sell next time. Studios can turn around and say, "Well have you ever done anything?" and it's like, "Yeah, here's the first 10 episodes of *Hypernauts*. Take a look at that."

PW: Did you also shoot the live action in Hypernauts?

RT: Yes, it was interesting. I mean we had a very, very tight schedule. Each episode in three days which is extremely tight when you consider usually a one-hour show is 7-10 days, well 10 days, so I mean 3 days for a half hour is really pushing it. It becomes difficult, but it worked out very well.

PW: I noticed that in the past year or so you've been doing a lot more feature film work, too.

RT: Yes.

PW: Specifically the machine in "Contact?"

RT: Yes, we did some of that and also we've been working on *The Jackel* with Bruce Willis and Richard Gere which was released in November of 1997. We've done about 21 shots for that.

PW: Is that one of the directions that you see Foundation Imaging going? Producing more and more film work and less TV?

RT: Yes and no. I'd like to do more film work, but that area of the business is very well-catered for. It just so happens that right now it's really busy and I think we do better with the television work. In television we're able to give people value for money plus we're more unique. You know, we're a bigger fish in a smaller pond. In the feature business there's ILM, Digital Domain, etc., and you just can't turn around and compete with them. If you're charging the same amount of money as somewhere like ILM, they'll go with ILM, because we don't have stacks of Academy Awards, plus it's very much an "in" thing at the moment in this town for a producer to turn around and say, "Hey, I'm having my effects done at ILM" at one of these power breakfasts or something.

PW: I'd always seen working in television as one of the ways to break into film, but you're saying it's a little bit more of a closed shop than that?

RT: Well, it's just that we choose not necessarily to compete heavily in that arena because ultimately our goal is not to service a movie, it's to make them. Our goal is to eventually service our own movies.

PW: Have you thought about virtual reality or theme parks?

A fully rendered scene from the Hypernauts television series.

RT: We've actually been working on some stuff for the *Star Trek* attraction in Las Vegas. Virtual reality, I don't know. Nothing has crossed our desk that is interesting yet. Mostly because of the fact that we very much like photorealistic artwork. We like doing photoreal stuff and there still really isn't the power there to be able to do it in realtime.

PW: Most art directors and designers are relatively unimpressed with VRML and virtual reality. Do you look at VRML and see any future in that? Do you see that as something you'd ever get into or do you see that as more hype than it's worth?

RT: Right now I see it as more hype than it's worth, but you know these things change. I mean in leaps and bounds these things change. For heaven's sake, we've only been in existence for five years. We only had our fifth anniversary about three weeks ago. Enormous strides have taken place in those five years. For example, there was barely a color printer to be seen that was any good when we started off. Now you've got all these different photorealistic choices around. I mean just a huge number of different things that have been going on. And just slightly off topic, I bought a vinyl cutter this last week for like $600. I mean most vinyl cutters have been $8,000 until recently. You know it's just incredible how this stuff is getting more accessible, faster, cheaper. It's insane. So, I don't believe that it's going to slow down anytime soon.

PW: That actually leads me to another question I had: Since your partner also comes from a computing background, does Foundation Imaging use any custom code, or do you stick to mostly off-the-shelf stuff?

RT: No, no we do have custom code, but mostly what we do is write the occasional plug-in for the software and the major thing is our rendering environment. We have an automated rendering system that's very, very intelligent and it's also our production management system that keeps track of the shots and what stage their at, automatically outputs a picture when you print a record of what particular shot you're viewing. It runs all of the machines in the facility. When everybody leaves, they just click an icon and their machine goes onto the render stack.

PW: You have a full distributed renderer that works with LightWave?

RT: Oh, totally and it's totally automatic. It has redundancy checks so that if a computer crashes while it's rendering a frame, the controller is intelligent enough to see it and it reboots the computer via software and then reassigns the frame that it was working on and deletes any temporary files associated with it. It's all really very, very elegant.

PW: So you'll have something like 20 machines rendering all night?

RT: Yes, we have sixteen 500 megahertz Alphas that are just rendering all the time, 24 hours a day. Then we have another 20 Alphas and another 15 or 16 PC's that go onto the stack at night.

PW: You've just made me incredibly jealous.

RT: Well, I keep saying to Paul that if ever the company goes down, we're each going to have a hell of a home system.

PW: You guys definitely put your finger on where the industry was going five years ago and positioned yourselves right. In the next few years, where do you see the 3D industry going, aside from all the technical innovations?

RT: More content. That's where it's got to go. One of the things that's very interesting about Siggraph this year — although I didn't go, I got most of this from reports from people — is that there was nothing particularly interesting, new, or anything there. It seems as if the industry has reached a maturity level where you can get and do just about most of the things that you need to and now it's an issue of "well what are you going to do?" So it's an issue of content. It's getting towards that time where companies are going to start looking around and saying, "Well what are we going to do here? Are we going to be a service business? Are we going to do visual effects or are we just going to do the old commercial flying logos or are we going to try to make movies?" Because you know you've got a movie studio on your desk. There's no reason why you can't make movies. You can put a PC together with multiple processors, sound cards, and all this stuff and literally can do just about every aspect of production, even in terms of digitizing live video at D1 quality. I mean Hollywood Board does just that.

PW: I guess I've heard a lot of hype about "the kid in his garage" producing his own film. Do you see a large trend towards that single freelancer working out of his house or do you still think there will be a strong need for small and mid-sized studios?

RT: I think that people will start making stuff out of their homes but the distribution medium is going to be different because the bigger companies are still going to want the comfort factor of a company that they can go to and they can see that there are employees working there. There'd be nothing worse for a producer to walk into someone's house and be led into the garage where there's just a few computers hanging around and this one guy. Even though the guy may well be capable of producing everything that's wanted for the show, it will be a difficult sell. We have a difficult enough time selling ourselves. We don't spend an awful lot of money on lush leather sofas and sponge-textured walls and things like that, and we find that we lose business to companies that have exactly that, that have invested a lot of money in very expensive equipment, but the actual work they do isn't very good. So, a lot of it is a producer education if you're going to be able to serve this business. Personally, I prefer just not to educate them. I prefer to just make the movies. You know, several people have come to us recently about doing children's shows and we've said, "Well, you know, the amount of money that's involved, we would want some participation" and they're like, "Well, you'd be able to do the effects on a major children's show." It's like, "Yea, we can think up our own children's show. Why should we do yours?"

PW: I wanted to ask you about how you organize Foundation Imaging. Do you work with a few different art directors, junior designers, split up your people into teams? Or, would it be reasonable for a single animator to make a 3 or 4 second clip totally themselves?

RT: Absolutely, each of the animators do shots, because that was the one thing that I always enjoyed, the fact that I would look at one of the shots and I'd say, "That one's mine." I think any artist enjoys that. They don't enjoy saying, "You see the texture map on that thing? I painted that." It doesn't quite have the same feel to it. And it simplifies it a lot when you're showing a demo reel and you say, "I did these shots." "What did you do on them?" "I did everything." It's much better from an artist's point of view, and I think it gives everybody a lot more job satisfaction and that helps you get better results.

PW: *How do you keep a consistency to a project if you have each individual artist doing different shots?*

RT: Well, you still have supervisors. For example, I'll look at shots, John Tesca will look at shots. Any of the senior animators or supervisors will watch over a particular project to make sure that it's staying within the bounds of what's required by the client. But, in general, every animator works on his own shots. It's very, very rare that we just make one person model and someone else light...almost never.

PW: *Doesn't each person have something they're a little bit better at...lighting or texture mapping, modeling...?*

From the Star Trek: Voyager television series. The Voyager spacecraft amidst battle debris.

185

RT: Absolutely, but you still let them deal with the whole thing from start to finish. And if there is someone who just clearly cannot model, then we don't give them models to do, but when it comes to lighting and choreographing a shot, we always just leave that with one person.

PW: *I saw a project on your website that looked like cel animation.*

RT: Yes, it's called *Batman and Mr. Freeze Subzero*. It's an animated hour-long video for home video release.

PW: *It's all done with LightWave again?*

RT: Not all of it. We've done certain sequences in it with LightWave just to add a little bit more dimension to the show and it works really well. I think it's a pretty spectacular production value and we've managed to match the look of the animated, the cel animated, stuff perfectly.

PW: *So there's a combination?*

RT: Yes, I mean there are instances in it where I'm looking and it's like, "Did we do that one or did they do that one?" It was difficult to tell.

PW: *So just like you're matching in with live action, now you're matching in with cel animation, too.*

RT: Yes, which is just fabulous. I've always been an animation fan so it was very interesting and quite a challenge to get the look of

Foundation Imaging composited 3D computer graphics with 2D cel animation for the made-for-video film **Batman vs. Subzero.**

what is a very, very well-established TV series. And they pushed us a little bit. I mean there were some things we had to do on it that were very difficult, but I'm pleased that we did. We know a lot more about how to deal with matching certain looks and certain environments. We had to make the backgrounds themselves look as if they'd been painted by someone, and then any characters and foreground elements had to look like they were done on a cel. So we were simultaneously using two different rendering techniques in the same shot.

There were some shots where the Japanese provided us with filmed cel animations against either green or blue or red and then we'd composite that with some of our backgrounds, which was very interesting.

PW: Knowing what you know now, what do you think you would do differently creatively, technically? How would you approach the whole thing differently?

RT: Oh boy, do you know what? I wouldn't. I think every mistake that we've ever made has been valuable. I'm a great believer in making big mistakes from time to time because it gives you big kicks up the butt and makes you watch a little bit more carefully where you're treading in terms of how you're designing stuff, how you're making stuff. I can't say that I regret a minute of it. I think we've done really well.

PW: You answered a little bit of this before, but what will you be doing next and what would you like to be doing?

RT: I'd like to do more cel animation stuff.

PW: In-house?

RT: Yes, computer-generated, film-look animation. By the end of the year, I'd like to have a fairly well-developed CG show, be it a TV show, cable, single feature – whatever it might be. I'd also like to have a couple of other live action/TV shows in development... you know, maybe a film, a one-hour show and a half-hour kids show, something like that.

PW: You're going to need more animators.

RT: That's not a problem. Just build out the back. It's one of those things they say, "It's not a problem, it's just an expense." Since LightWave has gone onto the PC platform, a lot more people are learning it because the Amiga was a very restrictive computer. Not a lot of people had them. A lot more people are getting their hands on LightWave now that it's on the Mac and PC. We've got one young guy who's going to Cornell at the moment. He's around 18 I think, and his demo reel just knocks the socks off everybody. It's phenomenal. This kid is just amazing. And the point is, once he's finished at Cornell, he's coming to work for us.

PW: *Whether he likes it or not.... So what kind of advice would you give a person trying to get into the industry? Would you suggest film school or just developing a reel on your own?*

RT: Well, if you can pick up filmmaking on your own, great. Film school will teach you how to pass film school. It's kind of like taking Driver's Ed. Driver's Ed will teach you how to pass the driving test. It won't necessarily teach you how to drive. I think the best thing to do is to make little pieces and let people see them. Let people who know see them, and be open to criticism and try to develop your techniques that way. Watch movies, watch how they go together. One or two of the more recent reels I've been seeing have been doing things like hand-held camera work in them and doing focus changes and things like that that directors of photography do. I love to see that. It shows they're thinking. Even if it's just a cube doing stuff, so long as it's choreographed well and they tell a visual story, that's the way to go.

Believe me, we get some horrendous demo reels. We get some demo reels where someone puts a model they made of a cigarette, you know, tough, and they spin it around for half a minute. It's like "okay, we've seen that already." Some of it's pretty hideous.

PW: *Have you ever thought of changing careers?*

RT: I don't know, I've kind of got my eye set on being an airport bum right now. I want to hang around airports and be the bore that tells the stories, "Yeah, I had one of those...." That's kind of an aside. I don't think I'll ever be out of this business, in general, because it's so much fun.

All the time you do not have to deal with the execs involved, it's a lot of fun. As soon as you have to deal with them, then it becomes real boring.

PW: Do you want me to edit that out for you?

RT: Oh, no, leave it in, never mind.

PW: Is there anything else you wanted to talk about.

RT: The most important thing that I can say is that it's the art, not the
technology. That's all it comes down to. It's the artistry of filmmaking, the knowledge of lighting, composition, things like the
golden mean. They are all really important. Being a computer
programmer isn't so important in terms of making this stuff happen. They've done all the work for us. They've written the
programs. And they're really great. They do the job. Everything
from LightWave to 3D StudioMax, to SoftImage...they're all
really great. You know, some people swear by Milwaukee drills,
some people swear by the Keifers. They both do the same thing;
they both drill holes. And when it comes down to it, in the long
run, paint brushes and paint have been available for centuries,
but you don't see that many Mona Lisa's. So, it's the art.

  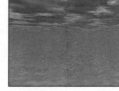 

Chuck Carter:
National Geographic

After leaving the U.S. Navy, Chuck Carter worked as an illustrator. Since 1979, he has done everything from designing greeting cards to editorial illustrations and caricatures. He discovered the computer in 1987 while working as an editorial artist in Kentucky. Told to make a map on an old Mac Plus without any manuals for the computer or the software, Chuck quickly figured out the Mac interface and MacDraw, and was soon applying what he learned to illustrating portraits and informational graphics. He was one of the first artists to make realistic-looking drawings with MacDraw and his artwork was picked up by the Knight-Ridder Graphics Network, appearing in newspapers across the country. In 1989, Chuck began dabbling in 3D on Macintosh computers.

In 1990 he met Rand and Robyn Miller of Cyan and in 1991 he went to work for Cyan as one of the two artists responsible for creating the graphics for Myst. *After* Myst, *Chuck created the 3D version of the popular Cyan children's game,* The Manhole: The Masterpiece Edition. *He left Cyan in 1995 to begin a freelance career designing graphics for a variety of well-known clients including Heliotrope Studios, Westwood Studios, Reactor, Inc., HyperQuest, Inc., National Geographic, Rockwell International, and US News and World Report. His work can be seen in numerous websites, and he recently began designing digital matte paintings and preproduction designs for the science fiction show* Babylon 5 *and an upcoming fantasy series.*

Chuck can be reached via e-mail at chuck@chuckcarter.com.

In 1992, while I was working on the art for the popular computer game, *Myst*, I was asked by a friend at Knight-Ridder to take on a digital illustration project for *National Geographic* magazine. It was a quarter-page illustration that needed to be done in PhotoShop and would use some 3D elements. After talking to the art director, Allen Carroll, the image turned out to be a three-page spread showing a timeline of the evolution of dinosaurs etched in stone. At the time, I was working on a Quadra 700 with 20 megs of RAM and was wondering how I would produce such a high resolution, complex image. Fortunately, I had no idea that the job would be so hard, so I just plowed through (slowly) and began my relationship with *National Geographic*. I was also working on *Myst* at the time, so in addition to spending about 12 hours a day on Myst graphics, I was working four hours on the *National Geographic* illustration. Sometimes that four hours was spent just moving a section of the image from one side to the other. Working with large images was very slow going back then. I was lucky I had a friend who did some of the rendering for me.

In June, 1996, *National Geographic* made the jump from the printed page to electronic publishing on the World Wide Web when they launched nationalgeographic.com. Like many companies who saw the potential of the Internet, *National Geographic* saw this as a way to tell a story interactively and decided to open up with a large interactive project and environment. Having produced nearly a dozen high-resolution illustrations for the magazine, I was called on to use the skills I learned working on *Myst* for the new website. The story was about a Spanish Galleon that sank in shallow water during a storm and the efforts to find the remains of the ship and its cargo, long covered by corals and sand.

My job was to digitally produce a series of images recreating the 300-year-old ship as it existed prior to the sinking and to design a virtual walkthrough of the deck. Making an accurate interactive environment of a sailing ship is a difficult enough proposition. It becomes even harder when the users will be looking in all directions at the deck and will see objects from many angles. I've seen numerous 3D models of ships and even built one myself for Cyan's children's game, *The Manhole: The Masterpiece Edition*, and I was amazed at just how wrong and inaccurate these 3D models were when compared to the real thing. But for this project I had to be sure of the accuracy of the final model and images as this project was one where computer-generated, three-dimensional environments really should shine. The only problem we encountered was no one really knew what

Original sketches by Richard Schelct.

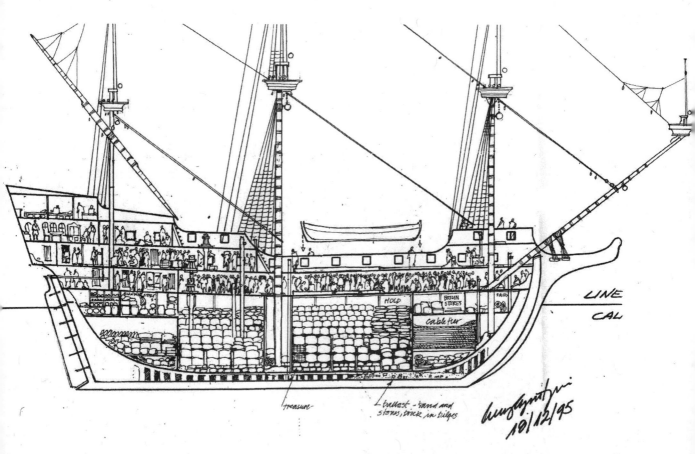

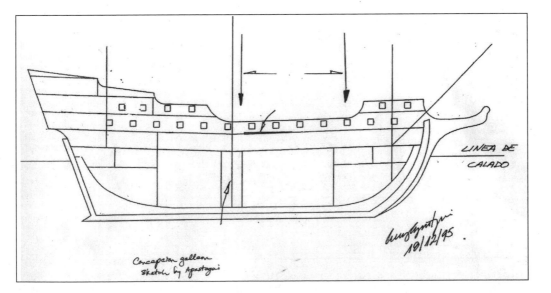

a box of silver bars

Concepcion galleon Schlecht 3/8/96

encased in a sewn canvas cover

Economy class.

Casks in hold

Terracotta wine pipes — stacked in straw (in hold)

a lot of the ship looked like and we had no idea what many of the objects should look like from various directions. Working for *National Geographic* means that every nut and bolt, every rope and door hinge will be checked for accuracy. So as I began the project I made a list of the hundreds of objects that needed to be modeled, even things that might not show up in the final images, just in case they could be seen from one of the interface shots.

When I began to get information and resources about the structure, materials and cargo of the ship, I had the good fortune to

LINEA DE CALADO

19/12/95.

Concepcion galleon Sketch by Apostegui

be assisted by an illustrator, Richard Schelct, who specializes in historic sailing ships. His paintings and illustrations are found throughout the world in galleries and magazines including *National Geographic*. Richard's knowledge of the field and of life on the seas throughout history is unsurpassed. He was wonderful to work with and as I look back, I know the job could not have been done in the two weeks I had without his generous help and his offbeat sense of humor to keep me sane during the long hours of modeling and texturing.

Our working arrangement consisted of a phone, a fax machine, and America Online. Richard was on the East Coast and I'm in Southern Utah. When I came to some part of the ship that I had insufficient reference materials for or when I wanted to check on the accuracy of my work, Richard would draw that part of the ship or that object and fax it to me. I would make changes in my models and send him a rendered image on America Online. He would then look at the image in PhotoShop and return it with suggested changes drawn over the original rendering, sometimes painting over the image to show me how it should really look.

In a number of instances I had an object with only one view showing only one side. I sent this to Richard who took it, figured out what it should look like on all sides and sent me a series of sketches. We went back and forth with some objects perhaps 10 times until we had something that looked correct, and even then we were never 100 percent sure we had the exact shape. We did this on more than a few objects until *National Geographic* and their researchers and scientists finally approved of the final images. We were lucky there was

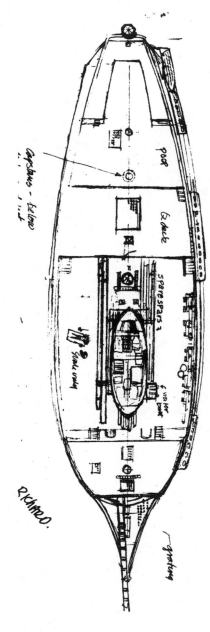

File   Edit   Windows   Keyframe   Tools   Select   Help   12:42 PM

Camera View of SilverBanks Project

00:00:00:00   0

View of the ship model inside the ElectricImage interface.

a huge body of knowledge concerning sailing ships from this time period and we had lots of other historic artifacts in museums and books to use as reference. The problem was we did not have all of the exact data about this particular ship, so we needed to make a number of assumptions referencing other ships from that time period.

Creating a digital environment with more than a thousand objects, structures, and shapes along with their associated textures, we found that even Richard was hard pressed at times to think in 3D on some shapes. For most of his career he illustrated objects from one viewpoint. Working in 2D, he did not have to worry about how things looked from all angles. It was when we put the objects together in the context of the deck of the ship that things clicked for us and we made corrections, some of which took an entire day to get right such as getting the deck curved just right. You don't necessarily think about things like a ship's deck is curved down and crowned from the center so that water spills off when it rains or is washed up during rough seas. This little fact necessitated that I replace every object on the deck to be sure the shapes were angled to sit on a curved surface. Elements like canons and crates had to be rotated to accommodate the curvature of the deck so they wouldn't stick oddly through the surface.

When building in 3D you find, after a while, that you get real nitpicky about how an object would really work if it was not computer-generated. A sense of scale and function is developed, and objects that look difficult come together when you start thinking like the person who would have made it in real life. You turn it over in your head until it takes on a sense of reality and you intuit its design. You find you can usually get it right without complete references so long as you understand its use, interpolating its construction from limited resources.

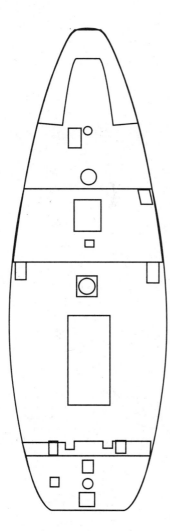

I worked on a Power PC 8100/80 with about 100 megs of RAM and a 17-inch and a 13-inch monitor. I used a Zip drive to ship files and keep backups of the models. I also have a recordable CD-ROM drive that I used to back-up files. I have a Hewlett Packard ScanJet IICX used for scanning my photographic textures and templates. I used the Macintosh version of Form•Z to model the ship and its objects and rendered all the images in ElectricImage Broadcast. Bryce was used for the background ocean and sky images. PhotoShop 3.0, Illustrator 5.5 and Painter 3.0 were used to create textures and manipulate scanned, drawn, and canned textures. Illustrator was used for creating templates for

the models and details for some of the textures. In Form•Z, I used layers extensively to keep track of my objects and to make the editing process less painful. ElectricImage allowed me to quickly render very highly-detailed images for editing purposes.

The production began with a series of ship cross sections supplied by *National Geographic*. I started the process by scanning the cross sections and using them as forms for making Adobe Illustrator outlines and templates which were later imported into Form•Z for modeling.

I decided to approach the models and images as a set designer, concentrating only on the visible areas of the exterior decks. This way I did not need to model the hull or any interior areas short of the forward kitchen area because they would not be used in the Internet module. *Geographic* only wanted to walk across the deck to get the feel of the environment. This made the process simpler, but not easier considering one week was used to do the bulk of the modeling and the subsequent week was used for editing. A massive amount of detail was still needed and as the list of objects grew, I felt the pressure of this deadline hanging over my head like an axe.

Most *National Geographic* illustrations have a six-month or longer deadline. The Internet has changed that in a big way with most stories having just a couple of months or less to turn around a module, leaving even less time to produce the artwork. The fact that this model was concentrating on just the deck gave me more time to work on individual models so I could add more detail to each shape.

A two-week deadline on a project like this means you have to make sacrifices and use Photoshop to make corrections at the end if time is too short for small changes.

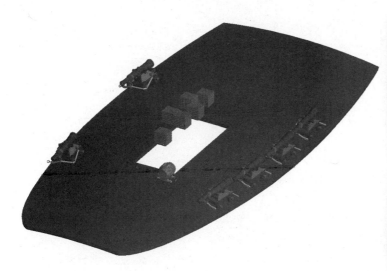

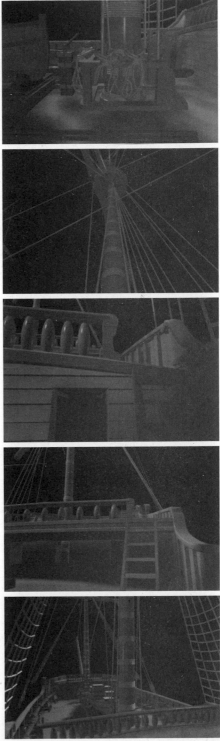

My painting and illustration background helped me here as it was easy to just paint in corrections when needed.

The first part of the model I worked on was the deck structure, rails, and masts. Working on the main elements of the environment and its surrounding areas made it easier to move on to the additional objects that filled up the environment and added realism.

The first object I created was the ship's deck. Using a template created in Illustrator, scanned from a set of drawings used to build similar ships from roughly the same time period, I imported the shapes into Form•Z and began the modeling process.

(One note about using Illustrator: I've found it faster and easier to create all of my outlines in Illustrator prior to beginning work in Form•Z. Once you create all of your shape outlines in Illustrator, you can import them directly into Form•Z and use them as is for creating the model outlines that will eventually be used for skin objects, extrusions, lathes, or paths. This saves time simply because Illustrator is designed for drawing and is easier to use at times than the tools provided by most modelers.)

I extruded all of the Illustrator shapes, including the boolean shapes I would use to cut holes into the deck for hatches and openings. I then created a layer called "Deck Main." All of my shapes were moved there and I continued refining the deck shape.

I added yet another Illustrator template, one with some notations and scale indicators with a light-blue texture as a reference, on a separate layer that was locked so as not to confuse it with the models in a top planar view. I placed all the objects in the correct positions and began cutting out my holes and resizing the various depths of the objects to match those of the ship.

Since there were basically five deck levels, I imported another template for reference, this time to be used as a side reference. I adjusted the decks by moving and rotating them around the side-view template. I then created new layers for the additional decks and moved them accordingly.

Going back to the side-view template, I imported my

mast outlines. I created all of the mast segments as lathed shapes and placed them in their proper positions using the top and side references I already had imported into the file. The templates served a dual purpose here: They were used for creating the actual shapes and as a positional guide for object placements. This sped up the entire process considerably and had the added benefit of assuring a more accurate outline to begin the modeling process.

After the deck was finished, I began the process of building each object that would be placed on the deck. I started with the masts and the various ropes and supports that connect the mast and the sails to the ship. I duplicated the lines in Form•Z. The amount of detail I built into each line and its anchor was pretty high as it might be seen in the final image. There are dozens, if not hundreds, of lines in the rigging of an old sailing ship. Knowing where each line is to be connected and strung made the modeling a bit harder. Lucky for me, most 3D programs have an alpha channel, and PhotoShop lets you select the image and composite it over another image. In my case I created a few rope models and rendered them each with their own alpha channel. This allowed me to composite many of the ropes in PhotoShop, each in its own layer. I moved, rotated, and resized them until they were in the correct position and scale. This was much easier to do in post-production than in the model file which, by this time, was pushing my machine's limits. And since I was working with still images, I did not have to worry about keeping every detail in a single model file.

While ElectricImage can easily handle models of more than a million polygons, it gets a little cumbersome to keep track of such large files, so I divided the primary models into specific views like looking forward or backward, deleting what was not seen from each view. This

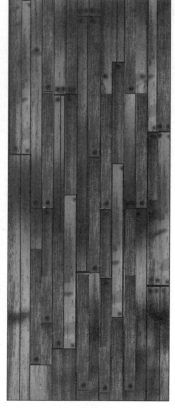

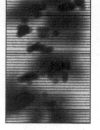

simplified the final images making it easier to do the final composite work in PhotoShop.

This whole process took about three days. Another solid day was spent placing all these objects on the deck itself.

After the ship and its structural elements were completed, I added all the props and textures. Because

Texture maps used for the Galleon.

these props and textures would be viewed closely, they needed to be highly accurate. At this stage, I began importing all the models into ElectricImage. I exported them as DXF format from Form•Z, a personal preference.

(Note: The great thing about working with Form•Z and ElectricImage is that any changes I make in the final models while in Form•Z will remain in exactly the same position in

ElectricImage, provided nothing changes in Form•Z as far as scale, position, or orientation are concerned. For instance, if you got the canons wrong in the working ElectricImage project file, you would delete them from ElectricImage, make the changes in Form•Z, and export out just the canons to be reimported into ElectricImage. You might also try exporting them with the same name as the fact file.)

In the deck texture map, I added shadows for each one. I figured it would solve two problems: time and final placement of objects. I saved in rendering time by turning off shadows for certain passes in the final images. I took screen shots of the initial placements of everything and used them to create the final deck textures. By taking a snapshot of the wireframe, I was also able to create additional maps and textures to simulate water stains coming from the bilge pumps, seams, hatches, and the water barrel, as well as other stains and textures from the daily wear and tear of a ship's crew and the weathering that occurs at sea. These snapshots were also used in addition to the information supplied by the researchers to adjust the final placement of objects.

As for textures, I created base textures like a primary wood which would be used to fabricate everything from the deck to the wood that makes up the rails and mast. I referred to photos of existing ships and created my textures from existing scrap files, or by going out and taking pitures which I later manipulated in PhotoShop. I created textures using Adobe Illustrator, then brought them into PhotoShop for more manipulations that help them appear more photographic.

Once the ship, and its various objects and textures were in place in ElectricImage, it was time to adjust the final lighting and camera compositions. I used a strong, yellow-tinted light source from the right side for the primary sunlight in the scene to match the fact that the camera was on the port side of the ship and I was working toward the rear. I used two fill lights — one a light-blue and another a light-violet — to match the mood of the sky which was cloudy and slightly threatening. I also used a few

small spotlights on the masts and on some of the objects on the deck to fill in darker areas. Unlike the primary light, the secondary lights or the spotlights did not have shadows associated with them.

The background scene of the ocean and clouds was done in Bryce 2.0 and composited in PhotoShop. Again, I needed to be sure the light sources were correct and that the shots matched my camera views for each of the 22 interface shots requested by *National Geographic*. I also added a touch of fog in the scene in ElectricImage to create depth throughout the renderings. This enhanced the illusion of realism in each scene when the background was added.

It would have been easy to add dozens of interface shots simply because of the detail I built into the final models and scene files.

But the Internet is still used by people with slow connections and the *National Geographic* still designs for the lowest common demoninator of modem and IP so all users can quickly download each screen and not get lost when graphics are loading slowly during peak hours. Each shot of the ship was about 12k (12 kilobytes) when finally included in the website and each had a sound file attached to it detailing the sounds of a creaking ship and lapping ocean and breezes.

It was a successful opening, evidenced by the fact that the first day the *National Geographic* site was launched, demand was in the millions, quickly bringing down the entire system. It's fixed now and I believe the project can still be found in the site archives.

Richard Dubrow, Jon Kletzien:
Advanced Media Design, Inc.

The elusive feel and liveliness of a hand-crafted rendering has escaped many 3D artists leaving most computer-generated architectural renders with a sterile feel. Jon Kletzien and Richard Dubrow set out to tackle this problem and disprove the misconceptions about computer artwork when they founded Advanced Media Design, Inc. (AMD). Their Providence, Rhode Island-based firm produces dramatic and attractive architectural renderings using 3D Studio Max software on desktop computers. In 1997, Jon and Richard won the prestigious Hugh Ferriss Memorial Prize for excellence in architectural rendering for their work on the World War II Memorial planned for the center of the Mall in Washington, D.C. This was the first time this prize was awarded to computer-generated artwork.

In his own words, Jon Kletzien talks about his company and the World War II Memorial project:

As a digital media studio dedicated to the artistic vitality of architectural illustration, Advanced Media Design, Inc., balances the flexible precision of digital media with the subtle aesthetics of hand rendering.

Perhaps more than any other project with which AMD has been involved to date, rendering Friedrich St. Florian's World War II Memorial competition entry focused substantial pressures on the firm. These pressures pushed AMD to evolve beyond their concern with experimentation towards more mature considerations of method and purpose. It proved to be a pivotal assignment: More sound, efficient production practices were established, and clearer aesthetic goals were defined.

The project occurred in two stages. However, it was only after the architect's design proposal was selected for the final round that AMD was able to reflect on the value of the work they had done during the first stage — and understand just how important this project would be. Going into the first stage, the opportunity to do something truly different from the work they had been doing — to break the monotony, so to speak — was incentive enough. Afterwards, though, it was clear to the personnel in the firm that they had come together as a team, forced to operate more efficiently and in a more professional manner.

The first stage of the project was completed in less than three days. In one way, this extraordinarily tight timeframe was an unexpected boon because it allowed for rather spontaneous artistic freedom. A sharply-focused creative discussion took place within the office, concentrating primarily on the architect's need to have dramatic points of view rendered in a way that did not overstate the proposed memorial's influence on its surroundings. It was obvious that the design would have a significant impact on the visual integrity of what is, unquestionably, the nation's most important memorial site. The American Battle Monuments Commission, who was sponsoring the competition, had set certain requirements for the illustrations that implied their concerns. Preserving the long-established spatial perspectives was a paramount concern of both the commission and the architect. Thus, it became AMD's responsibility to exercise absolute control over the aesthetic impact suggested in the illustrations.

Three renderings were executed for the preliminary competition: one day view and two night views. With the architect, it was decided not to push for great detail, but rather to focus on accurately blocking out the proposed memorial, and to stress how it would work with existing buildings and monuments. By keeping it simple at this stage, AMD focused the commission's attention on the aesthetic sensitivity of the design.

The decision to render two night views was suggested by existing night views found in design books about Washington furnished by the architect, as well as the initial renderings AMD produced. The greenery represented in the day views tended to diminish the architectural impact of all the monuments, whereas the reflections and the subdued, ambient lighting characteristic of the night views greatly enhanced the inspirational presence of the memorial. For that reason, as much as anything, the one day view chosen for the first stage was an aerial perspective from the top of the Washington Monument. The scale was consistent with minimal detail, the memorial itself rendered as hardly more than a painted model. And since the presentation format for the first round of the competition was to be a single board featuring three renderings (each 8x10 inches), along with the architect's plans and a text describing the project, the decision to go with simple, inspirational renderings was more than justified.

To maximize the efficiency of the production process, systematic tasks were assigned to the four people working at AMD: James Kuhn was responsible for modeling, performed in AutoCAD R12; Jay Forrest was responsible for painting the texture maps; Richard Dubrow (partner and co-founder of AMD) determined viewpoint and lighting, applied materials, and rendered all stills; and, finally, Jon Kletzien (partner and co-founder of AMD) painted on top of all the stills.

Other measures of economy were also put into place. Data structures were organized according to the various levels of design cohesion. The stone piers (which eventually became columns) of the colonnades were instanced so that their definition could be changed at will. The back wall was constructed as one solid form. This saved AMD time and allowed them to easily change the texture map to reflect the latest coursing condition. The texture-mapping phase was taking place concurrently with the modeling. Paintings were created, based on the material specifications and the likely stone patterning plans, and then applied to the model. The paintings, which were executed in HRQ4, were then brought into 3D Studio R2 and associated with a material definition used during the rendering phase.

AMD's notable control over digital media is particularly evident here, at the rendering phase. Disciplined strategic thinking and superior artistic sensibility took shape as Dubrow brought model and materials together, introduced lighting, and determined potential points of view. After several low-resolution images were critiqued with the architect, high-resolution renderings of the optimum views were produced and saved to disk. Before being sent to the architect, however, each 3D Studio rendering was carefully painted by Kletzien. Pedestrians were pasted in, sky and trees were added, and highlights were adjusted. Kletzien was also responsible for adding last-minute design modifications.

Given the unusually tight timeframe for the first stage, it helped enormously that the final, approved design was quite close to the original concept. A few details were changed, but the original vision remained basically intact. Still, important decisions were made during the first stage — decisions that highlight the advantage digital illustrators provide an architect before designs are finalized. While visiting AMD once or twice a day, the architect was able to view the design from several different viewpoints (in printouts, as well as fresh images on the screen). Thus, even within such a constrained timeframe, the architect was able to make subtle, but critical, design changes because of the flexibility afforded by AMD's digital capabilities.

Upon reflection, the tight schedule had as much to do with what was downplayed as with what was emphasized. While the lighting plan was pretty well confirmed with these renderings, the

front steps of the memorial were merely suggested graphically when it became apparent that they were hardly visible in the three views rendered for the initial phase of the competition. The most noteworthy change resulting from AMD's ability to quickly offer the architect a selection of spatially-accurate views of the memorial's design was the shape of the columns forming the colonnades in front of the walls of the memorial, echoing their curve. Originally designed as piers, or rectangular shafts, fluted columns were used instead when the piers failed to satisfy the architect's conceptual vision.

With the second stage, AMD orchestrated a far more serious approach. There was, after all, a great deal riding on the final outcome. It helped, too, that the deadline for the second, and final, round of the competition was six weeks away. Creative discussions were again conducted to establish clear aesthetic expectations and to articulate strict process guidelines. Tasks were, once again, assigned primarily by phase. Kletzien was put in charge of modeling the memorial. Dubrow was responsible for creating the materials, as well as redoing the lighting for the night views. A variety of tasks fell to Kuhn, not the least of which was modeling the surrounding monuments as they appeared in the selected views to be rendered. It was agreed that the tone of the views, their emotional impact on the historical sight lines between the Lincoln Memorial and the Washington Memorial, was as important as — if not more so than — the details. A number of views were considered, with five selected for the final presentation.

The most coherent way to understand and, thus, control the model was to create discrete surfaces in the modeling phase, not the rendering phase. The wireframe model of the memorial, therefore, was completely rebuilt for the second phase of the competition, with each stone individually constructed as a 3D component of the whole. The unique geometry of each stone required individual texture maps. All of the materials were

redone, as well. While the angle of the lighting in the night views was retained, the lighting was redefined, and great care was taken to strengthen the impression of depth through strict application.

Commission requirements for the final round called for two standing-height views, one from 17th Street and one from the Lincoln Memorial, as well as an aerial view. Both AMD and the architect were satisfied with the aerial point of view chosen for the first round. They felt strongly, as well, about the points of view represented by the two night views already chosen. Fortunately, none of the three posed a problem in regard to the sight-line issue.

Considerable attention, therefore, was focused on selecting eye-level points of view that would best illustrate the full symbolic power of the architect's design, without overemphasizing the height of the berms sloping away from the walls of the memorial.

It was especially important to create informational day views that would both support and substantiate the architect's argument that the berms would not adversely affect the natural sightlines of the landscape. The two illustrations resulting from this effort typify the refined artistic sensibilities that distinguish all of AMD's work.

To achieve the sensitive aesthetic values found in the illustrations that helped win the World War II Memorial competition, images still must be manipulated substantially, even after they have been fully rendered. In truth, computers generate fairly hard, sterile images. Therefore, renderings must be further enhanced during the post-production phase. AMD's experimentation with various methods of digital painting, for instance, enabled them to associate surprisingly subtle reflections and shadows with the pedestrians and architectural features found in Evening Colonnade View, winner of The Hugh Ferriss Memorial Prize. Counter-changing the light values in the sky further enhanced the dramatic impact of the design. Perhaps the most significant breakthrough was achieved in View from Mall, where digitally-generated grass appears surprisingly real. As Richard Dubrow likes to say, "We've learned how to make the machines work for us."

References

BOOKS

Becoming a Computer Animator by Mike Morrison. Indianapolis, IN: SAMS Publishing, 1994.

Designing 3D Graphics by Josh White. New York, NY: John Wiley & Sons, Inc., 1996.

Exploring Moving Worlds: Discovering Virtual Motion on the Web by Ed Dille. Research Triangle Park, NC: Ventana Communications Group, Inc., 1996.

Film Directing Shot by Shot: Visualizing From Concept to Screen by Steven D. Katz. Studio City, CA: Michael Wiese Productions, 1991.

MacWEEK Guide to Desktop Video by Erik Holsinger. Emeryville, CA: Ziff-Davis Press, 1993.

Possible Worlds–The Social Dynamic of Virtual Reality Technology by Ralph Schroeder. Boulder, CO: Westview Press, 1996.

Proceedings of SIGGRAPH 96, Computer Graphics Proceedings, Annual Conference Series. New York, NY: ACM SIGGRAPH, 1996.

Proceedings of SIGGRAPH 97, Computer Graphics Proceedings, Annual Conference Series. New York, NY: ACM SIGGRAPH, 1997.

3D Computer Graphics, Second Edition, by Alan Watt. Wokingham, England: Addison-Wesley Publishing Company, Inc., 1993.

3D Graphics & Animation: From Starting Up to Standing Out by Mark Giambruno. Indianapolis, IN: New Riders Publishing, 1997.

Virtual Reality Systems by John Vince. Workingham, England: Addison-Wesley Publishing Company, Inc., 1995.

Virtus® VRML Toolkit by David Smith, Richard Boyd, and Alan Scott. Indianapolis, IN: Hayden Books, 1995.

VRML–Browsing & Building Cyberspace by Mark Pesce. Indianapolis, IN: New Riders Publishing, 1995.

PERIODICALS

CGW (Computer Graphics World), PennWell Publishing Company, 1670 S. Amphlett Boulevard, Suite 214, San Mateo, CA 94402.

Digital Magic, PennWell Publishing Company, 1670 S. Amphlett Boulevard, Suite 214, San Mateo, CA 94402.

DV (Digital Video), Miller Freeman, Inc., 411 Borel Avenue, Suite 100, San Mateo, CA 94402.

Innovation3, Silicon Graphics, Inc., 2011 N. Shoreline Boulevard, Mail Stop 21L-415, Mountain View, CA 94043.

InterActivity, Miller Freeman, Inc., 411 Borel Avenue, Suite 100, San Mateo, CA 94402.

Millimeter, Intertec Publishing, 5 Penn Plaza, 13th Floor, New York, NY 10001

NewMedia, HyperMedia Communications Inc., 901 Mariner's Island Boulevard, Suite 365, San Mateo, CA 94404.

3D Design, Miller Freeman, Inc., 525 Market Street, Suite 500, San Francisco, CA 94105.

Wired, Wired Ventures, Inc., 520 3rd Street, 4th Floor, San Francisco, CA 94107-1816

Glossary

ABSOLUTE VALUE • To use absolute values (for size, position, color, etc.) is to define objects in terms of the world: For instance, 5" in diameter, at position X33, Y21 on a grid. If you express the change in absolute values, you specify the new size in similar terms: 7" in diameter, position X44, Y21. You can also express the change in relative values: 40% larger, 10 ticks up from the original position.

ACTIVE WINDOW • The window in which the user is currently working. When a window is active, its title bar is highlighted.

ADAPTIVE SMOOTHING • Smoothing that is applied only where it is needed, rather than to an entire object.

ADDITIVE COLOR MODEL • Using light to create colors, as opposed to pigment. In a lighting (or additive or RGB) model, red, green, and blue light are added together to create other colors; if all three are projected at 100%, the result will be bright white. Compare CMYK, RGB, and SUBTRACTIVE COLOR MODEL.

ALGORITHM • A more or less involved mathematical procedure that can be used repeatedly to produce predictable results. Mathematical algorithms are used when RENDERING a final image from a WIREFRAME MODEL.

ALIGN • A command that lines up the centers or edges of multiple objects along one or more AXES.

ALPHA CHANNEL • A layer of image data that provides additional visual information about a file such as a transparency map. It is often used for image compositing. In a 32-bit image, 24 bits are used for color and 8 bits are for the alpha channel.

AMBIENT COLOR • The HUE an object reflects in the areas that are not directly affected by a light source.

AMBIENT LIGHT • A light that is generally set as a global value that is even throughout an entire scene. An ambient light is often used to simulate the effect of diffuse light bouncing off multiple surfaces. Since an ambient light affects all surfaces equally, a 10% ambient light would make the darkest possible value in the scene 90% of black.

ANAMORPHIC LENSES • A system of lenses for cameras and projectors that records a horizontally-squeezed image onto film, then corrects the image when it is projected on a wide screen in a theater.

ANGLE OF INCIDENCE • The angle at which a light ray strikes a surface and is reflected toward the viewer.

ANGLE OF VIEW (also called FIELD OF VIEW or VIEWING PYRAMID) • The angle between the limits of the camera's view, encompassing everything the camera can see. The angle of view, given in degrees, increases as the perspective becomes more extreme.

ANIMATIC • A rough animated sketch used to resolve composition and general pacing. In 3D design, animatics are often created by utilizing PRIMITIVE SHAPES and flat images instead of the final complex GEOMETRY.

ANIMATION • Literally means "giving life or motion." It is the creation of simulated movement with inanimate objects.

ANIMATION CAMERA • A camera mounted on a vertical stand above a table on which animation artwork can be recorded. A good animation camera is usually hooked up to a stand with precise controls for motion and lighting.

ANIMATION CONTROLLER • A method used to create or modify animated objects or animation keyframes. Expressions, constraints, and bézier curves can all be used as controllers.

ANIME • A Japanese word (pronounced ANNI-MAY) for animation. Anime has become a popular cult-art form.

ANTI-ALIASING • A method of softening rough edges in a rendering by modifying the jagged lines or edges in an image. With anti-aliased rendering, adjacent pixels with sharp variations in color and brightness are averaged, giving the effect of a smooth curve or diagonal. If the resolution of the image is greater than the resolution of the display, the anti-aliasing can be done on the fly by the software, video card, or monitor.

APERTURE • The opening behind the lens of a camera. Traditionally, aperture is controlled by adjusting the f-stop of a camera lens. The f-stop is the ratio of the width of the opening through which light passes to the focal length of the lens.

ARMATURE • The underlying structure of a sculpture. A STOP-MOTION puppet has an armature, which works like a skeleton to constrain and dictate more natural movement.

ASPECT RATIO • The ratio of height to width of an image. Aspect ratio can be expressed as a decimal value. For example a 500-pixel by 300-pixel image would have a ratio of 5:3 or 1.6667.

ATMOSPHERE • A setting that lets the user control the amount of aerial occlusion in a rendered image. Fog, mist, and haze effects can all be adjusted and created by manipulating the atmosphere.

ATTACH • The command used to join two separate objects into a single object. This is very different from the Group command, which allows separate objects to be selected and moved together, but doesn't actually connect them.

ATTENUATION • The gradual reduction in the intensity of light as it gets farther from its source (also called FALLOFF). This is mostly a function of distance, but in part it is caused by light dissipating in the atmosphere. When working on a computer, the user attaches the attenuation parameters to the actual light source.

AXIS • An imaginary line in three-dimensional space that defines a direction. The axes (the plural, pronounced AX-eez) used in 3D programs are usually x axis (width), y axis (height), and z axis (depth).

B-SPLINE • A curve (or spline) drawn in 3D space whose control points (which determine its shape) do not lie along the path of the curve.

BACK-FACING POLYGONS • POLYGONS whose surface normals point away from the viewer.

BACKGROUND PLATES • In optical photography of traditional animations, the background (usually a soundstage set or a location) over which foreground elements are composited.

BALL-JOINT LINK • A link in which the CHILD OBJECT can rotate and change size independently, but cannot move in space independently of its parent.

BANK • A camera's or object's roll as it moves along a curve.

BEAM SPLITTER • A semi-reflective mirror (or fifty-fifty mirror) that is placed in front of a camera lens at an angle, so that the camera sees both the image reflected in the splitter and the image behind it. It allows a camera to record both the image straight ahead of it and the reflection of an image at the side of the camera.

BEAUTY PASS • In multiple-pass photography, the beauty pass is the exposure that captures the subject's details. In computer graphics it is a rendering that shows textures, reflections, and fine details.

BEHAVIOR • A control that can be attached to an object that simplifies the animation process. Usually behaviors are associated with simple movements such as "spin," "bounce," and "look at."

BEVEL (OR CHAMFER) • A narrow, angled plane, sometimes found on the edge of a mirror or furniture. In 3D design, bevels are often used to soften the hard edge of an object.

BÉZIER SPLINE • A type of line that can be curved by adjusting its vertices or control points.

BIAS • In a TCB (Tension, Continuity, and Bias) animation controller, bias adjusts the peak of the motion path in relation to the keyframe.

BIPACK • Bipack cameras and projection systems are equipped to run two separate pieces of film simultaneously — often one for the action and one for a complementary matte.

BITMAP • A 2D image that is composed of pixels. Common bitmap formats are BMP, PICT, TIFF, and TARGA.

BLUESCREEN • A "replaceable" background. Objects and actors photographed in front of a bluescreen can be optically or digitally composited into any background later on. Objects with blue or purple elements (which would otherwise be discarded along with the bluescreen) are photographed in front of a green background.

BONES DEFORMATION • A method of animation in which the user defines and animates a skeleton; its moving bones automatically deform the surrounding mesh for an animation.

BOOLEAN OPERATION • A function used to create a new shape by adding one shape to another, or to make a hole in an object by subtracting another shape from it.

BOUNDING BOX • An imaginary box that is used to represent an object or group of objects. It can be used to move and adjust the objects contained, and it can be used as a stand-in for the objects during many phases of 3D work, speeding up the work by simplifying the calculations in the computer and the redrawing on screen.

BROWSER • A WINDOW that organizes and displays the individual elements in a scene.

BUMP MAP • A BITMAP file that is used like a texture map to modify a surface, the light areas forming hills and the dark areas valleys.

CAD/CAM (Computer-Aided Design and **Computer-Aided Manufacturing)** • CAD programs are used to design everything from bolts to buildings; CAM uses CAD drawings to control the equipment that makes the smaller object.

CAMERA MOTION • The path of a virtual camera through space in an animated sequence.

CAMERA MOVEMENT • The mechanism that alternately advances and holds the film during motion photography. The movement of a camera must hold each frame of film perfectly still for 1/24th of a second before advancing to the next frame.

CAMERA TARGET • A small external OBJECT attached to a virtual camera that marks the center of its FIELD OF VIEW.

CCD (CHARGE-COUPLED DEVICE) • A light-sensitive electronic chip that converts color and brightness information to the binary digits that form the digitized image. CCD's are basic components of digital cameras and scanners.

CD-R DRIVE • A drive capable of recording most CD-ROM formats on special CD-R (CD-Recordable) media. These drives are used to burn individual CD-ROM's while a program or sequence is being developed, so it can be checked from its destination format.

CEL ANIMATION • Animation created by painting figures on clear acetate (originally cellophane) sheets, then photographing them frame by frame on an animation camera. A moving subject is drawn with incremental changes in successive cels, so that the finished sequence gives the illusion of motion.

CENTER POINT (OR PIVOT POINT) • The point around which an object ROTATES. By default it is in the geometric center, but it can be moved. It also determines how the object will be LINKED or ALIGNED.

CG • See COMPUTER GRAPHICS.

CHAIN • A series of linked objects, extending the parent-child relationship through further generations — grandchild, great-grandchild, and so forth.

CHAMFER • See BEVEL.

CHANNEL • An adjustable attribute of an object or surface, such as OPACITY or REFLECTIVITY.

CHARACTER ANIMATION • Giving animated objects not only movement, but personality.

CHEAP MESH • A slang term for an object whose surface mesh is made up of a small number of polygons; one that can be rendered very efficiently and quickly.

CHILD OBJECT • The subordinate object in a linked pair. Until an object is linked to another object it is positioned relative to the world's coordinate system. When linked, the child moves relative to its parent.

CHROMA • The color of an object, determined by the frequency of the light it reflects or emits.

CHROMA KEY • A process that electronically removes all areas of a single color or color range from an image, so the area can be filled with another image. The process is often used to place actors photographed in front of a bluescreen into a virtual environment.

CLICK • To press the mouse button. Clicking while a tool cursor is on an object will launch a process or operation related to the tool's function.

CLICK AND DRAG • To press the mouse button and hold it down while moving the mouse. This can be done to move an object within the view, or to select an area or a group of objects.

CLIPPING PLANE • The plane beyond which an object is not rendered. A view of the world has six clipping planes: top, bottom, left, right, near, and far.

CLOSE-UP • A tight shot of a subject that shows all its detail, as opposed to a long shot that shows

an entire setting. A medium shot is between these two extremes.

CLOSED SHAPE • A shape with an inside and an outside.

CMYK • The four colors of ink — Cyan, Magenta, Yellow, and Black — used in the normal four-color printing process. They are applied as tiny dots to form full-color images.

CODEC (COMPRESSION-DECOMPRESSION) • Any technique for compressing and decompressing a digital file so it takes up less disk space and can be played back at a lower transfer rate.

COLLISION DETECTION • The feature that prevents the geometry in a 3D model from intersecting during movement. This will keep the user in a walkthrough from passing through walls and other solid objects.

COLOR • A property of lights and materials. The color of an object is determined by the frequency of the light it emits or reflects. In computer graphics, color is determined by the combination of hue, saturation, and value in the HSV color model, or of red, green, and blue color levels in the RGB color model.

COLOR CALIBRATOR • An external device used in adjusting the color settings of a computer monitor.

COLOR DEPTH • The number of bits used to define the color of each pixel in an image. Black-and-white images use 1 bit per pixel. Grayscale images normally use 8 bits (which can record 256 shades of gray). Eight-bit color images provide 256 colors. A 24-bit image can provide millions of colors (usually 8 bits each for red, green, and blue), while a 32-bit image has an additional 8 bits for an ALPHA CHANNEL.

COLOR SELECTOR • A tool that shows a range of colors that can be assigned to objects or surfaces.

COLOR TEMPERATURE • A value used to differentiate between spectrums of light; the measurement is given in degrees Kelvin.

COMPONENT SOFTWARE • A software architecture in which add-on modules can be linked to the core program as needed, so they will work together as if they were a single program.

COMPOSITING • Any process of combining different elements — still photographs, bluescreen video, computer graphics, or whatever — into a single scene.

COMPRESSION • Any technique for storing a large file so it takes up less disk space. See also CODEC.

COMPRESSION RATE • The speed (in kilobytes per second, or KB/s) at which digital video data is to be played back. For the movie to be viewed as intended, the target system must decompress and display it at that speed.

COMPUTER GRAPHICS (CG) • Images and animation completely generated in a computer.

CONE ANGLE • Angle at which the light from a spotlight expands in a cone of light.

CONSTRAINT • A restriction placed on the way an object moves, usually in order to make it behave realistically.

CONSTRUCTION OBJECTS • Such objects as axes, grids, and lines, that are used in sizing and aligning components while constructing a 3D model. They do not appear in a final render.

CONTINUITY • In filmmaking, continuity maintains consistency in props, costumes, and action from shot to shot in a scene. In a TCB CONTROLLER, it is an adjustment how close a curving path comes to the control point.

CONTROL VERTICES (CV's) • Control points that influence a flexible surface by pulling them in one direction or another.

COORDINATES • Numbers that use a grid to identify a given point on a plane (see XY COORDINATES) or in space (see XYZ COORDINATES).

CROSS HAIR • A reference point in the center of a view, used for navigation; it represents the center of the angle of view.

CROSS SECTION • A means of creating a surface from two profiles by stretching one profile (the cross section) along the shape of the second profile (the face).

CUBIC MAPPING • A method of placing a texture map on an object, as if projected from each of six sides. On a cube, each face is covered by one copy of the map.

CUBIC REFLECTION ENVIRONMENT • A digital environment that represents the way light will interact with a computer-generated subject. It enables the computer to shade the elements of the scene appropriately.

CURRENT TIME FIELD • The field on animation controls that displays the current animation time.

CURSOR • An icon indicating the selected tool in the active window. The cursor is normally controlled by a mouse, but can also be controlled by a keyboard, touchpad, or other pointing device.

CUT (OR SHOT) • The smallest segment of an animation or film — anything from a single frame to an entire unbroken sequence. Also, an edited version of the entire film, as in rough cut or final cut.

CUT SCENE • In computer gaming, a predetermined sequence played in response to a user action to show its results or to advance the story.

CYBERSPACE • In 3D graphics, the virtual space inside the computer where scenes are constructed; also called the WORLD. Cyberspace is also used to describe the intangible world of digital information that can be accessed through the Internet.

CYCLE • A segment of animation that is repeated to create repetitive motions: a ball bouncing, a child running, a tail wagging.

CYLINDRICAL MAPPING • A mapping coordinate system that wraps an image or texture map around one of the object's axes, like a label on a can, and then "shrinks" it to fit.

DAILIES • The rough, unedited film, developed immediately the day of the shoot. With computer graphics and image processing, works in progress can be viewed at any time.

DATA • In the computer world, any information recorded, stored, manipulated, or transmitted as binary digits. It may represent images, text, statistics, or whatever.

DATABASE • Broadly, a program and an area of memory used to store and organize data. In a graphics program, the database keeps track of objects within an image or model.

DATASET • The various information that describes a 3D object. A dataset may contain coordinates, material attributes, textures, animation, and anything else needed to describe the object.

DECAL • A "paste-on" image that can be moved around on an object without affecting any other attributes.

DEFAULT • A parameter or setting that a program will use if not instructed otherwise. Many defaults may be changed by the user.

DEFAULT LIGHTING • The lighting a 3D program presents at startup, so a user can start a model before defining a light source.

DEFAULT MATERIALS • A set of basic materials which can be used to generate custom materials.

DEFINING GEOMETRY • The profiles and settings used to create a surface.

DEFORM • See DEFORMATION GRID.

DEFORM FIT • A type of DEFORM MODIFIER that lets the user define an object's shape using an X-axis outline, a Y-axis outline, and one or more cross-sections.

DEFORM MODIFIER • A procedure for changing the outline of a cross-sectional object as it moves along a path.

DEFORMATION ANIMATION • A method of animating an object by using deformation tools to change its shape.

DEFORMATION LATTICE (OR GRID) • A usually invisible object that defines an area in 3D space that deforms objects passing through its influence. There are many deforms, such as Ripple, Wave, Gravity, and Explode.

DEFORMATION MAP • See DISPLACEMENT MAP.

DELTA CHANGE • The amount an object has moved (in position or orientation), expressed as the numerical difference between the former values and the new values for the relevant coordinates and angles.

DEPTH OF FIELD • The part of a view or image that is in focus; it can range from very shallow to infinite, but with normal vision is moderate. In a camera, depth of field gets shallower as the aperture gets larger. In 3D graphics, depth of field is normally infinite — everything's in focus — but some programs allow it to be adjusted.

DESIGN VIEW • A 2D window where the user can draw 3D objects, usually from the front, top, and sides.

DESKTOP VIDEO • The ability to edit video and add effects digitally on a desktop computer usually equipped with special video cards and software.

DETACH • To disconnect an element of a larger object, making two separate objects. The opposite of ATTACH.

DIFFUSE COLOR • The hue of an object, which is reflected to the camera when the object is illuminated by a direct lighting source.

DIFFUSE MAP • A mapping channel used to alter the texture of an object.

DIFFUSE REFLECTION • The light reflected from a dull surface, which reflects the light striking it at random angles over a broad range, making the surface look equally bright from many directions.

DIFFUSION DITHER • A type of dithering in which differently colored pixels are placed randomly (rather than in a pattern), smoothing the blend.

DIGITAL CAMERA • A camera that records images through CCD's onto built-in memory, flash memory cards, or tiny disks. The image data can be downloaded directly into a computer for processing and manipulation.

DIGITAL COMPOSITE • A composite made up of separate image elements manipulated in a computer, as opposed to the photochemical process of traditional optical composites.

DIGITAL REALM • The data-based environment within a computer.

DIGITAL RETOUCHING • The use of 2D paint programs such as Photoshop to change still photos or movies.

DIGITAL SOUND • Audio that has been converted to binary format so it can be edited and played back by computer.

DVD (Digital Versatile Disk or Digital Video Disk) • A new optical-disc format for video and computer files; it can hold much more data than a CD-ROM.

DIGITIZING • Translating images, objects, or sounds into the digital (or binary) form that a computer can process.

DIRECT INPUT DEVICE (DID) • A device that can feed information directly to a computer in digital form. A popular DID is the "monkey" which is an armature with encoders at pivot points which guides the animation of a wireframe figure inside the computer.

DIRECTIONAL LIGHT (or Distant or Global Light) • Virtual illumination that simulates faraway light sources such as the sun. All its light rays (and resultant shadows) are parallel.

DISPLACEMENT MAP (or Deformation Map) • A grayscale image applied to an object that distorts its mesh, deforming it according to the gray values of the image. Often used to make models of terrain.

DISSOLVE • A transition in which one image fades in while another fades out.

DISTRIBUTED RENDERING • The process of rendering one or more files over a network simultaneously to use the processing power of several machines.

DITHERING • A way of arranging numerous pixels of a limited range of colors to create the appearance of other colors, blends, and shadings.

DOLLY • A camera motion made with a film or video camera by moving the camera smoothly forward or back on a wheeled platform called a dolly. In 3D software, such a movement can easily be simulated.

DONGLE (or Hardware Key) • A physical device plugged into a computer that unlocks high-end software for use. Unlike software, it cannot be illegally copied.

DOUBLE-CLICK • To click a mouse button twice in rapid succession while the cursor is on an object, icon, or menu item. This usually launches a process rather than merely selecting the item.

DOUBLE EXPOSURE • Making two separate shots on the same area of film.

DOUBLE-SIDED OBJECT • An object with normals on both sides of its faces, allowing it to be seen from any viewpoint, even inside.

DOWN TREE • All hierarchically linked objects below a given parent object — children, grandchildren, and so forth.

DPI (Dots Per Inch) • The number of dots or pixels a medium can display in one inch. Most computers display an image at dpi; modern laser printers generally print at 300 to 600 dpi.

DRAWING TOOLS • Tools for creating 2D shapes, which, in a 3D program, can be interpreted as 3D objects or 2D surface features.

DUMMY OBJECT • See NULL.

DUPE (for Duplicate) • A copy.

DVE (Digital Video Editing) • Digitally editing a video and adding special effects using a desktop video system.

EASING (Ease In and Ease Out) • A parameter that controls the way animation is interpolated between keyframes. Easing in gradually accelerates the animation from a standstill; easing out gradually decelerates it to a stop.

EDITING • The process of assembling the various scenes created and rendered during production, turning them into a cohesive whole.

EFFECTS ANIMATION • Effects traditionally hand-drawn (on cels or rotoscopes) to produce fantasy visuals.

EMBEDDED TEXTURES • Textures stored in a model when the file is saved, rather than being linked from a separate texture file.

EMITTER • A simple (and usually invisible) shape that marks where particles emerge in a particle system.

EMULSION • The gelatinous substance that holds the light-sensitive silver halide on the acetate or polyester film base. Color films have three layers of emulsion, one sensitive to each primary color.

END TIME • In animation controls, the time a playback is to stop, usually given in minutes:seconds:hundredths.

ENGINE • In 3D software, the part of the program that deals with the real-time 3D graphics.

ENVIRONMENT MAP • A bitmap image that gives something for a reflective 3D surface to reflect, in place of a complete 3D environment around the reflective object.

EPS (Encapsulated PostScript) • A file format for turning a page design into graphics, or for saving an image. The format contains the code necessary to print a file on a PostScript printer.

ESTABLISHING SHOT • A shot that sets the scene for the action to come, usually by showing the entire set.

EXCLUDE • A command to omit listed objects from the influence of a selected light source.

EXPORT • A command to save a file in a format that can be read in another program.

EXTENSION • The letters or numbers after the dot in a filename (three in Windows, often four on a Mac), usually indicating the format of the file, such as .BMP and .PICT.

EXTRUSION • The process of extending a 2D shape to make a 3D object. In reality, pasta is made through an extrusion process of pushing dough through shaped holes in a template. In 3D graphics the user can extrude a 2D profile along a specified path to make a 3D object.

EYE POINT • A term for the location of the viewer relative to the 3D scene; the point at the tip of the angle of view.

FACE • The polygon that forms one side of an object.

FACE MAPPING • A type of image mapping in which images are applied to pairs of faces that share an invisible edge.

FACIAL-MOTION CAPTURE • A system designed to record the motions of faces, especially lips.

FADE • A scene-transition effect. When a scene fades out, it darkens to black; when one fades in, a black screen lightens to reveal the scene.

FALLOFF • Same as ATTENUATION. Also, a transparency option that sets how much more or less transparent an object is at its edges.

FIELD OF VIEW (FOV) • See ANGLE OF VIEW.

FIELD RENDERING • Output that renders images the way they would be displayed on TV — in two passes, one for even-numbered lines, the other for odd. Compare FRAME RENDERING.

FILE COMPRESSION • Any process that reduces the size of a file for storage or playback.

FILE FORMAT • The way data is organized in a computer file, usually indicated in the filename's extension: BMP, PICT, and TGA are common bitmap formats; 3DS, DXF, and OBJ are some 3D formats.

FILLET (or Radius Edge). • A curved transition between two planes or lines.

FILL LIGHT • A light source used to lighten shadowy areas of a scene.

FILM FORMAT • Either the width of a film, such as 16 mm, 35 mm, or 70 mm, or the aspect ratio of the image.

FILM GRAIN • The silver halide particles in a film emulsion that are visible in the projected image. The finer the grain, the sharper the picture. Some high-end renderers have simulated film grain to match the digitally created image with live action footage.

FILM GRAMMAR • The storytelling methods developed by film pioneers like D.W. Griffith to use the medium to its fullest.

FILTER • In computer graphics, a routine for altering images, originally in imitation of photographic filters. Another sense is the part of a program used to read a foreign file format.

FINAL RENDERING • The last, and often the highest-quality rendering of a scene, using all materials and effects specified, rather than the stand-ins and shortcuts used during development.

FIRST VERTEX • The vertex in a shape that is used for orientation during skinning operations. Any vertex can be specified as first; by default, the first one created is used.

FLAT SHADING • A mode of displaying or rendering a scene rapidly by filling each facet of a surface with a single color. A curved object will show as a faceted polyhedron because the different facets are not smoothed together as in a FINAL RENDERING.

FLIPPING • A method of placing a TEXTURE MAP on an object, with one copy on one side of a specified AXIS, and its mirror image on the other. or replicating or changing geometry to mirror the original.

FOCAL LENGTH • In film, the distance from the center of the lens to the image it forms of the subject. A short focal length produces wide-angle images, while long ones produce telephoto shots. Most programs allow the user to adjust focal length to extremes well beyond the range of real lenses.

FOG • A lighting effect that simulates fog or haze by bleaching and diffusing objects in the distance.

FOLEY STAGE • A soundproof room containing many objects and materials for creating sound effects.

FORCED PERSPECTIVE • In traditional set design (and CEL ANIMATION), the use of painted perspective and the placement of smaller objects behind larger foreground elements to give the illusion of great depth in a limited space.

FORWARD KINEMATICS • A mode of animating LINKED objects, in which the parent's movement affects all children and more distant offspring. Compare INVERSE KINEMATICS.

FOUR-PERF FORMAT • The standard 35 mm film format in which the film passes vertically through the camera, with the space four perforations, or sprocket holes, for each frame; as compared to the horizontal eight-perf format of vistavision.

FRAME • In filmmaking or animation, a single still image, one of the many that make up a sequence. Also, a scene as viewed through a camera or viewport; compare FIELD OF VIEW.

FRAME RENDERING • The normal output, with the entire image rendered in one pass. Compare FIELD RENDERING.

FRAMES PER SECOND (FPS) • The rate at which frames of a film are exposed or projected. Live action is normally simulated at 24 fps, but other rates can be used.

FREE-FORM DEFORMATION • A way of changing the shape of an object. Free-form deformation tools are usually used on relatively simple objects.

FREE LINK • A LINK in which the CHILD OBJECT can move independently of its parent, but moves and changes scale when the parent does.

FREEZE (or Templated) • A command that leaves an object visible but unable to be selected or changed.

FRESNEL FACTOR • An optical effect that makes an object look more realistic by brightening the edges.

FRONT-FACING POLYGON • A POLYGON whose NORMALS point forward, toward the viewer or camera.

FULL SCREEN • A command to expand a view to cover the entire monitor screen, suppressing other windows and the menu bar.

FUNCTION CURVE • A graph showing the parameters of object transformations and the like.

GAMMA • A measure of the overall brightness of a computer screen, and by extension a measure of brightness for all output technologies.

GAMUT • The more or less limited color range that any particular display or printing technology can represent.

GARBAGE MATTE • An animated matte used to block out unwanted elements such as cables captured during photography.

G-BUFFER (or Geometry Channel) • An additional channel that uses a grayscale image to describe the GEOMETRY, SURFACE NORMALS, and other information in a 3D file.

GEL • In traditional stage and film work, a colored filter placed over a floodlight or spotlight. By extension, sometimes used for projection map.

GENERATION • A level of duplication in film: the original negative is first-generation, a dupe of that is second-generation, a copy made from the second-generation negative is third-generation, etc. The image degrades with successive generations. In the DIGITAL REALM an image can be copied hundreds of generations with no degradation of quality.

GEOMETRY • 3D objects in general; the mathematical description of such objects.

GEOMETRY CHANNEL • See G-BUFFER.

GIMBAL LOCK • The unintended inability of an object to rotate around one or more of its axes.

GLASS SHOT • An old-fashioned way of creating a composite shot where an image is painted on a sheet of glass with certain areas left clear. When the camera shoots the image, the objects in the background show through the glass, creating an in-camera effect.

GLOW • A soft halo of light around an object, produced by a setting on a light source or by post-production manipulation.

GOBO • See PROJECTION MAP.

GO-MOTION • Traditional frame-by-frame stop-motion animation doesn't produce the blur of a normally moving object, instead producing stroboscopic effects. In the go-motion technique, rods attached to a stop-motion puppet move it while the camera shutter is open, producing motion blur on the film.

GOURAUD SHADING • A shading calculation that computes shading only at polygon vertices and averages that color information across polygon faces. The result is a smooth rendered look that gives a fairly accurate idea of the effect of lights. A type of smooth shading.

GRADIENT • A smooth blend from one color or brightness to another.

GREENSCREEN • Similar to BLUESCREEN, used when objects have blue or purple pigments.

GRID • A regular pattern of squares like graph paper, used for scale when creating objects.

GRID SCALE • A scale that shows what size an object would be in the real world.

GROUND PLANE • A grid on the horizontal plane,

which serves as a reference for the ground of the scene.

GROUP • A command that temporarily collects several selected objects without permanently attaching them, allowing them to be treated and moved as a unit.

HANDLE • A small cube that represents the meeting of two or more planes or sides. When an object is selected, its handles become visible and can be used to manipulate the object.

HARDWARE • In computer work, the physical equipment, as opposed to the software programs and binary data that run the computer and record the work.

HARRY • A high-end video editing and compositing tool made by Quantel. Its real-time interactive capabilities make it an excellent tool for commercial film production.

HEADS-UP ORIENTATION AXIS • An axis that indicates the orientation of the view with respect to the world's coordinate system.

HIDDEN LINE • A display or rendering mode that draws only the edges of an object, as a wireframe does, but hides the edges that would not be seen if the object were opaque.

HIDE • A command that makes an object temporarily invisible.

HIERARCHICAL OBJECT • An object shape created in a separate workspace; when an instance of the shape is inserted into the model, its retains a link to the shape. Changes made to the shape are automatically applied to the instances.

HIERARCHY • The full set of parent-child linkages in a scene.

HIGH-RESOLUTION IMAGE • Usually determined by the pixel density. Images produced for print and commercial film must have a very high resolution so pixilation (or blockiness) is not apparent.

HOME • A base location or reference point in some 3D programs.

HOTSPOT • The portion of the light projected from a source that is at the full intensity specified.

HSV (Hue, Saturation, Value) • An interface in which hue (or chroma), saturation (or intensity), and value (or brightness) can be adjusted to produce a color.

HUE • The property of COLOR that corresponds to the frequency or wavelength of the light; and to what most people would consider color itself.

ILM (Industrial Light and Magic) • Prestigious special effects house founded by George Lucas.

IMAGE LIBRARY • A collection of professionally photographed and scanned images, often on CD-ROM, that can be used free or for a one-time fee.

IMAGE MAP (or picture map) • A bitmapped image, either scanned or painted, that gives qualities not available simply by varying surface attributes.

IMAGE PROCESSING • The computerized manipulation of a digital image — commonly a scanned photograph or painting, or a video capture.

IMPORT • To load a file saved in a format not native to the active program; it may be a cross-program or cross-platform format, like DXF.

IN-CAMERA EFFECTS • In-camera effects composite multiple elements on a single film negative inside the camera, thus retaining first-generation quality. In CG there is less advantage to generating all of the effects at once since there is no degeneration in quality in post-production.

INCLUDE • A light-source option; the user can select which objects the specified light will affect. All other objects in the scene will be ignored.

INSTANCE • A replica of an original shape; it will change if the original is changed, even though it isn't in the same window. See HIERARCHICAL OBJECT.

INTENSITY • A measure of the brightness of a light source. Also, a synonym for saturation.

INTERACTIVE RENDERER • A tool that quickly renders an approximation of the scene, including shapes and colors but omitting details like shadows.

INTERPOLATE • To calculate the unknown values that fall between two known values. The animations between two keyframes are interpolations done by the computer.

INTRINSIC MAPPING • Placing a texture map on a surface using the object's own geometry as a guide. Other placement techniques, such as spherical and cylindrical mapping, assume a fixed extrinsic geometry to guide the placement.

INVERSE KINEMATICS (IK) • Controlling linked objects by moving the far end of a hierarchical chain, causing the rest of the chain to conform. Compare FORWARD KINEMATICS.

INVERTED LIGHT (or Negative or Dark Light) • A setting that makes a light source lower the illumination level of whatever is in range.

JAGGIES • See STAIRSTEPPING.

JPEG (Joint Photographic Experts Group) • A committee that has developed compression standards for still images; also the compression methods and file formats developed by that group.

KEY LIGHT • A scene's main source of illumination, which usually casts the most apparent shadows.

KEYFRAME • In computer animation, a user-defined point where a specific animation event takes place, such as the beginning or end of a motion. The computer then interpolates (or "tweens") the events from keyframe to keyframe. In a digital video file, the keyframe contains the entire image; other frames contain only the information that changes from the previous frame.

KEYFRAMING • The process of defining keyframes for animation.

LATHING • Also called revolving. A method of creating a 3D object by revolving a 2D profile about a designated axis. Though the approach is the inverse, the results resemble those from a woodworker's lathe, where a solid is rotated and cut away by a negative of the desired profile.

LAYER • A means of organizing objects in a graphics program. In a 2D program, the layers are strict, and something on a front layer will block anything behind. Since a 3D scene can be viewed from various angles, the grouping can be free-form.

LENS FLARE • The bright circles and rays seen when a camera lens is pointed at a bright light.

LIBRARY • A collection of objects, images, or shapes that can be used in a model or scene. Also, a collection of code that enables programmers to create links to perform specific tasks.

LIGHT EDITOR (or Lights Browser) • A window that displays the properties for lights and lets you organize and edit them.

LIGHT OBJECTS • The objects in the workspace that represent various lights and spotlights.

LIGHTS BROWSER • See LIGHT EDITOR.

LINEAR ARRAY • A series of identical objects duplicated from an original along a straight line. Compare RADIAL ARRAY.

LINEAR EDITING • See NONLINEAR EDITING.

LINEAR-MOTION STYLE • A method of interpolation, in which the unknown frame values between two known keyframe values are calculated for the shortest distance between the two values, resulting in linear motion. Compare SMOOTH-MOTION STYLE.

LINEAR WEIGHTING • Animation control method in which tweening is done in a continuous, even manner, with no variation in speed or direction.

LINK • A hierarchical connection between two objects, parent and child. A parent can have any number of children, but a child (which can have its own children) can have only one parent.

LOCAL COORDINATES • A coordinate system that

centers its axes on the object itself.

LOCAL LIGHTS • The generic term for omni light and spotlight objects.

LOCK LINK • A link in which the child object is bound to its parent, changing scale, orientation, and position in response to corresponding changes in the parent. Neither object can move nor be scaled independently of the other.

LOCKED-OFF CAMERA • A camera that remains stationary during a shot. Special effects photography used to require a locked-off camera.

LOOK-AT POINT • The center of a view or the focus of a camera.

LOW-RESOLUTION IMAGE • During development, digital images and computer-generated animation are produced at low resolution, which requires less memory to store and less time to process. Compare HIGH-RESOLUTION IMAGE.

LUMINANCE • The value (or brightness) of a color; the amount of light emitted by an object or a computer monitor.

LUMINOSITY • See SELF-ILLUMINATION.

MAGNET TOOL • A tool for 3D modeling available in some programs that attracts or repels vertices when brought close to an object.

MAGNIFY TOOL • A tool that increases the apparent size of a drawing when the mouse is clicked.

MAINFRAME • In older networked systems, the large central computer to which all terminals were connected, and where all computations were made.

Mapping (or Texture Mapping) • The process of assigning attributes to the surface of an object.

MAPPING COORDINATES • Parameters that specify the scale and placement of textures on an object.

MAQUETTE • A small but detailed sculpture used to visualize a character or object in three dimensions.

MARQUEE (or Selection Rectangle) • A dotted-line box created by clicking and dragging the cursor with any of several tools to select or define an object, area, or group. It provides visual feedback during various operations.

MASK • A custom-shaped element used to prevent a specific area of an image from being affected by a process. Compare MATTE.

MATCHED MOVE • A shot matched frame-by-frame to another. A 3D artist will often match camera movement from a live shot to help the composited image look seamless.

MATERIAL • A general term for any images and settings assigned to an object's surface.

MATTE • An opaque image that prevents exposure in a particular area of film, which can later be filled with another image. See MASK.

MATTE LINES • The undesirable visible edges of an element that has not been seamlessly matted into a shot.

MATTE PAINTINGS • Matte paintings are usually used to provide expansive establishing shots and extend physical sets. Traditional matte painting is rendered with brushes and oils on glass. Digital matte painting has gained a great deal of popularity in Hollywood and has (in most cases) replaced traditional methods.

MEMORY • Programs and files are loaded from disk (or any other input) into random-access memory (RAM) for easy access during all phases of processing. Computer graphics need both powerful processors and huge amounts of RAM. If RAM is insufficient, it can be supplemented with VIRTUAL MEMORY.

MENU BAR • A bar at the top of the monitor screen that contains lists of commands for EDITING, viewing, and so forth.

MERCATOR MAP (or Mercator Projection) • A 2D map in which meridians are drawn as straight north-south lines. A Mercator map of the world distorts areas near the poles, but when mapped to a sphere, these features are seen as they should be.

MESH • The surface of a 3D object or scene, called that because (especially in WIREFRAME view) it looks like a sculpture made of wire mesh.

MESH OPTIMIZATION • Combining closely aligned faces of a mesh object to reduce its complexity (or density) and speed up RENDERING.

MESH SURFACE • A surface made up of many POLYGONS, each of which shares VERTEX points with several neighbors. Mesh surfaces are used to define complex forms; they provide smoothing information for the rendering ALGORITHMS.

METABALLS • A type of modeling in which spheres are built into forms that the software then blends into a single mass.

MIRROR • To reverse an object or copy a reversed version of it along a given axis.

MODEL • A broad term used to describe any grouping of geometry from a simple sphere to an entire complex stage set.

MOIRÉ • A wavy pattern first produced in watered silk, hence the term. Elsewhere, it's undesirable. It occurs on screen when narrow striped patterns are seen at an angle and become aliased on screen. By extension, any similar optical artifact — a pattern that appears in video images that contain small repetitive textures, or in scans when the scanning resolution doesn't match the printing resolution, or on screen when a halftone is displayed at the wrong resolution or angle.

MORPHING • Animated 2D or 3D technique that smoothly transforms one form into another.

MOTION BLUR • The smearing of an image when either the subject or camera is moving; the effect can be imitated digitally to give the appearance of motion.

MOTION CAPTURE • Any process that enables a performer's actions to be digitized and used to drive a bones-deformation system for 3D character animation. Also see DIRECT INPUT DEVICE, OPTICAL TRACKING.

MOTION CONTROL • A system that uses computers to program cameras, props, and models to move in repeatable ways so that separately shot elements can be synchronized into a single composite.

MOTION LIBRARY • A stock collection of animated movements (usually motion-captured) — reaching, bending, eating, and so forth — for use in bones-deformation systems.

MOTION PATH • A line or curve that represents the path of an object.

MULTIPLANE EFFECTS • A traditional animation technique that allows separate pieces of two-dimensional artwork to be positioned relative to each other beneath a moving camera, creating the illusion of depth of field when photographed. The same effect is relatively simple to replicate with digital techniques.

MULTIPLE EXPOSURES (or Passes) • Several different exposures made on a single strip of film.

MULTIPLIER • A setting that pushes the intensity of a light source past the limits of the RGB setting.

NAVIGATION • The process of moving through a view or scene.

NEGATIVE LIGHT • See INVERTED LIGHT.

NOISE • Static or white noise in radio is caused by random signals interfering with the transmission; on television the result is called snow. In computer graphics, the noise function randomly places pixels of variants of the desired color on a surface, thus improving photorealism.

NONLINEAR EDITING • An editing system that lets the user edit scenes in any order; in LINEAR EDITING, the operator must start at the beginning and work through to the end.

NONPLANAR POLYGON • A polygon at least one vertex of which is on a different plane from the others; this can cause problems in rendering.

NONREPRODUCING GUIDELINES • Guidelines are

used to help align objects; nonreproducing ones don't show up on a final print.

NON SEQUITUR • A statement or action that doesn't follow logically or flow organically from what came before.

NORMAL • A marker (usually a little line or arrow, visible when an object is selected) that shows which direction a polygon is facing in 3D space; also the numerical value that defines the direction precisely. Normals are attached either to each polygon or to each vertex.

NUDGE • To make a change in position, orientation, or scale in small increments, usually using the arrow keys. Often the size of the increments can be specified by the user.

NULL (or Dummy) **OBJECT** • An invisible object used as a reference point for establishing remote axes of rotation.

NURBS (Non-Uniform Rational B-Spline) • A type of spline whose control points are visible away from the resulting curve, which is controlled with weights.

OBJECT • In a 3D program, usually something constructed in three dimensions; more broadly, any guideline, profile, or model that can be manipulated in the workspace.

OBJECT AXIS • The axis, visible on command, that indicates the orientation of an object. Compare NORMAL.

OBJECTS BROWSER • A window used for organizing and manipulating 3D objects and 2D profiles.

OBSERVER • A marker to represent the viewer — for example, a circle with a line to indicate the viewing direction, shown in a design window.

OCTREE • An internal data structure which subdivides the three-dimensional space for more efficient rendering. Increasing the octree height of a render may bring out more detail but increases processing time.

OFFSET THE ANIMATION • To move the beginning and ending times of an animation, without changing the duration.

OMNI LIGHT • See POINT LIGHT.

OPACITY • The degree to which an object blocks light rays; the opposite of TRANSPARENCY. If an object's opacity is 100%, it is totally opaque; no light can penetrate it and nothing can be seen through it.

OPACITY MAP • A grayscale image that can be mapped to an object's surface to make some areas more opaque than others.

OPERAND • An object used in a boolean operation.

OPEN GL (Open Graphics Library) • A collection of low-level code developed by Silicon Graphics, Inc., which enables fast redraw of 3D objects on screen. Open GL is quickly becoming an industry standard.

OPTICAL COMPOSITING • The traditional method of combining two or more separately filmed elements onto a fresh piece of film using an optical printer.

OPTICAL PRINTER • An elaborate device made of one or more projectors that can project filmed elements into the lens of a camera loaded with fresh film, in order to composite several previously photographed elements onto the same strip of film.

OPTICAL TRACKING • A method of motion capture in which the performer has numerous little targets (usually white disks or balls) on hands, feet, limbs, head, and body, and a video camera is used to record and digitize their motion as the performer moves.

OPTIMIZE • In 3D graphics, to simplify a mesh object by combining adjacent polygons, thereby speeding up rendering. In computers generally, to reorganize a hard drive by placing all of a single file in contiguous sectors, speeding access to the data.

OPTIMIZED PALETTE • The best selection of colors to display a given image. This is important with the 256 colors available in 8-bit images, which is the practical limit of most older monitors.

ORIGIN POINT • The center of the workspace, where the x axis, y axis, and z axis cross at the coordinates 0,0,0.

ORTHOGRAPHIC PROJECTION • In 3D graphics, a display mode in which all lines along the same axis are parallel (rather than converging as they do in a perspective drawing) and all dimensions remain undistorted. Working windows with top, side, and front views are orthographic in two dimensions; an orthographic projection shows the third dimension by viewing the object from an angle.

OUTPUT • Anything — file, slide, videotape, CD, or other medium — used to store or publish an image or animation.

OUTPUT DEVICE • Any hardware, such as a laser printer, that produces output on a final medium.

PAINT SYSTEM (or Painting Program) • Any graphics software that, with the aid of digitizing tablets or pens or other input devices, can simulate the effect of paintbrushes and ink pens.

PALETTE • The range of colors used in an image. See OPTIMIZED PALETTE.

PALETTE FLASH • A flaring or color shift sometimes seen when an image's palette changes.

PAN (short for PANORAMIC) • A shot in which the camera moves horizontally across a scene, rotating on its y axis (vertical). Compare TILT, ROLL, TRACKING SHOT.

PARAMETRIC MODELING • A 3D modeling system in which objects retain their base geometry and can be extensively modified by varying the defining parameters.

PARENT OBJECT • In a chain of linked objects, the object closer to the top of the hierarchy than the object or objects below it (its CHILD or children).

PARENT-CHILD LINK • A connection between two objects, in which the child is linked to the parent to constrain it. Most commonly used in animations.

PARENT-RELATIVE MOTION • An object's motion governed by its parent's coordinate system.

PARTIAL LATHE • A lathing operation in which the 2D profile is revolved less than full circle.

PARTICLE (or Particle-Generating) **SYSTEM** • An animation module for generating and controlling the semirandom behavior of numerous tiny objects (particles), to simulate bubbles, flames, sparks, and the like.

PASTE-REPLACE • A command to paste an object in place of another one, copying the latter's position and orientation.

PATCH • A curved shape, usually a lattice of splines or polygons, that helps model a 3D image.

PATCH MODELER • A 3D modeling system that uses a network of control points to define and modify the shape of a patch.

PATH • The line or curve along which an object or PROFILE moves in an animation or a process such as EXTRUDE.

PENUMBRA • A partial shadow, often between a full shadow and an illuminated area.

PERSISTENCE OF VISION • The tendency of the eye and mind to retain an image for a moment after seeing it, allowing steps of action (as in movie frames) to be perceived as continuous movement. Films project 24 individual frames a second and videos project 30 (or more accurately 29.97 fps); slower rates may produce an unpleasant flicker and seem jerky.

PERSPECTIVE • A way of representing 3D objects on a screen or canvas that shrinks and distorts them according to their distance from the eye of the viewer (real or virtual), with parallel lines converging at a distant vanishing point, simulating the perspective of the real world. The shorter the view distance, the wider the perspective and the more distorted the objects appear. Compare ORTHOGRAPHIC projection.

PHONG RENDERING (or Shading) • A smooth rendering method, with specular highlights added for more realism; it computes shading at every pixel, thus creating better surfaces than GOURAUD SHADING but taking longer to render.

PICT • A standard file format for storing graphics on a Macintosh.

PICTURE ELEMENT • See PIXEL.

PITCH • Rotation around the x axis (horizontal).

PIVOT POINT • See CENTER POINT.

PIXEL (short for Picture Element) • The smallest component of a computer image or display; each dot on a bitmap or monitor screen is a pixel. An SVGA monitor has a resolution of 800x600 pixels, so a bitmap designed for it has 480,000 pixels (each of which has up to 32 bits of data to define its color); much higher resolutions are necessary for computer animations to be projected on a movie screen.

PLANAR MAPPING • A type of mapping best used on flat objects, since it applies an image from a single direction.

PLANE • A flat surface, theoretically infinite in two dimensions, defined by any three points that aren't in a single line; it has two axes, usually represented as x and y. Compare POINT.

PLAYBACK CONTROLS • In animation programs, the buttons that work like standard VCR controls: play, stop, rewind, and so forth.

PLAYBACK HEAD • The marker in the score that indicates the current time. In most programs the user can adjust the playback head to go to any point in an animation.

PLAYBACK MODES • Settings for playing an animation or segment: Normal, from start time to end time, once; Loop, from start to end, repeatedly; and Reverse, from start to end and back, repeatedly.

PLUG-IN OR EXTENSION • A modular software program that expands the capabilities of COMPONENT SOFTWARE; it functions as if part of the base program.

POINT • A location without dimension (though represented by a 2D dot onscreen), defined by one coordinate on each of the three axes. Compare PLANE.

POINT CLOUD • A very fast method of rendering that shows only the vertices of an object, often used in the modeling window.

POINT (or Omnidirectional or Omni) **LIGHT** • A light source that shines equally in all directions from a single point. Compare AMBIENT LIGHT, SPOTLIGHT.

POLYGON • A closed plane bounded by three or more line segments; in 3D work, most surfaces are made up of numerous abutting polygons.

POLYGON NORMAL • See NORMAL.

POLYGON RESOLUTION • The number of polygons used to represent an object's surface, clearly seen in wireframe.

POLYGONAL MODELING • The fundamental type of 3D modeling, in which an object is made up of polygons.

POLYLINE • A line with more than one segment (and therefore at least three vertices).

POLYMESH • An array of vertices that describe a surface.

POST-PRODUCTION EFFECTS • In 3D graphics, the transitions, color adjustments, or special effects applied to an animation after rendering. Sometimes referred to as just "post."

PREFERENCES • Settings that can be adjusted to customize an application.

PRELIMINARY COMPOSITE (or Precomp) • A rough composite of the primary elements of a shot, used as a reference for producing further shots.

PRERENDERED ANIMATION • An animation that is rendered beforehand and then stored as a series of digital images.

PREVIEW • A rapid output mode that produces a simplified version of a work in progress.

PREVIEW FPS • A temporary frames-per-second rate for previewing animations.

PRIMITIVE • A basic 3D geometric form, such as a cube, sphere, cone, or cylinder, that can be modified or combined with others in a model.

PROCEDURAL TEXTURE • A texture produced through mathematical procedures. It can simulate wood, marble, and other materials, but is rarely as convincing as the scanned images of an actual texture.

PROFILE • The fundamental defining geometry of many 3D objects. A 2D profile is created, then manipulated through the third dimension with a procedure such as extrusion or lathing.

PROJECTION • Often used as a synonym for mapping (see MERCATOR PROJECTION); confusingly, it is also what is done with a projector, which is used in projection mapping.

PROJECTION MAP OR GOBO • An image added to a light source that changes the light's shape or causes it to throw a pattern onto objects it illuminates. (In filmmaking, a gobo is a steel cutout that changes the shape or quality of a spotlight.)

PROJECTION MAPPING • Placing a texture map on an object by projecting the texture on the object's surface, often from behind.

PROJECTION TOOL • A tool that projects a profile onto a surface so the surface can be trimmed to shape.

PROJECTOR • A light source that can use a gobo or projection map.

PROPERTY • An attribute of an object that can be animated or modified, such as COLOR or visibility.

PULLING POINTS • Slang term for modeling or deforming an object by adjusting its vertices.

PYLON • Elaborate custom-made supports, usually connected to a motion-control system, used to mount and move models and props during bluescreen photography.

PYROTECHNICS (or Pyro) • The creation of fireworks and explosives; the simulation of them and other smoke and fire effects.

QUADRANGLE (or Quad) • A four-sided polygon (irregular or rectangular) commonly used in 3D programs.

RADIAL ARRAY • A series of objects duplicated from the original along an arc, circle, or other rotation-based trajectory. Compare LINEAR ARRAY.

RADIOSITY • A rendering method which calculates the transfer of light between surfaces based on their color and proximity. Adding radiosity to the calculations can increase realism markedly.

RADIUS EDGE • See FILLET.

RAM • (Random Access Memory) See MEMORY.

RAYTRACING • A 3D rendering method that simulates the properties of light rays reflected off objects toward the viewer. Typically, a ray of light is traced from the imaging plane back to the object, and then to the light source.

REALTIME • On a computer that's powerful enough, input data and graphics can be processed in real time — as the work is going on, or as the game is being played — so that any changes result in near-instantaneous adjustments to the image.

REFLECTION • Light from an external source that is thrown back from the surface of an object toward the observer or another object.

REFLECTION MAP • A 2D image of an environment for a reflective object, used to simulate the effects of raytracing on reflective objects.

REFLECTIVITY (or Shininess) • A measure of the portion of the total amount of light striking the surface that reflects from its surface; gloss.

REFRACTION • The change in direction of light

rays as they pass from one transparent material (say glass) to one of a different density (such as air). This causes an apparent shift in an image seen through the material.

REFRACTION MAPPING • A way of simulating the effects of light refraction in programs that don't offer raytracing.

REFRESH RATE • The frequency with which a screen image is repainted, measured in cycles per second, or Hertz (Hz).

REGISTRATION PINS • In a camera or projector, pins that position and hold the film at each frame in turn.

RENDERING • The process in which the computer combines all the specified object and light data to create an image, either a still or a frame in an animation. There are many types of rendering, among them field rendering, final rendering, frame rendering, flat shading, smooth shading.

RENDERMAN • Pixar software used to create 3D images.

RGB • Red, green, and blue are the three primary colors in the additive color model. Computer monitors use pixels of these colors, varying their intensity to create the display. Compare CMYK and SUBTRACTIVE COLOR MODEL.

ROLL • Rotation of an object or camera around the z axis. Compare PITCH, YAW.

ROTATE • To spin an object around any selected axis.

ROTOSCOPE • An old animation technique in which individual film frames were projected onto a surface and the outline of selected images were traced by hand, in order to create traveling mattes or animation effects. Hence, rotoscoping is the process of adding film or video to animation, as either a finished element or a working reference.

ROUGHNESS • An attribute that scatters the reflections from an object, corresponding to physical roughness of a real surface.

ROUGHNESS MAP • A texture map that is used — often along with a specular map — to control highlights.

SABRE SYSTEM • An interactive digital tool for compositing and editing that emulates the freedom of a HARRY and other such digital video tools. An open-architecture system, it can accept both off-the-shelf and proprietary software to work on SGI hardware.

SATURATION • The degree of color intensity. A highly saturated color is vivid; as it loses saturation, it turns gray.

SCALE • The ratio between the size of a real object and the size of its representation on paper or in 3D. In computer graphics, to scale an object is to make it proportionately smaller or larger in all three dimensions. To scale an animation is to lengthen or shorten it.

SCANLINE RENDERER • A typical rendering method that draws the image in a series of horizontal lines. Scanline is a very fast renderer that produces images at a slightly lower quality than raytracing.

SCANNER • A device that converts film or flat images into digital information.

SCENE • A 3D space customized with models, lights, materials, and possibly animation.

SCORE • The window that contains all the time information about each object and property in the scene.

SEGMENT • A step or division in an object or line.

SELF-ILLUMINATION • The quality of being lit from within.

SELF-ILLUMINATION MAP • A grayscale image that governs which parts of an object appear to be lit from within, and how strongly.

SGI (Silicon Graphics, Inc.) • Maker of powerful workstations for which much high-end 3D-graphics software is written.

SHADER • A combination of surface attributes

such as COLOR, TEXTURE, REFLECTIVITY, and SMOOTHNESS.

SHADING • The varied coloration of a surface that results from the way light strikes it. See FLAT SHADING and SMOOTH SHADING.

SHADOW MAPPING • A method of creating shadows by use of a grayscale texture map applied to an object.

SHININESS • See REFLECTIVITY.

SIMPLIFYING GEOMETRY • The process of reducing the complexity of a model by eliminating unseen structural elements and reducing polygons to the minimum.

SINGLE-SIDED POLYGON • By default, a polygon can be "seen" only from the side with the normal; it has only one side.

SKATING • A common problem in animation in which a character's feet seem to slide around on the ground instead of remaining firmly planted.

SKELETON • The internal structure of linked bones (perhaps a simplified version of a human skeleton) used to deform the surrounding mesh in a bones-deformation system.

SKEW • A command that pushes one side of an object one way along the selected axis, and the other side in the opposite direction.

SKIN • A surface stretched over a series of profile ribs, rather like the way a model airplane wing is made.

SKINNING • A method of generating a skin over a group of cross-sectional profiles to create a 3D object.

SLICE • The appropriate tool can slice a piece off a 3D object, adding a corresponding surface to each piece.

SMOOTH MOTION • A type of interpolation that calculates the unknown frame values between two known keyframe values as a curve rather than as a straight line. Compare LINEAR-MOTION STYLE.

SMOOTH SHADING • A rendering type that gives a smooth appearance to curved surfaces. See GOURAUD SHADING.

SMOOTHING • A technique that allows you to increase the polygon resolution of a surface for a final render. In general, the more polygons there are, the smoother the curved surface.

SMPTE (Society of Motion Picture and Television Engineers) • In video and 3D animation, a time format giving minutes:seconds: frames; thus 15:42:11 means 15 minutes, 42 seconds, and 11 frames.

SNAP • A feature that causes the cursor to snap to the nearest position on a grid or guideline, or to the objects' edges and vertices.

SNAPSHOT • A way of saving a view (or sometimes a sequence) on screen, at screen resolution.

SOFTIMAGE • A popular commercial animation software system owned by Microsoft. SoftImage is considered to be the leading commercial package for character animation.

SOFTWARE • The programs and data that make a computer work.

SOLID MODELING • A form of 3D modeling that includes information about weight, density, and tensile strength of a material; useful in engineering.

SOLITAIRE • An output device for scanning digital images onto film.

SPECULAR • Having to do with the direct (not diffuse) reflection of light off a surface. The specular color determines the color of the specular highlight of a material.

SPECULAR HIGHLIGHT • The bright reflections on glossy objects in high-level final renderings.

SPECULAR (or Specularity) **MAP** • A texture map used (sometimes along with roughness maps) instead of a specular color to control highlights. Some specular maps are created with noise filters; others are images composed of cross-hatches or scratches.

SPECULAR REFLECTION • The component of the light reflecting from a surface caused by its shininess (or gloss). Shiny surfaces reflect light striking them without diffusion, resulting in hot spots corresponding to the direction of the light sources.

SPECULARITY • The COLOR and INTENSITY of an object's highlights, which can be adjusted with a specularity setting.

SPHERICAL MAPPING • A method of placing a texture map on an object by first wrapping the map cylindrically around the object, then reducing the top and bottom into single points at the ends of the object's axis, and finally shrinking the map onto the object. You can create a geographical globe by thus mapping a Mercator projection of the world onto a sphere.

SPLINE • A curve defined by three or more control points. The tightness of a curve can be controlled by adjusting the tangent lines at a control point. BÉZIER, B-spline, and NURBS are common types of splines.

SPOTLIGHT • A local light source that shines in only one direction, from a single point out into a user-defined cone; compare AMBIENT LIGHT. DIRECTIONAL LIGHT, POINT LIGHT.

SQUASH AND STRETCH • Operations that treat an object as though it had a set volume. Squashing an object flattens it along one axis but makes it spread out correspondingly along the others; stretching an object makes it thinner in the middle.

STAIRSTEPPING (or Jaggies) • In a screen display or bitmap image or rendering, the jagged edges formed by square pixels trying to form a diagonal or curved line. They can be smoothed by anti-aliasing.

START TIME • The beginning point of the animation playback, set on the animation controls.

STATUS BAR • A help bar, usually at the bottom of the screen, that gives information about currently selected tools, menu items, controls, and the like.

STEPS • Additional vertices generated between control points on a spline or vertices on a polygon.

STOP-MOTION ANIMATION • The animation technique of manipulating puppets or props and shooting a single frame of film for each incremental position, resulting in the illusion of motion when played.

STORYBOARDING • Planning a film or animation by breaking a scene down into a sequence of sketches (on a storyboard) that illustrate the key movements and compositions.

STREAK PHOTOGRAPHY • A technique in which a moving camera and a long exposure gives a streaking effect to an image.

SUBSTITUTION ANIMATION • A method of animating instant changes, in which one object replaces another at a given frame.

SUBTRACTIVE COLOR MODEL • The familiar color model — applicable to pigments or reflected light — in which red, yellow, and blue are the primary colors, and mixing the three together results in a muddy brown. Compare CMYK, RGB, and ADDITIVE COLOR MODEL.

SURFACE ATTRIBUTE • A setting, such as color or transparency, that affects all parts of a surface equally.

SURFACE COLOR • The assigned color of an object; it is combined with other values to calculate the final rendered color.

SURFACE EDITOR TOOL • A tool with which to edit an object's surface.

SURFACE FEATURE • A 2D polygon applied to a surface to represent a door, window, or surface feature; it can have attributes such as transparency and color, but no depth.

SURFACE GEOMETRY • The exposed geometry on

the outside of an object.

SURFACE MAPPING • A process by which a BITMAP image can be used to define such properties as color, texture, and reflectivity on an object's surface.

SURFACE NORMALS • The set of values that determine the direction of the surface geometry of a model.

SURFACE OBJECTS • 3D objects built from one or more 2D profiles.

SWEEP • A method of creating a geometrically complex 3D object such as a coiled spring from a 2D profile or template, using a combination of extrude with lathe to simultaneously push the profile through space and revolve it around an axis, or with another command along a different curved path.

SYSTEM PALETTE • The set of colors defined by the operating system of the computer.

TANGENT LINE • A line that touches a curve at a control point; it is used to adjust the curve of a spline.

TANGENT POINT OR WEIGHT • The portion of a NURBS or B-SPLINE system (in which control points are held away from the spline) that acts like a magnet to pull the spline toward it.

TAPER • A transform that expands or shrinks a 3D object along one axis.

TARGET • A marker that shows where a camera or light is aimed.

TCB (Tension, Continuity, Bias) **CONTROLLER** • A means of adjusting keyframe control points.

TEETER • A deformation modifier that allows a cross section to be rotated around the axes perpendicular to the path.

TENSION • In a TCB CONTROLLER, it is the influence the keyframe exerts on the curvature path before and after the keyframe.

TERRAIN MODEL • A 3D landscape model. It can

be made through displacement mapping, using a grayscale topographical map.

TEXTURE MAP • A scanned or painted BITMAP that can be applied to a surface to give qualities not available simply by varying surface attributes. There are several types, including ROUGHNESS MAPS and BUMP MAPS.

TEXTURE MAPPING • The process of applying a texture to an object's surface, relating the features of a bitmap image to the internal coordinates of the object.

THREE-DIMENSIONAL (3D) • Relating to objects that have the three dimensions of height, width, and depth. Computer-generated 3D objects can be freely manipulated in computer space.

3D ACCELERATION • Enhancements to video hardware that can speed up the display of 3D scenes.

3D DIGITIZER • A mechanical arm that determines the position of key points on a physical object and records them as xyz coordinates that can generate a 3D computer image of the original. Compare 3D SCANNER.

3D OBJECT • Any three-dimensional object created or used in 3D graphics or animation.

3D OBJECT LIBRARY • A collection of stock 3D objects that can be used in 3D graphics and animation, as an alternative to creating them from scratch. Such a library may come with a program or can be bought separately in a variety of file formats and resolutions.

3D OBJECT SELECTOR • A tool used to select an object in a 3D view.

3D PAINT SOFTWARE • A software program or plug-in that enables the user to paint texture maps directly on a 3D model.

3D SCANNER • A device that uses optical or laser technology to scan a physical object, in order to generate a wireframe mesh or full-color map of the object in a computer graphics program. It can create accurate models of complex objects or people. Compare 3D DIGITIZER.

3D SURFACE SELECTOR • A tool used to select a surface of an object in a 3D view.

THROUGHPUT • The process by which a digital image is processed and turned into output; the term is often used in discussions of speed.

TIFF (Tagged-Image File Format) • A file format, developed by Aldus and Microsoft to store bitmaps; widely used in 2D graphics.

TILE • To fill an area or surface with numerous duplicates of a small, regular shape or a block of pattern or texture.

TILT (or Vertical Pan) • The vertical equivalent of a pan, created by rotating the camera up or down, usually less than 180 degrees, on its x axis. Compare PITCH.

TIME MODE • A setting that governs the way time is displayed in an animation program. See SMPTE.

TIME VALUE • The keyframe value that represents the moment in the animation in which a change takes place. The time value component along with the animation value determines the movement of the object.

TIME ZERO • The point at which an animation begins. Compare START TIME.

TIMELINE • A scale that displays the time continuum of an animation, along which keyframes and animatible features are indicated.

TITLE SAFE • The part of the screen where text should be placed if the image is output to video.

TOOL PALETTE • A small window that shows the tools available for use in a graphics program.

TRACK • A line of data in an animation file, which stores and displays all the information for a single property throughout the animation.

TRACK CAMERA • A camera used to film pylon-mounted models or miniature sets. It is mounted on a boom equipped for pan, tilt, and roll movements, and the whole unit rides on a steel track.

TRACK FILTER • A filter that allows you to select the properties whose track of animation information will be displayed.

TRACKING (or Trucking) **SHOT** • A shot in which the camera glides smoothly past the subject and parallel to it. Compare PAN.

TRANSFORM • Any operation, such as move, scale, or rotate, that affects the position, size, or shape of an object.

TRANSLUCENCY • The quality of letting some light, but not an image, pass through. A translucent material can be anything from nearly opaque to nearly transparent.

TRANSPARENCY • The quality of letting most light through, enough to see an image clearly. In computer graphics, a single control sometimes governs relative transparency (or translucency) from transparent at one end of the scale to opaque at the other. Compare OPACITY.

TRAVELING MATTE • A matte that forms the silhouette of a moving subject on frame after frame, providing the space into which the positive image of the subject can later be optically composited.

TRIANGLE • Any three-sided polygon, a basic shape used in 3D software. Compared to other polygons, it has the advantage that it cannot become nonplanar, and therefore is unlikely to cause problems in rendering.

TRIM CURVE • A curve that allows parts of a surface to be trimmed away; it may be created by projecting a profile onto the surface or intersecting it with another object.

TRUCKING SHOT • See TRACKING SHOT.

TUMBLE EDITOR • A window in which you can rotate an object in 3D, slice off a piece of it, or edit a selected surface.

TWEENING • Process in which the software interpolates action between keyframes.

TWIST • A transform effect that twists an object around a selected axis by rotating the two ends unequally.

Two Dimensional (2D) • Having height and width, but not depth. When film and artwork are scanned, the result is a 2D bitmap image, which cannot be manipulated in all the ways a 3D object can.

Up Vector • A line perpendicular to the view-distance line of the camera that allows the camera to be rolled around the eye point. The up vector is useful in stabilizing the camera view when attached to a path or moving object.

User Axis • An axis that the user can define, whether aligned to an existing axis or at any other position.

UV Coordinate System • A 2D coordinate system imposed on a 3D surface in order to match a texture map to it. UV coordinates run along the surface of an object and conform to the mesh no matter how it twists or bends.

UVW Coordinate System • Like UV coordinates, but adding the W coordinate for depth. UVW coordinates are used for mesh objects. They are used for precise positioning of maps on an object.

Value • The brightness of a color in an HSV color system; more generally, the lightness or darkness (or tinting or shading) of a color.

Velocity • Speed; the rate (relative to time) at which an object's position changes.

Vertex • In geometry, the highest point, the tip of an angle, the corner of a polygon. The last sense is the main one used in 3D graphics. Like any point in space, it can be identified by its xyz coordinates. Vertices can define polygons or be control points of any 3D figure.

Vertex Animation • A method of animating the shape of an object by moving its surface control points.

Vertex Normals • See NORMALS.

Vertices • Plural of VERTEX.

Video Acceleration • Hardware enhancements such as specific chip sets and video RAM that enable a video card to display digital video more efficiently.

Video Capture • The process of converting a signal from a nondigital video source (TV, video camera, VCR, etc.) to digital form and saving it into RAM or as a file on disk.

Video Post Effects • See POST-PRODUCTION effects.

Video Safe (or Boundary) • The cropped portion of the monitor screen that will safely appear on an average television if the image is output to video. This boundary can be superimposed on a viewport. Compare TITLE SAFE.

Video-Safe Colors • Colors within the standard limits of saturation and luminance set for television broadcast. Unsafe colors may bleed into each other, causing the image to blur.

View • What the user sees of a 3D scene on screen. Most programs allow several different simultaneous views enabling the user to shift from one view to another, changing the relative position.

View Angle • See ANGLE OF VIEW.

View Distance • The distance from the eye point to the target or look-at point.

View-Distance Vector • The control point on a virtual camera that adjusts the camera's viewing distance and perspective.

Viewing Direction • The direction the observer is looking at any given time, at the center of the field of view; a line from the eye point to the look-at point.

Viewing Plane • A flat plane perpendicular to the viewing direction that defines the limits of the user's field of view.

Viewing Pyramid • See ANGLE OF VIEW.

Viewpoint • A position in 3D space that represents the viewer's current location. Compare OBSERVER.

VIEWPOINT DATA LABS • A company that creates and sells libraries of models for 3D artists.

VIEWPORT • A window that looks into 3D space when using 3D software.

VIRTUAL • Not actual, but well-imitated. A 3D object is a virtual object: It doesn't exist outside of the computer's memory, but the user can manipulate it (within the computer) as if it actually did exist.

VIRTUAL (or Synthetic) **CHARACTERS AND SETS** • Digital 3D characters and sets that are usually composited with live-action elements.

VIRTUAL MEMORY • Hard-drive space used to supplement the RAM (random-access memory) on the computer. It takes about 10 megabytes of hard-drive space to do the work of a single meg of actual RAM. Virtual memory can run up to a hundred times slower than actual RAM.

VIRTUAL REALITY (VR) • Any of various forms of computer-generated 3D environments, the more interactive and immersive the better. Virtual reality can be used to describe simple walkthroughs on desktop computers to complex systems using stereoscopic images in head-mounted displays (HMD), and sensor gloves for manipulation of objects in virtual environments.

VISTAVISION • An eight-perf film format that has twice the image area of a standard four-perf 35 mm film frame. VistaVision film runs through a projector horizontally, allowing for a larger frame, unlike four-perf film which runs vertically through a standard projection system.

VOLUMETRIC LIGHT • A light source with an adjustable 3D volume that simulates the behavior of natural light as it reacts to particles in the atmosphere.

VOLUMETRIC MAPPING • A process in which a map is defined in 3D space, though it is visible only on the surface of an object. The object displays the part of the map it is intersecting.

VRML (Virtual Reality Markup Language) • A coding language that works with a Web-browser plug-in to enable the user to explore simple 3D environments.

WALK VIEW • A window that displays a 3D rendering of a scene, and allows the user to walk through it.

WATCH LINK • A link in which the z axis of one object stays oriented to, and "watches," the center of another object. When the latter moves, the watcher rotates to keep its z axis oriented to the watched object's new position; other than that, both objects can move independently, and they can be part of other linked hierarchies. This link is most useful for making the camera and lights follow an animated object.

WEIGHT • See TANGENT POINT.

WELD • A term sometimes used to describe the process of joining objects with overlapping vertices.

WINDOW • Any rectangular workspace smaller than the whole computer screen, usually defined by an adjustable frame. In most 3D graphics programs, several windows can be visible at once — commonly top, front, side, and 3D views — but only one is active.

WIPE • A transition from one scene to another, with one image replacing another as if a blade were wiping the first off the screen and revealing the second.

WIREFRAME • A method used to render or display geometry that draws objects using lines to represent the polygon or spline edges.

WIRE REMOVAL • The process of digitally cleaning up a filmed live-action scene by removing wires, props, and other unwanted elements.

WORKING PLANE • The drawing grid (usually but not necessarily horizontal) on which a 3D scene is built.

WORKSPACE • The portion of 3D space that is visible through a window, where it is possible to interact directly with the objects.

WORKSTATION • A high-end computer system designed as a complete solution for a single user — centrally a powerful computer with its monitor, keyboard, and input devices, but also including necessary peripheral devices.

WORLD • The simulated 3D space in which models are built and scenes are created.

WORLD COORDINATES • The basic coordinates of 3D space, which do not change when the user changes views.

WORLD SCALE • The size an object is on the screen, as opposed to the size represented by the grid.

X AXIS • Usually the horizontal axis, representing width.

XY COORDINATES • The coordinate system usually for two-dimensional geometry; normally the x axis is horizontal, and the y axis is vertical.

XYZ COORDINATES • The coordinate system for 3D images and shapes. Typically, the x and y axes are the same as for 2D images; the z axis represents depth.

Y AXIS • Usually the vertical axis, which represents height.

YAW • Rotation around the Y AXIS.

Z AXIS • The z axis usually represents depth, from front to back.

Z-BUFFER RENDERER • A renderer that temporarily stores in a buffer all the pixels that would go in each location where objects overlap, along with information about how far each overlapping pixel is from the camera. It then renders the pixel that corresponds to the object closest to the camera last (on top).

ZOOM • The effect of going from a wide shot to a CLOSE-UP by adjusting the lens on a stationary camera in one continuous move — zoom in or, vice versa, zoom out.

Index